GCSE AQA
Music

There's a lot to be excited about in GCSE Music, and CGP is here
at every step to make sure you know the score...

This brilliant all-in-one book covers the AQA course, and it explains everything
you'll need to do well in your coursework and exam. Musical knowledge,
study pieces, compositions — you name it... we've got it covered.

What's more, each section has warm-up questions and exam-style practice,
plus plenty of online audio. And to help you finish the course on a high note,
we've even included a realistic practice paper at the end!

Complete
Revision & Practice

Includes Free Online Edition and Online Audio!

Contents

Section Seven — Popular Music

Section Eight — Traditional Music

Section Nine — Western Classical Tradition since 1910

You'll see QR codes throughout the book that you can scan with your smartphone.
It'll take you to the audio tracks for this book.
You can access all the audio by going to cgpbooks.co.uk/tempo or by scanning
this code here. You'll need to redeem your Online Edition first using the code
on the first page of this book if you haven't already done so.

Published by CGP

Editors: Sammy El-Bahrawy, Caley Simpson, Hannah Wilkie.

Contributors: Catherine Baird, Michelle Bird, John Deane, Elena Delaney, Hannah Grainger,
Rob Hall, Angela Major, Peter Maries, Sam Norman, James Reevell.

With thanks to Helen Clements, Katherine Faudemar and Delyth Medi Lloyd for the proofreading.
With thanks to Beth Linnane for the copyright research.

For copyright reasons, this book can only be sold in the UK.

ISBN: 978 1 83774 201 1

Clipart from Corel®
Printed by Bell & Bain Ltd, Glasgow.

Based on the classic CGP style created by Richard Parsons.

Text, design, layout and original illustrations © Coordination Group Publications Ltd. (CGP) 2024
All rights reserved.

What You Have To Do For GCSE Music

GCSE Music doesn't cover every single aspect of music — if it did it would take forever. Instead you focus on four main 'Areas of Study' (AoS for short).

You Learn About Four Areas of Study

For each Area of Study you'll learn the basics of that style or period — e.g. the musical structures, the instruments used, the context the music was originally created in, etc.

You have to be able to answer questions on all four Areas of Study, but you only need to look at study pieces for two Areas of Study. One of these has to be AoS1, but you (or your teacher) can choose which of the other pieces you study. The four Areas of Study are:

> **AoS1 — WESTERN CLASSICAL TRADITION 1650-1910** (covered in Section 6)
> Your study piece is the First Movement of Beethoven's *Symphony No. 1 in C Major*.

This is the compulsory piece — you have to study it.

> **AoS2 — POPULAR MUSIC** (covered in Section 7)
> Your study pieces are 'Bohemian Rhapsody', 'Love of My Life' and 'Seven Seas of Rhye' by Queen.

> **AoS3 — TRADITIONAL MUSIC** (covered in Section 8)
> Your study pieces are Esperanza Spalding's 'Little Fly', 'I Know You Know' and 'I Adore You'.

> **AoS4 — WESTERN CLASSICAL TRADITION SINCE 1910** (covered in Section 9)
> Your study pieces are Bartók's 'An Evening in the Village', 'Bear Dance', 'Slightly Tipsy' and 'Swineherd's Dance' from *Hungarian Pictures*.

There's another movement called "Melody", but you don't need to study that one.

They Test You With a Listening Exam...

worth 40% of the total marks

At the end of Year 11 you do an exam. You listen to excerpts of pieces from all four Areas of Study and answer questions on what you hear. You'll also have questions on your study pieces.

...And With Coursework

The coursework is work done during the course. Obviously. It's split into two chunks:

PERFORMING

worth 30% of the total marks

1) You do two performances.
2) One has to be a solo performance. This can be a piece you play or sing, a DJ performance or a realisation using music technology (e.g. sequencing).
3) For the other, you have to perform as part of an ensemble. There must be 2 or more players in the ensemble, with distinct and separate parts.

COMPOSING

worth 30% of the total marks

1) You compose two pieces. One is based on a composition brief. You'll be given a choice of four composition briefs, which might have a stimulus (e.g. a poem, photo or some notation).
2) Your second composition can be anything you like — it's a free composition.

Err, Miss... Is it too late to change to Physics?

Welcome to the wonderful world of GCSE Music. Breathe in the cool clear air. Listen to the birds. Relax.

Component 1 — Understanding Music

At the end of the course, you have the joy of a **listening exam**. All **1 hour and 30 minutes** of it.

The **Exam** Tests All Four **Areas of Study**

1) The listening and understanding music exam is worth 96 marks (40% of your total mark). It's divided into two sections — Section A and Section B.

2) Section A is the listening section — it's worth 68 marks. You have to listen to and answer questions on excerpts of music. You'll be told which Area of Study each excerpt is from and how many times it'll be played. You'll be given writing time for each question.

3) You have to answer all 8 questions in this section — they're on unfamiliar pieces from all four Areas of Study (most only need short answers). One question will probably require musical dictation.

4) Section B is the contextual understanding section — it's worth 28 marks. You have to answer the first question, which is on the study piece from AoS1 (Beethoven's Symphony No. 1, Movement 1).

5) You then have to answer one of the next three questions — on whichever other AoS study pieces that you've looked at. There aren't any excerpts to listen to in this section — it's all based on your own knowledge. One part of each question needs a longer answer (it's worth 8 marks).

Some Questions are **Multiple Choice**

⌐ If you're stuck — guess the answer. There's a chance of getting it right. ⌐

Don't mess these up by rushing — read all the options carefully.

What is the texture of this excerpt? Put a cross in the correct box. *[1 mark]*
☐ homophonic   ☐ monophonic   ☐ contrapuntal   ☐ antiphonal

Some Questions Just Need a **Short Answer**

These questions are only worth a few marks so don't waste time writing your answer out in a nice long sentence — just write down one good word for each mark.

Name two instruments playing the theme in this excerpt. *[2 marks]*

⌐ For questions worth 3 or 4 marks, you'll have to write a bit more. ⌐

They Sometimes Give You an **Outline** of the Music

You'll be given an outline of part of the music called a 'skeleton score'. It will just show part of the music — the melody, rhythm or lyrics, say. The skeleton score will help you with answering the question. You might be asked to fill in the pitch, rhythm or chords of a short section of the music.

Fill in the missing notes in bar 4.
The rhythm is given above the stave. *[3 marks]*

Some Questions in **Section B** Need **Longer Answers**

There are a couple of questions where you have to write a longer answer — a few paragraphs of writing. Make sure you cover all the key points of the question in your answer.

Explain how the first movement of Beethoven's *Symphony No. 1* is typical of the Classical period. *[8 marks]*

 EXAM TIP

Shiver me timbers — 'tis the skeleton score...
Concentrate on answering just a few of the questions each time the music's played — it's less confusing. Have a go at the Practice Exam on p.167 to give you an idea of what it'll be like.

Component 2 — Performing

Pick your pieces carefully and **practise** till your neighbours beg for mercy.

You Have To Do **Two Performances**

The <u>combined time</u> of both your performances must be at least <u>four minutes</u>.
Your <u>ensemble</u> performance must be at least <u>one minute</u> long.

SOLO PERFORMANCE

You simply play <u>one solo piece</u> of your own choice. It can be a <u>traditional performance</u>,
a <u>DJ performance</u> or a <u>realisation</u> using <u>music technology</u> (if you're using <u>multi-tracking</u>, you must
have a <u>minimum</u> of <u>three tracks</u>, at least <u>one</u> of which must be performed <u>live</u>). Your solo can be
<u>accompanied</u> (if it was <u>written</u> with an accompaniment, you <u>have</u> to perform it with accompaniment).

ENSEMBLE PERFORMANCE

For your ensemble piece, there must be <u>at least two</u> of you playing or singing, and your part can't
be <u>doubled</u>. Like the solo performance, this can be a <u>traditional performance</u>, a <u>DJ performance</u>
(with <u>other DJs</u> or <u>live musicians</u>) or a <u>realisation</u> using <u>music technology</u>. For a <u>multi-tracked</u>
performance, <u>you</u> must perform at least <u>three</u> tracks (<u>one</u> must be <u>live</u>), and there must be <u>one or
more</u> other parts (<u>one</u> has to be <u>live</u>). You have to play a <u>different</u> piece than your solo piece.

You have to hand in the music you've worked from for <u>each</u> performance. This can be
a <u>score</u>, a <u>lead sheet</u> or a <u>recording</u> of the piece made by <u>someone else</u> — a '<u>guide recording</u>'.
(For <u>music technology</u> performances, you have to hand in an <u>annotation</u>, giving <u>details</u> of how
you produced your piece.) You also have to hand in <u>digital recordings</u> of your performances.

You Get Marks for the **Difficulty** of the **Piece...**

1) It's <u>obvious</u> really — a very <u>simple</u> piece will get <u>fewer marks</u> for difficulty than a <u>complicated</u> piece.
   But there's <u>no point</u> trying to play something that you're <u>not capable of</u> and then messing it up...

2) Choose your pieces <u>carefully</u> — ideally they should be the <u>hardest level</u> that you can
   play <u>well</u>. If you pick something <u>too easy</u>, you'll be throwing away <u>difficulty marks</u>.
   If you pick something <u>too hard</u>, you won't be able to play your <u>best</u>, and you'll lose marks
   for <u>musicality</u>. Get your music teacher or instrument teacher's <u>advice</u> on what to play.

3) If you choose an <u>easy</u> piece, you won't be able to get <u>as many marks</u> for the areas described below.

...And Marks for the **Quality** of Your **Playing**

Music technology performances
are also marked on balance,
panning, effects and style.

You need to show off your '<u>musicality</u>' and <u>technique</u> (how <u>well</u> you play your
instrument, including techniques <u>specific</u> to your instrument). You get marks for:

1) **ACCURACY**: Learn the <u>notes</u>, play them <u>in time</u> and <u>in tune</u>. Most importantly, <u>keep going</u>
   — your performance needs to be <u>fluent</u>. Lots of <u>stopping</u> and <u>starting</u> or <u>slowing down</u> for
   tricky bits will lose you marks. Don't worry about the <u>odd slip</u>, but start off <u>well prepared</u>.
   For <u>DJ</u> and <u>music technology</u> performances, this includes <u>pitch</u> and <u>balance</u> as well.

2) **EXPRESSION AND INTERPRETATION**: Your performance needs to be <u>expressive</u> — to make
   the audience <u>feel</u> something. Pay attention to stuff like <u>dynamics</u>, <u>tempo</u>, <u>mood</u>, <u>articulation</u>
   and <u>phrasing</u>. It's all about how well you <u>communicate</u> — i.e. how you <u>interpret</u> the music.

When you're playing in an <u>ensemble</u>, there are other things that you'll get marks for. Play <u>in time</u> and
<u>in tune</u> with the <u>other players</u>. Really <u>listen</u> to the other parts, so you know when you should be part of
the <u>background</u> and when you should make your part <u>stand out</u> — the ensemble should be <u>balanced</u>.

Practice makes perfect...

No doubt people have been going on at you about practising since you were knee-high to a piccolo.
It gets boring after a while. I expect you <u>know</u> that you need to do lots of practice. So I'll say no more.

Component 3 — Composing

For one composition, you can write whatever you like — but for the other, you have to follow a brief.

You Have to Write **Two Pieces** for **Coursework**

1) The total time for both pieces has to be at least three minutes
   (you'll lose marks if they're less than three minutes).

2) You don't have to perform your compositions yourself (but you can if you want to).

3) You can compose for any combination of instruments, voices or DJs and
   can use technology (unless the composition brief tells you otherwise).

4) One piece you write has to follow a composition brief:

   - The composition brief will be given to you by the exam board.
   - There will be four different composition briefs to choose from.
   - You can choose which one you do (though your teacher might suggest which one to pick).
   - The brief might include a stimulus — written words (e.g. a poem or some text),
     images (e.g. a photo or film clip) or some notation (e.g. a short melody or rhythm).

5) You should be given the composition brief halfway through your GCSE course — by which
   point, you should have studied the different areas (and looked at the study pieces) in detail.

6) The other piece you write is a free composition — it can be in any style you like.

Each Piece is Marked on **Six** Different **Categories**

Each composition is worth 36 marks, based on two different categories (there are up to 18 marks
available for each category — you need to use at least two different elements to get all 18 marks).

RHYTHM, METRE, TEXTURE, MELODY, STRUCTURE AND FORM:
To get top marks in this category, think about things like changing time signatures,
using compound metres, syncopated and dotted rhythms, cross-rhythms or tempo changes
(including rubato) — see Section 2. Try using homophonic and polyphonic textures,
imitation, canon or antiphony, ostinatos (or riffs), conjunct or disjunct melodies,
different ornaments or blue notes. Texture is covered in Section 3 and melody is covered
in Section 4. You could use one of the forms covered in Section 4, such as ternary,
rondo, theme and variation, ground bass, popular song form, or 12-bar blues (see p.130).

HARMONY, TONALITY, TIMBRE, DYNAMICS, PHRASING AND ARTICULATION:
Think about all four types of cadence, using major and minor keys, modes, different types of
harmony, changing key (modulation), dissonance or pedal notes. This is all covered in Section 3.
You should try and use both solo instruments/voices and groupings of instruments or voices,
synthesized or digitally-produced sounds, tremolo, vibrato, reverb or distortion (for appropriate
instruments or voices). You should also use a variety of dynamics (including crescendos and
diminuendos), as well as a range of phrasing and articulation (e.g. legato, staccato, tenuto or
marcato). See p.19-20 for dynamics and articulation and Section 5 for instruments and timbre.

For each composition, you have to produce a programme note — a written report that covers:

- The purpose or intention of the piece (you should specify the audience or occasion you wrote it for).
- The musical elements you chose (e.g. the texture, structure or rhythms you used — anything from the lists above).
- Any equipment you used to compose the piece.

Each programme note should be about 150 words long.

You have to hand in a recording of each composition, as well as a written version
and your programme note. There's more information about these on p.7.

Component 3 — Composing

Well, the **good news** is — the compositions you have to do for GCSE only need to be a total of **3 minutes** long. No one's expecting an opera. Something short will do.

Here Are Some **General Things** To Think About...

DEVELOPING YOUR MUSICAL IDEAS

Don't just use a good idea once and then forget about it. Build up and develop the good bits — e.g. by changing the rhythm from short notes to long notes or the key from major to minor. See Section 3 for loads more techniques and devices for developing your ideas.

MAKING THE STYLE CONVINCING

Listen to lots of music from the style you're composing in.
Make your piece sound like 'the real thing' by using similar musical ideas — e.g. in a Baroque gigue, use a lively tempo, regular beat and a harpsichord.

THE POTENTIAL AND LIMITS OF YOUR RESOURCES

Once you've chosen the instruments, think about all the ways they can make interesting and contrasting sounds — e.g. pizzicato bits for strings. But also remember the limitations — e.g. clarinet players need time to breathe. Think about the highest and lowest notes your chosen instruments can play — there's no point composing a brilliant piece if no one can play it.

> One of your pieces will have to meet the composition brief, so there'll be extra things you have to bear in mind to match the brief.

STRUCTURE

Organise your music with a clear, definite structure (there's lots of information on different structures throughout this book). Even if your composition doesn't follow a traditional form, you'll need to make sure it doesn't just ramble on aimlessly.

When You're Composing, Make Plans **Before** You Start

1) Making a musical plan helps to organise your ideas — it's a bit like writing an essay plan. It'll also help when it comes to writing your composing log.

2) Music's got to be organised, or it just sounds like a load of random notes. The most basic bit of organisation is the timing (beats in a bar). The next biggest chunk is the phrasing.

3) The overall shape is called the structure or form. The structure could be the verses and chorus in a pop song, or the movements of a symphony. Composers usually decide on the structure of a piece of music before they get into the detail.

4) It's OK to design your own musical plan, but a lot of people use 'tried and tested' structures like the ones described throughout this book — because they know they'll work.

5) 'Tried and tested' structures are like templates. The general organisation of your ideas is decided for you — you just need to add the details.

6) For the piece that follows the composition brief, it's probably a good idea to use a 'tried and tested' structure as your composition will need to be in a particular style or form.

7) Your plan should include ways to vary the different sections — have a look on the next page for some ideas.

COMPOSING TIP

Clarinet players need time to breathe? Amateurs...

So the main thing to take away from this page is 'be organised'. I'm not expecting you to be organised in all aspects of your life, just in your compositions — and planning really helps.

Component 3 — Composing

There are lots of things you need to think about when composing. This is not a complete list (just a few general ideas), but it'll give you a few things to bear in mind.

Most Music Uses Repetition Repetition Repetition...

1) <u>Repetition</u> means using a <u>musical idea</u> — a chunk of tune — <u>more than once</u>.

2) Repeating bits is a really good way of giving music <u>shape</u>. A recognisable tune works like a <u>landmark</u> — the audience recognises that tune <u>later</u> in the piece. That's how <u>choruses</u> work.

3) If you're planning <u>your own</u> piece of music, try repeating the best part of the tune.

4) You can even repeat <u>whole sections</u> — in <u>rondo form</u> (see p.93), one section is repeated lots of times.

...and Contrast

Repetition is really important — but <u>constant repetition</u> is <u>boring</u>. Good compositions balance repetition with <u>contrast</u>. The aim is to do something <u>different</u> from the repeated bits to add <u>variety</u>. Here are some ways you can <u>vary</u> your compositions:

These changes will get you extra marks for your compositions.

PITCH AND TONALITY

You can create contrast by changing the <u>organisation of pitch</u> — e.g. changing the melody from a <u>high register</u> to a <u>low register</u>, and swapping between <u>conjunct</u> and <u>disjunct</u> tunes (see p.54). You can also change the tonality by <u>modulating</u> between <u>major</u> and <u>minor keys</u>.

TEMPO AND RHYTHM

Changing <u>speed</u> from <u>fast</u> to <u>slow</u> (or vice versa) is a good way of creating contrast. You can also change the rhythms — try a mix of <u>dotted</u> and <u>straight rhythms</u>, or <u>long</u> and <u>short notes</u>. You can change the <u>articulation</u> too — try <u>legato</u>, <u>staccato</u>, <u>slurs</u> and <u>accents</u> to vary your piece.

DYNAMICS

Changes in <u>dynamics</u> (<u>loud</u> to <u>soft</u> and vice versa, and <u>crescendos</u> and <u>diminuendos</u>) will instantly create contrast.

TEXTURE

Changing between a thin, <u>monophonic</u> texture to a thicker <u>homophonic</u> or <u>polyphonic</u> texture (see p.45) will create contrast.

Decide How To Hand In Your Work

For each piece, you give in three things — a <u>written version</u>, a <u>recording</u> (though you won't be marked on the <u>quality</u> of the recording, just the composition) and a <u>programme note</u>. There are a few <u>options</u> for how you present your written version.

1) The **WRITTEN VERSION** can be either a <u>score</u> (either <u>handwritten</u> or <u>computer generated</u>), a <u>lead sheet</u> (e.g. a <u>vocal line</u> with <u>accompanying chords</u>) or a <u>written account</u> (a <u>guide</u> to what the listener should <u>hear</u> in the piece).

2) Give as much <u>information</u> as possible. <u>Dynamics</u>, <u>tempo</u>, <u>expression</u> and <u>articulation</u> will all improve your mark. There should be <u>enough detail</u> for someone else to be able to <u>recreate</u> your piece.

The **RECORDING** must be <u>saved digitally</u>.

Even though you don't get marks for the quality of the recording, good recordings are easier to mark. It's also in your best interests to produce an accurate one.

The **PROGRAMME NOTE** is a <u>written report</u>. It should be about <u>150 words</u> long.

The Basics

These two pages give the **essential basics** you'll need to get through GCSE Music.
Make sure you know everything here before you go on into the rest of the book.

1 **CLEF**

These symbols at the start of a line tell you how <u>high</u> or <u>low</u> to play the notes. All the different clefs are covered on <u>page 10</u>.

3 **TWO LINES OF MUSIC**

The top line of music has got a tune — it's the <u>melody</u>. The bottom line is the <u>accompaniment</u>.

2 **NOTE**

Each note is shown by a separate <u>oval</u>. The symbol also tells you how <u>long</u> or <u>short</u> the note is. The symbols are shown on <u>page 16</u>.

7 **TIME SIGNATURE**

The numbers tell you about the <u>beats</u> in a <u>bar</u>. Time signatures are covered on <u>page 12</u>.

9 **KEY SIGNATURE**

There are no flats or sharps, so this piece is in the <u>key</u> of C. Keys and scales are covered in <u>Section Three</u>.

8 **BEATS**

Each bar has the <u>same</u> number of <u>beats</u>. Beats, bars and rhythm are covered on <u>pages 13, 16 & 17</u>.

THE PIANO KEYBOARD

Some of the diagrams in this book make more sense if you know what's what on a <u>piano keyboard</u>. The white keys play <u>natural notes</u>.

F G A B C D E F G A B C D E

Note: The white notes from C to C make the scale of C major (p.24).

The black keys play <u>SHARPS</u> and <u>FLATS</u>. Sharps and flats are covered on <u>page 11</u>.
The C in the middle of a piano keyboard is known as <u>MIDDLE C</u>.

The Basics

5 STAVE
The five lines are called a stave. Notes can go on or between the lines, or on separate short lines above or below.

4 BAR
The vertical bar lines split the music into bars.
bar line

6 TRIPLETS
The '3' and the curved line show these notes are triplets. They're explained on page 17.

11 PITCH
Notes higher up the stave have a higher pitch. Notes lower down have a lower pitch. Look at page 16 to see where the different notes go.

12 CHORD
More than one note played together makes a chord. See Section Three for more about chords.

13 DOUBLE BAR LINE
You get a double bar line at the end of a piece (or section of a piece).

10 STRUCTURE
The melody's built out of two different tunes — phrases and structures are covered in Sections Three and Four.

TONES AND SEMITONES

Tones and *semitones* are the gaps between notes.

On a piano, a semitone is the gap between any key, black or white, and its immediate neighbour.

The gap from any key to a key two semitone steps above or below is called a tone.

Clefs

Clefs are the **curly symbols** that you find right at the **start** of most written music. The treble clef is used for high-pitched music. The bass and alto clefs are used for lower-pitched music.

The **Treble** Clef is the **Most Common** Clef

1) The treble clef is used for <u>higher-pitched melody instruments</u>, e.g. flute, oboe, clarinet, violin, trumpet and horn.

2) Music for <u>soprano</u> and <u>alto</u> voices is written on the treble clef, too.

3) The sign always goes in the same place on the stave, with the curly bit wrapped around the line for the <u>G above middle C</u>.

MIDDLE C

The **Bass** Clef is used for **Low-pitched Instruments**

1) The bass clef is used for <u>lower-pitched instruments</u> like the tuba, trombone, bassoon, cello and double bass.

2) It's also used for <u>bass voices</u>.

3) The big blob always goes on the line for the <u>F below middle C</u>, and the two little dots go either side of the line.

MIDDLE C

The **Vocal Tenor** Clef is for **Tenor** Voices and **Lead Guitar**

MIDDLE C

Here's the 8.

1) Each line and gap in the vocal tenor clef stands for exactly the same note as it does in the <u>treble clef</u>, BUT that little '<u>8</u>' underneath means that the notes are played <u>one octave lower</u>.

2) It's used by <u>tenor voices</u> and <u>lead guitar</u> parts.

The **C** Clef can **Move** Up and Down on the Stave

The C clef always has its <u>middle point</u> on <u>middle C</u>. It can be used as two different clefs, depending on its <u>position</u> on the stave.

1) When its middle point is on the <u>middle line</u>, it's the <u>alto clef</u> and is used for <u>viola</u> parts.

MIDDLE C

2) When the middle point is on the <u>fourth line up</u>, it's called the <u>tenor clef</u>, which is used for the <u>higher notes</u> in <u>bass instruments</u> like trombones, bassoons and cellos.

MIDDLE C

Make sure you know your clefs...

You don't see the vocal tenor or C clefs very often, but you've got to know what they are when they <u>do</u> turn up. The treble and bass clefs are used all the time — aim to get so good at reading and writing them that it's easier than English. The only way is to practise. The notes are written in full on page 16.

Sharps, Flats and Naturals

On a piano, **natural** notes are the **white** ones. **Sharps** are the **black** notes to the **right** of the white notes. **Flats** are the blacks to the **left** of the whites. So each black is both sharp **and** flat.

♯ A **Sharp** Makes a Note One Step **Higher**

1) A sharp sign next to a note tells you to play it one semitone higher.

> When you're writing on the stave, put sharps, flats and naturals before the note they affect. If you're writing text, put them afterwards — F♯.

2) A double sharp — 𝄪 — makes a note two semitones higher. If you see C𝄪 you play D — it's the same note going by a different name. The fancy name for notes that sound the same but have different names is enharmonic equivalents.

♭ A **Flat** Makes a Note One Step **Lower**

1) A flat symbol next to a note means you have to play it one semitone lower.

2) A double flat — 𝄫 — makes a note two semitones (a tone) lower.

The **Key Signature** is Shown with Sharps or Flats

KEY SIGNATURE

- Sharps or flats written at the start of a piece, straight after the clef, tell you the key signature.
- The key signature makes notes sharp or flat all the way through a piece of music.
- Sharps and flats that you see by individual notes — but not in the key signature — are called accidentals. Once an accidental has appeared in a bar, it applies to all notes of the same pitch for the rest of the bar, unless it's cancelled out by a natural sign...

> There's more about key signatures on p.24-26.

> This key signature's got one sharp — on the F line. You have to play every F in the piece as an F♯.

♮ A **Natural** Sign **Cancels** a Sharp or Flat

A natural sign before a note cancels the effect of a sharp or flat sign from earlier in the bar or from a key signature. You never see natural signs in the key signature, only in the music, as accidentals.

This stuff should all come naturally in no time...

Double sharps and flats are uncommon and quite peculiar — it doesn't seem that logical to write C𝄪 when you could write D, but sometimes you just have to, I'm afraid. It all depends what key you're in.

Time Signatures

Those **two numbers** at the beginning of a piece of music tell you **how many beats** there are in a bar and **how long** they are. Whatever you're playing, don't ignore them.

Music has a **Regular Beat**

1) You can tap your foot along to the <u>beat</u> of any piece of music, as long as it hasn't got a horribly complicated rhythm. The beat is also called the <u>pulse</u>.

2) If you listen a bit harder, you can hear that some beats are <u>stronger</u> than others.

3) The strong beats come at <u>regular intervals</u> — usually every <u>2</u>, <u>3</u> or <u>4</u> beats.

4) The strong beat is the <u>first</u> beat of each <u>bar</u>. If the strong beat comes every 3 beats, then the piece of music you're listening to has <u>three beats</u> in a bar.

The **Time Signature** Shows **How Many** Beats are in a Bar

- There's always a <u>time signature</u> at the beginning of a piece of music.
- It goes to the <u>right</u> of the clef and the key signature.
- It's written using <u>two numbers</u>.

TOP NUMBER goes between the middle line and the top line

BOTTOM NUMBER goes between the middle line and the bottom line

The <u>top number</u> tells you <u>how many beats</u> there are in each bar, e.g. a '2' means two beats in a bar, a '3' means three beats in a bar and so on.

The <u>bottom number</u> tells you <u>how long</u> each beat is (see <u>page 16</u> for the names of the different notes).

If you see a big '**C**' in place of the time signature, it stands for 'common time', which means it's in $\frac{4}{4}$. If it's **¢**, then it's 'cut common time' — $\frac{2}{2}$.

A <u>2</u> at the bottom means each beat is <u>1 minim</u> long.

A <u>4</u> at the bottom means each beat is <u>1 crotchet</u> long.

An <u>8</u> at the bottom means each beat is <u>1 quaver</u> long.

A <u>16</u> at the bottom means each beat is <u>1 semiquaver</u> long.

If the **Beat Changes**, the **Time Signature Changes**

1) The time signature usually <u>stays the same</u> all the way through a piece of music. If it does, it's written just <u>once</u>, at the beginning.

2) Sometimes the beat <u>changes</u> during a piece. If it does, the new time signature's written in the bar where it <u>changes</u>.

3) Not all pieces start on the first beat of the bar — some start on an <u>unaccented beat</u> called an <u>anacrusis</u> (or <u>upbeat</u>).

You can practise listening for the beat any time...

Every time you listen to music, practise <u>listening for the beat</u> and work out the time signature.

Counting the Beat

Counting the beat's fairly easy, but it's a crucial skill. It can help you work out how to **play** a new piece and how to **write a tune down** when you've only heard it played aloud or in your head.

In **Simple Time** You Count **All the Beats**

1) <u>Simple</u> time signatures have <u>2</u>, <u>3</u> or <u>4</u> as their <u>top</u> number.

2) In simple time, if you're counting to the music, you count <u>every beat</u>. For $\frac{4}{4}$ you'd count, "<u>One, two, three, four</u>." For $\frac{3}{2}$, you'd count, "<u>One, two, three</u>."

3) If you want to count out the rhythm of <u>smaller notes</u> as well as the beats, try using "<u>and</u>", "<u>eye</u>" and "<u>a</u>" — it seems to make the rhythm come out just right.

> Count "<u>One and two and</u>" for quavers, and "<u>One eye and a</u>" for semiquavers.
>
> $\frac{2}{4}$ [musical notation]
> 1 2   1 and 2 and   1 eye and a 2 eye and a

2) Any shorter notes are usually a <u>half</u>, a <u>quarter</u>, an <u>eighth</u> or a <u>sixteenth</u> of the main beat.

In **Compound Time** Only Count the **Big Beats**

1) Compound time signatures have <u>6</u>, <u>9</u> or <u>12</u> as their <u>top</u> number — you can always divide the top number by <u>three</u>.

2) If the music is fairly fast, it's too <u>awkward</u> to count to nine or twelve for every bar. You end up with so many little beats that the rhythm sounds <u>mushy</u>.

3) To make the rhythm <u>clear</u>, you can just count the <u>main beats</u>:

4) If you were counting out the main beats in $\frac{6}{8}$, you'd count "One, two". $\frac{9}{8}$ would go "One, two, three".

$\frac{6}{8}$ [musical notation]
1 2

5) To count the <u>in-between notes</u>, use "<u>&</u>" and "<u>a</u>".

6) Shorter notes are made by dividing by three — so they're <u>thirds</u>, <u>sixths</u>, <u>twelfths</u>, etc. of the main beat.

$\frac{9}{8}$ [musical notation]
1 2 3   1 & a 2 & a 3 & a

7) Music in compound time <u>sounds different</u> from music in simple time because the beat is divided into threes — <u>practise</u> spotting the difference.

The **Patterns** the Beats Make are Called the **Metre**

Depending on the time signature, the beats make different <u>patterns</u>. The pattern is known as the <u>metre</u>. Metre can be:

Regular	Irregular	Free
The strong beats make the <u>same pattern</u> all the way through. <u>two</u> beats per bar = <u>duple</u> metre <u>three</u> beats per bar = <u>triple</u> metre <u>four</u> beats per bar = <u>quadruple</u> metre	There could be <u>five</u> beats in a bar grouped in twos and threes, or <u>seven</u> beats in a bar grouped in threes and twos or fours.	Music with <u>no particular metre</u>. This one's fairly unusual.

> You can describe a time signature based on its beat and metre — e.g. a piece in $\frac{4}{4}$ is in simple quadruple time, and a piece in $\frac{6}{8}$ is in compound duple time.

One and a, two and a, three and a, four and a...

Counting the beat's not really that hard. The tricky bit on this page is the stuff about <u>metre</u>. You could get asked about the metre of a piece in your listening exam, so learn <u>all three sorts</u>.

Rhythms and Metres

When **different rhythms** are played at the **same time**, some of them **fit together** well, but some of them **don't**. Rhythms that **don't fit** can create interesting and crazy **effects**.

Hemiola Gives the Impression of a Different Metre

1) Hemiola is a rhythmic device used to create contrast within a piece. Music written in duple metre (see p.13) is temporarily accented to make it feel like it's in triple metre, or vice versa.

2) In $\frac{6}{8}$ time there are two beats in a bar, each the length of a dotted crotchet. Hemiola is created by playing a bar of three crotchets, giving the impression of $\frac{3}{4}$ time instead.

3) In $\frac{3}{4}$ time, hemiola is created by accenting every other beat for two bars. This gives the impression of three bars of $\frac{2}{4}$ time, rather than two bars of $\frac{3}{4}$.

Different Rhythms Can be Played at the Same Time

1) When two or more contrasting rhythms are played at the same time, the music is polyrhythmic. A polyrhythm made up of just two different rhythms is known as a bi-rhythm. Lots of African music is polyrhythmic — see p.133.

2) Polyrhythms can be created by a number of performers playing different instruments. A drummer can also create polyrhythms by playing a different rhythm with each hand.

- The rhythms will often have accents in different places. Hemiola might be used in one or more parts, giving the impression of instruments playing in different time signatures (this is known as vertical hemiola).

- Another polyrhythmic device is to use triplets against standard notes, e.g. triplet quavers played at the same time as two normal quavers.

- Cross-rhythm occurs when the accents are 'out of sync' over a number of bars. This can be used to create tension in the music.

Drum Fills are Little Drum Solos

1) Drum fills are fairly short — they often only last for a few beats.
2) Fills are normally used to build the music up, or to change between sections.
3) They give the drummer a (very short) chance to show off.
4) Most rock, pop and jazz pieces will have drum fills in them.

Rhythms make me very cross...

Listen to 'Skyfall' by Adele and see if you can pick out the drum fills.

Warm-up and Exam Questions

Now have a crack at some questions to see how much you've learnt so far.

Warm-up Questions

1) Draw the symbols for a treble clef, bass clef, vocal tenor clef and C alto clef.

2) Explain what a sharp sign, a flat sign and a natural sign do.

3) Draw a time signature describing three minim beats per bar.

4) How many beats are there per bar if the time signature is $\frac{9}{8}$?

5) What's the difference between simple and compound time?

6) Name the three main types of metre.

Exam Question

This is the type of question you could get in your listening test. To access the tracks for the listening questions, go to cgpbooks.co.uk/extras and use your Online Edition code to log in.
Use this question to test your understanding of the last few pages and as practice for the real thing.

Play the following excerpt **four** times.
Leave a short pause between each playing of the excerpt.

Remember, you can find all the tracks for the listening questions at cgpbooks.co.uk/tempo.

Track 1

a) Fill in the **8 missing notes** from the vocal part, using the rhythm supplied.

Listen carefully for the direction of the notes — this really isn't as difficult as it seems at first.

[8 marks]

b) Draw a circle around the key signature.

[1 mark]

c) Fill in the time signature.

[1 mark]

d) Here is another part of the same excerpt.

Label the following features:

- the note A#
- two notes a tone apart
- two notes a semitone apart

[3 marks]

Notes and Rests

Let's face it, you'd be a bit lost reading music if you didn't know what all those funny little dots and squiggles meant. Make sure you know all this stuff **better than the alphabet**.

The **Symbols** Tell You **How Long** Notes and Rests Are

- Notes tell you how many beats to hold a sound for.
- Rests tell you how many beats to hold a silence for.
- Notes and rests have names, depending on how long they are.
  Two beats is a minim note or rest. A half-beat is a quaver note or rest.

Learn this table now — you need to know exactly how to write these out, and how to play them.

The length of a note or rest is also called its duration.

NAME OF NOTE	NUMBER OF CROTCHET BEATS	NOTE SYMBOL	REST SYMBOL
semibreve	4	o	▬
minim	2	♩ (hollow)	▬
crotchet	1	♩	𝄽
quaver	½	♪ or ♫ if there are 2 or more	𝄾
semiquaver	¼	♬ or ♬ if there are 2 or more	𝄿

A semibreve rest also indicates a full bar's rest, no matter what time signature the piece is in.

The **Position** of the Note Tells You the **Pitch**

Just in case you don't know, this is where the notes go in the bass and treble clefs:

In the bottom half of the stave, the tails on the notes go upwards.

There is some overlap — e.g. these are the same note written in different clefs.

In the top half of the stave, the tails on the notes go downwards.

The tail of the note on the middle line can go up or down.

These lines are called ledger lines. You use them to work out how high or low notes above and below the stave are.

'Leger lines' is an alternative spelling for 'ledger lines'.

There's no excuse for not knowing this stuff...

Those of you who were playing the church organ before you could crawl might be feeling a bit like you know this stuff already and you don't need to be told. It's still worth checking over though, I reckon.

Dots, Ties and Triplets

You can only get so far with the note lengths from **page 16**. If you use **dot**, **tie** and **triplet** symbols you can create more complicated, interesting and sophisticated rhythms.

A **Dot** After a Note or Rest Makes It **Longer**

1) A dot just to the right of a note or rest makes it half as long again.

2) A second dot adds on another quarter of the original note length.

Count these really carefully when you're playing — don't just "add a bit on".

3) In dotted quaver rhythms, you have a dotted quaver (worth ½ + ¼ = ¾ of a beat) followed by a semiquaver (worth ¼ of a beat). Dotted quaver rhythms are common in marches. They're usually written like this:

¾ beat   ¼ beat

4) In a Scotch snap, the rhythm is the other way round — the semiquaver is on the beat (and accented), followed by the dotted quaver, like this: Scotch snaps are used in Scottish music (e.g. dances) — hence the name.

A **Tie Joins Two Notes** Together

1) A tie is a curved line joining two notes of the same pitch together.
2) It turns them into one note.
3) Ties are often used to make a long note that goes over the end of a bar.

...sounds the same as...

...sounds the same as...

Ties are not the same as slurs. See page 19.

A **Triplet** is **Three Notes** Played in the Time of **Two**

1) A triplet is three notes, all the same length, squeezed into the time of two.
2) Triplets are marked with a '3' above or below the middle of the three notes. Sometimes there's a square bracket or a curved line as well as the three.

3) The notes don't all have to be played — part of a triplet can be rests.

Stick with it, even the tricky bits...

Triplets look so straightforward on the page, but they can be tricky to get just right. The only way to make sure you're playing them properly is to practise with a metronome. Have a go right now.

Tempo and Mood

Composers don't just tell you the notes — they tell you **how fast** to play them, and what the **atmosphere** of the piece should be too. You need to understand all the different **terms** they use.

The **Tempo** is the **Speed** of the Music

Tempo is Italian for "<u>time</u>". In a lot of music the instructions for how fast to play are written in Italian too. Here are the words you're <u>most</u> likely to come across:

> 60 beats a minute means each crotchet lasts one second. 120 beats a minute means each crotchet lasts half a second. And so on...

Italian word	What it means	Beats per minute
largo	broad and slow	40-60
larghetto	still broad, not so slow	60-66
adagio	bit faster than largo	66-76
andante	walking pace	76-108
moderato	moderate speed	108-120
allegro	quick and lively	120-168
vivace	very lively — quicker than allegro	168-180
presto	really fast	180-200

This is where you put the <u>tempo</u> and <u>beats per minute</u> on the stave. ♩ = 112 means there are 112 crotchet beats per minute. This is called a <u>metronome marking</u>.

These words tell you how to <u>vary</u> the speed. The <u>words</u> go <u>underneath</u> the stave. The <u>pause</u> symbol goes <u>above</u>.

> Rubato means 'robbed time' — you can slow some bits down and speed others up.

Italian word	Abbreviation	What it means
accelerando	accel.	speeding up
rallentando	rall.	slowing down
ritenuto	rit.	holding back the pace
allargando	allarg.	slowing down, getting a bit broader
rubato	rub.	can be flexible with pace of music
⌢		pause — longer than a whole beat
a tempo		back to the original pace

To give the <u>impression</u> that the tempo has changed (without actually changing it), composers can use <u>augmentation</u> or <u>diminution</u>. Augmentation is where note lengths are <u>increased</u> in a melody (e.g. by <u>doubling</u> the length of every note — so a <u>crotchet</u> becomes a <u>minim</u>). This has the effect of making the music sound <u>slower</u>. Diminution is the <u>opposite</u> — note lengths are <u>shortened</u>, so the music sounds <u>faster</u>.

Mood is the **Overall** Feel of a Piece

The <u>mood</u> of a piece is usually described in Italian too.

> Sometimes parts are marked obbligato, which means they are <u>really important</u> and can't be missed out (obbligato means 'obligatory').

Italian word	What it means
agitato	agitated
alla marcia	in a march style
amoroso	loving
calmato	calm
dolce	sweetly
energico	energetic

Italian word	What it means
giocoso	playful, humorous
grandioso	grandly
pesante	heavy
risoluto	strong, confident, bold
sospirando	sighing
trionfale	triumphant

To describe the <u>overall mood</u> put the word at the beginning of the piece.

To describe a <u>change of mood</u> write the word under the stave.

Yes, you do have to learn it all — even the Italian bits...

When you're learning this page, start with words that sound a bit like English — they're easy.

Dynamics and Articulation

More ways for composers to tell players **exactly** how they want their music to sound...

Dynamic Markings Tell You How Loud or Quietly to Play

Music that was all played at the <u>same volume</u> would be pretty dull.
To get a <u>variety</u> of different volumes you can use these symbols:

Symbol	Stands for	What it means
pp	pianissimo	very quiet
p	piano	quiet
mp	mezzopiano	fairly quiet
mf	mezzoforte	fairly loud
f	forte	loud
ff	fortissimo	very loud
◁ (crescendo symbol)	crescendo	getting louder
▷ (diminuendo symbol)	diminuendo	getting quieter

You might also see dynamics combined together in other ways. E.g. *fp* means you play a sudden loud bit followed by a sudden quiet bit.

For more extreme dynamics, composers might use *ppp* or *fff* (or even *pppp* or *ffff*).

The markings go <u>underneath</u> the stave.

Crescendos and diminuendos are sometimes called <u>hairpins</u> when they're written like this.

Articulation Tells You How Much to Separate the Notes

In theory all the notes of a bar should add up to one <u>continuous</u> sound — but actually there are <u>tiny gaps</u> between them. If you <u>exaggerate</u> the gaps you get a <u>staccato</u> effect. If you smooth the gaps out, the notes sound <u>slurred</u>.

STACCATO — All the dotted notes are played slightly short.

SLUR — All the notes below or above the slur are played smoothly, with no breaks between.

<u>Tenuto</u> marks (<u>lines</u> above or below a note) tell you that a note should be held for its <u>full length</u>, or even played slightly <u>longer</u>.

If the articulation goes <u>all the way through</u> a piece, there's an overall instruction at the <u>beginning</u>.

If this piece was marked <u>legato</u> you would have to play smoothly all the way through.

Staccato

Nothing to do with articulated lorries then...

Don't just learn the symbols, learn what they're <u>called</u> too — it'll sound far more impressive if you write about the "dynamics" and "articulation" in your listening exam rather than "loudness and quietness".

More Instructions

Once a composer has told you how **fast** and how **loud** to play and how to **articulate** it, they sometimes put in **extra instructions**. Things like **accents**, **sforzandos** and **bends** make the music more **interesting**.

An **Accent Emphasises** a Note

1) An accent is a type of articulation that tells you to emphasise (or stress) a note.

2) On a wind instrument, this is often done by tonguing a note harder than normal.

3) Accents are usually written like this **>** or like this **∧**.

4) If a whole section should be accented, it can be marked '*marcato*' (which means 'marked').

5) A sforzando is a strongly accented note. It's shown by writing ***sfz*** or ***sf*** underneath the note.

6) A sforzando is often a sudden accent — e.g. a very loud note in a quiet section of a piece. This makes the music more dramatic.

A **Glissando** is a **Slide** Between Notes

1) A glissando is a slide from one note to another. Usually you're told which notes to start and finish on.

2) A glissando can be played effectively on a violin (or other string instrument), piano, harp, xylophone (or similar instrument), timpani and trombone. Other instruments can play them too, but they often won't sound as good.

3) On some instruments (e.g. piano, harp and xylophone), every note is played in the glissando. Think about it — if you were to play a glissando on a xylophone, you'd run your beater over every note, so they'd all be played.

4) On other instruments, like the trombone and strings, the notes you hear aren't fixed notes — the glissando covers all the tiny differences in pitch between the two notes. For example, you can't pick out individual notes in a glissando on the trombone.

> A portamento is similar to a glissando — it's more common in singing and on string instruments.

5) A glissando can be shown by writing *gliss.* underneath the stave, or by putting a line between two notes.

or

Notes can be **Bent**

- A bend (or bent note) changes the pitch of the note slightly — it sounds a bit like a wobble.
- They're often played by starting just above or below the note then bending to it.
- Bends are often used in jazz music.
- Bent notes can be played on most instruments — including guitars, trumpets, trombones and harmonicas. Singers can bend notes too.

COMPOSING TIP

Roundabouts, swings, climbing frames, glissandi...

All the things on this page are little extras composers can add to their music to make it more interesting — you could try adding some to your compositions too. I do love a good sforzando.

Warm-up and Exam Questions

Get your brain going with these warm-up questions before tackling the exam question below.

Warm-up Questions

1) Draw a 4-beat note, and write down its full name.

2) Draw a 4-beat rest.

3) Name the following notes and give the time value of each of them.

4) Explain the difference between a tie and a slur.

5) Look at the tempo words below. Write them out in order, fastest first.

Andante   Largo   Presto   Moderato   Allegro

Exam Question

Here's another exam-style question for you to try.

Play the following excerpt **three** times.
Leave a short pause between each playing of the excerpt.

Track 2

a) Listen to the rhythm of the opening melody.
Tick one feature that matches what you hear.

Staccato notes ☐

Triplets ☐

Dotted notes ☑

[1 mark]

Turn over

Exam Question

b) Which word best describes the tempo of this piece of music? Underline your answer.

largo   adagio   ~~andante~~   allegro

[1 mark]

c) Which word describes the dynamic at the opening? Underline your answer.

pianissimo   piano   forte   fortissimo

[1 mark]

d) Which of the following describes the mood of this excerpt? Tick the box.

agitato   ☑

dolce   ☐

energico   ☑

pesante   ☐

[1 mark]

Revision Summary for Section Two

That's it for Section Two — better test yourself to find out what you've learned.

- Try these questions and tick off each one when you get it right.
- When you've done all the questions for a topic and are completely happy with it, tick off the topic.

The Basics (p.8-11) ☑

1) Draw a stave with a bass clef at the beginning.
2) Which voices read music from the treble clef?
3) Name two instruments that read music from the bass clef.
4) What's the difference between the symbol for a treble clef and the symbol for the vocal tenor clef?
5) Where does middle C go on a vocal tenor clef?
6) Draw staves showing the C clef in both positions and write the correct name by each one.
7) Draw a sharp sign, a flat sign and a natural sign.
8) What does a sharp do to a note?
9) What does a flat do to a note?
10) Draw each of these signs and explain what you do if you see them by a note:
    a) a double sharp   b) a double flat
11) Draw a treble clef stave and add a key signature with one sharp.
12) What do you call a sharp, flat or natural sign when it's in the music but not in the key signature?

Time Signatures and Rhythms (p.12-14) ☑

13) What do you call the two numbers at the start of a piece of music?
14) What does the top number tell you about the beats?
15) What does the bottom number tell you about the beats?
16) When a time signature changes in a piece of music, where's the new one written?
17) What's the difference between simple and compound time?
18) What's the difference between regular and irregular metre?
19) What is meant by a cross-rhythm?

Types of Notes and Rests (p.16-17) ☑

20) Draw the symbol for each of the following notes and write down how many crotchet beats it lasts:
    a) semibreve   b) semiquaver   c) crotchet   d) quaver   e) minim
21) What does a dot immediately after a note or rest do?
22) What's the time value of:
    a) a dotted crotchet   b) a dotted minim   c) a dotted semibreve   d) a double dotted minim?
23) What does a 'tie' do?
24) How much time, in crotchet beats, does a crotchet triplet take up?

Musical Instructions (p.18-20) ☑

25) Where do you put the tempo marking on a stave?
26) Which is slower, *allegro* or *moderato*?
27) Where would you write the word *agitato* on the stave?
28) How does a composer show on the written music that the notes should be played smoothly?
29) How are accents usually indicated in a piece of music?
30) What's a glissando?

Major Scales

There are two main types of scales — **major** and **minor**. Once you've got the hang of how scales are put together, you should find keys and chords start to make a lot more sense.

Ordinary Scales have **Eight Notes**

The gap between the bottom and top notes of a scale is called an octave. See p.28.

1) An ordinary major (or minor) scale has 8 notes, starting and ending on notes of the same name, e.g. C major goes C, D, E, F, G, A, B, C.

2) Each of the eight notes has a name.

1st note	2nd note	3rd note	4th note	5th note	6th note	7th note	8th note
tonic	supertonic	mediant	subdominant	dominant	submediant	leading note	tonic
I	II	III	IV	V	VI	VII	VIII

3) You can just use the numbers or the Roman numerals to name the notes too.

Major Scales Sound **Bright** and Cheery

Whatever note they start on, all major scales sound similar, because they all follow the same pattern. This pattern is a set order of tone and semitone gaps between the notes:

I tone II tone III semitone IV tone V tone VI tone VII semitone VIII

This is how C major goes on a keyboard.

Major scales can start on any note, including the black notes, e.g. C♯ major.

All Major Scales Except C have **One or More Black Notes**

C major is the only major scale with no black notes.
All the others need at least one black note to stick to the 'tone-semitone' pattern.

- G major scale — you have to change F to F♯ to make the notes fit the major scale pattern.

- F major scale — you have to change B to B♭ to make the pattern right.

The **Set of Notes** in a **Scale** is Called a **Key**

1) The key tells you what sharps and flats there are (if any).

2) Most music sticks to one key. To show what key it's in, all the sharp or flat signs from the scale are written on the beginning of every stave of the piece. This is called the key signature.

3) A key signature can have sharps or flats but NEVER both.

4) If a piece changes key, it's called a modulation — see p.44.

The key signature goes between the clef and the time signature.

G major's got one sharp note — F♯. You put a sharp symbol on the F line.

Scales — dull but important...

Try playing some major scales starting on different notes. Even if you don't "know" them, you should be able to work out what the notes are, using the tone-semitone pattern and the sound. Give it a go.

Minor Scales

Minor scales have fixed patterns too. There are **three** different kinds you need to know.

Minor Scales All Sound a Bit Mournful

Minor scales sound <u>completely different</u> from major scales, because they've got a different tone-semitone pattern. There are <u>three</u> types of minor scale, and all of them sound a bit <u>mournful</u>.

1) The **Natural Minor** has the **Same Notes** as the **Relative Major**

These are easy. Start from the <u>sixth</u> note of any major scale. Carry on up to the same note an octave higher. You're playing a <u>natural minor scale</u>.

The sixth note of <u>C major</u> is <u>A</u>. If you play from <u>A to A</u> using the notes of C major, you're playing <u>A natural minor</u> (usually just called 'A minor').

Pairs of keys like <u>A minor and C major</u> are called "<u>relative</u>" keys.
A minor is the <u>relative minor</u> of C major.
C major is the <u>relative major</u> of A minor.

<u>All the notes</u> in a natural minor are <u>exactly the same</u> as the ones in the <u>relative major</u>. The <u>key signature's</u> exactly the same too.

2) The **Harmonic Minor** has **One Accidental**

- The <u>harmonic minor</u> has the same notes as the relative major, except for the <u>seventh note</u>.
- The <u>seventh</u> note is always raised by <u>one semitone</u>.
- You use the harmonic minor when you're writing <u>harmonies</u>. That <u>sharpened seventh note</u> makes the harmonies work much better than they would with notes from a natural minor. It's probably because it feels like it wants to move up to the <u>tonic</u>.

3) The **Melodic Minor** has **Two Accidentals**

- The <u>melodic minor</u> is just like a natural minor, using the notes from the relative major scale, <u>except for notes 6 and 7</u>.
- On the way <u>up</u>, notes <u>6</u> and <u>7</u> are each <u>raised</u> by <u>one semitone</u>.
- On the way <u>down</u>, the melodic minor goes just like the natural minor.

- The melodic minor is used for writing <u>melodies</u>. The accidental on note 6 makes tunes sound <u>smoother</u> by avoiding the big jump between notes 6 and 7 in the harmonic minor.

And not forgetting the Morris Minor...

All these scales have a <u>minor third</u> between the first and third notes in the scale — that's why they sound melancholy. You need to learn <u>all three</u> — names, notes and what they're used for.

The Circle of Fifths

The circle of fifths looks complicated but it's very **useful** once you understand how it works — it tells you **all the keys**, all the **relative keys** and their **key signatures**.

The **Circle of Fifths** Shows **All the Keys**

1) Altogether there are 12 major keys. They're all shown on the circle of fifths.
2) Don't expect to fully get it if this is the first time you've seen it. Just have a look, then read on.

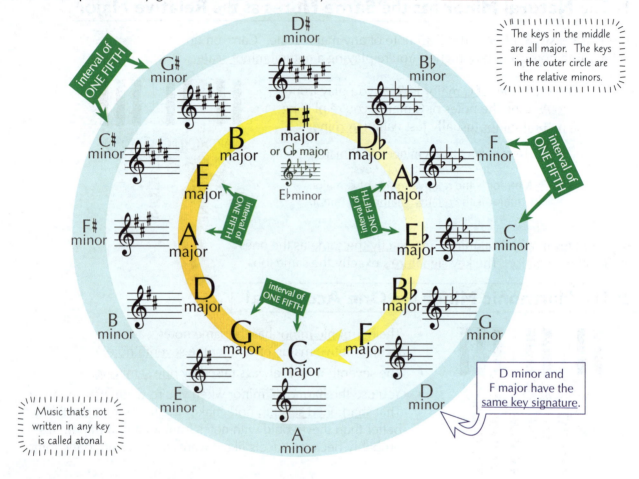

The keys in the middle are all major. The keys in the outer circle are the relative minors.

D minor and F major have the same key signature.

Music that's not written in any key is called atonal.

Each Key **Links** to the Next One

1) The circle starts with C major at the bottom. The next key round is G. G's the fifth note of C major.
2) The fifth note of G major is D, the next key on the circle. This pattern repeats all the way round. That's why the chart's called the circle of fifths.
3) As you go round the circle the number of sharps in the key signature goes up one for each key.
4) When you get to F♯ major at the top there are six sharps. From here, you start writing the key signature in flats — you don't need as many so it's clearer to read.
5) The number of flats keeps going down until you get back to C major, with no sharps and no flats.

The relative minors in the outer circle work just the same way as the major keys — the fifth note of A minor is E and the next minor key's E minor... and so on. Don't forget you can always work out the relative minor by counting up or down to the sixth note of a major scale, (see p.25) or the relative major by counting up to the third note of the minor scale.

Don't worry if it's making your head spin...

You need to be familiar with key signatures with up to four sharps or four flats (both major and minor). Don't worry too much about the others (but there's no harm in learning them too).

Modes and Other Types of Scale

Most music uses notes from a **major** or a **minor scale** — and they're the **most important** ones to learn, but there are a few **more unusual scales** and **modes** that you need to know about too.

Modes Follow Different Patterns of Tones and Semitones

Just like scales, you can start a mode on any note.

1) The most common mode is the one you get by playing a major scale (e.g. C major — just play the white notes on a keyboard from C to C). The pattern is tone-tone-semitone-tone-tone-tone-semitone.

2) Another mode can be formed by playing the notes of the same major scale, starting from the second note, e.g. D to D:

3) Starting on E gives you another mode...

This one is used a lot in flamenco music.

4) ...and so on. Each forms its own semitone / tone pattern and they all have different names. For example, G to G is the Mixolydian mode, and A to A is the Aeolian mode:

5) You don't need to know all the modes — it's more important that you can spot when something's modal. (E.g. the Mixolydian mode sounds like a major scale but with a flattened seventh.)

Pentatonic Scales are Used a Lot in Folk and Rock Music

Pentatonic scales use five notes. They're really easy to compose with, because there are no semitone steps — most combinations of notes sound fine. There are two types of pentatonic scale.

The major pentatonic uses notes 1, 2, 3, 5 and 6 of a major scale.

The minor pentatonic uses notes 1, 3, 4, 5 and 7 of the natural minor scale.

Whole Tone and Chromatic Scales Sound Spooky

Major and minor scales are known as diatonic scales.

Whole tone scales

Whole tone scales are pretty simple to remember — every step is a tone. From bottom to top there are only six notes in a whole tone scale.

Chromatic scales

Chromatic scales are fairly easy too. On a keyboard you play every white and black note until you get up to an octave above the note you started with. From bottom to top there are 12 notes. Basically, every step of a chromatic scale is a semitone.

You know the score...

Modal music could feature in the listening exam — for some examples of pieces written in modes, have a listen to the folk song Scarborough Fair, REM's Losing My Religion, and the theme tune to The Simpsons™. Modes are also used in some of the study pieces, e.g. Bartók and Spalding.

Intervals

Not the break halfway through a concert, but the **distance** between two notes.

An **Interval** is the **Gap** Between **Two Notes**

An interval is the <u>musical word</u> for the <u>gap</u> or <u>distance</u> between <u>two notes</u>.

Notes <u>close together</u> make <u>small</u> intervals. Notes <u>further apart</u> make <u>larger</u> intervals.

There are <u>two ways</u> of playing an interval.

Melodic interval
When one note <u>jumps</u> up or down to another note, you get a <u>melodic interval</u>.

ASCENDING interval   DESCENDING interval

Harmonic interval
When <u>two notes</u> are played at the <u>same time</u>, they make a <u>harmonic interval</u>.

- You can use the <u>melodic intervals</u> to describe the <u>pattern</u> of a <u>melody</u>.
- In some melodies, there are only <u>small</u> intervals between the notes — no bigger than a <u>tone</u>.
- When the notes are <u>close together</u> like this, the melody can be called <u>stepwise</u>, <u>conjunct</u> or <u>scalic</u> (because it moves up and down the notes of a <u>scale</u>).
- Tunes with <u>big</u> melodic intervals (larger than a tone) are called <u>disjunct</u>.

An Interval has **Two Parts** to its Name...

1) A <u>number</u>

an augmented fifth

2) A <u>description</u>

The **Number** Tells You **How Many Notes** the Interval Covers

1) You get the number by counting up the stave from the bottom note to the top note. You <u>include</u> the bottom and top notes in your counting.

2) C to E is a <u>third</u> because it covers <u>three letter names</u> — C, D and E.

3) C to F is a <u>fourth</u> because it covers <u>four letter names</u> — C, D, E and F.

4) The number of an interval is sometimes called the <u>interval quantity</u>.

The "description" bit is covered at the top of the next page...

The interval between G and D is a <u>fifth</u>.

G	A	B	C	D
1	2	3	4	5

An interval covering eight letters (e.g. A to A) is called an octave.

The interval between D and F sharp is a <u>third</u> (you can just <u>ignore</u> the accidentals when counting).

D	E	F♯
1	2	3

Intervals

The **Description** Tells You How the Interval **Sounds**

There are <u>five names</u> for the five main sounds:

> perfect   major   minor   diminished   augmented

1) To work out the <u>description part</u> of an interval's name, think of the <u>lower note</u> of the interval as the <u>first</u> note of a <u>major scale</u>.

2) If the top note of the interval is part of that major scale it's either <u>perfect</u> or <u>major</u>:

PERFECT	MAJOR	MAJOR	PERFECT	PERFECT	MAJOR	MAJOR	PERFECT
unison	2nd	3rd	4th	5th	6th	7th	octave

The perfect intervals are the ones that sound 'best' — the notes go together very cleanly.

3) If the top note <u>doesn't</u> belong to the major scale, then it's <u>minor</u>, <u>diminished</u> or <u>augmented</u>.
   If the interval is <u>one semitone LESS</u> than a <u>major interval</u>, then it's <u>minor</u>.
   If the interval is <u>one semitone LESS</u> than a <u>minor</u> or a <u>perfect interval</u>, then it's <u>diminished</u>.
   If the interval is <u>one semitone MORE</u> than a <u>major</u> or a <u>perfect interval</u>, then it's <u>augmented</u>.

Work Out the **Full Name** of an Interval **Step by Step**

1) **HOW MANY LETTER NAMES DOES IT COVER?**
   <u>Six</u> — G, A, B, C, D and E. So the <u>quantity</u> is a <u>sixth</u>.

2) **ARE THE NOTES FROM THE SAME MAJOR SCALE?**
   The bottom note's G. E <u>is</u> in G major — it's the <u>sixth</u> note.

3) **WHAT TYPE OF INTERVAL IS IT?**
   It's the <u>sixth note</u> of G major, and the sixth note always gives a major interval — so it's a <u>major sixth</u>.

1) **HOW MANY LETTER NAMES DOES IT COVER?**
   <u>Three</u> — C, D and E flat. So the <u>quantity</u> is a <u>third</u>.

2) **ARE THE NOTES FROM THE SAME MAJOR SCALE?**
   No.

3) **WHAT TYPE OF INTERVAL IS IT?**
   A third in the major scale is a <u>major</u> interval.
   This interval's one semitone smaller, so it's a <u>minor third</u>.

The **Tritone** Interval **Sounds Odd**

1) The tritone is an interval of <u>three tones</u>. It's <u>dissonant</u> — i.e. it sounds awkward, some would say terrible. It's used in some twentieth century Western art music.

2) <u>Diminished fifths</u> (e.g. G to D flat) and <u>augmented fourths</u> (e.g. G to C♯) are both <u>tritones</u>.

3) Try playing some, so you know what they <u>sound</u> like.

Take it one step at a time and you'll get there in the end...

The tritone interval used to be called '<u>the Devil's interval</u>' — because it has such an awkward, clashing sound. It's supposed to be unlucky, so use it in your composition at your own risk...

Examples

You need to <u>hear</u> the difference between different types of scales and chords. Tracks 3-9 are practical examples of the theory on pages 24-29. Listen to the tracks as you read the info below.

Examples

Tracks 3-9

Track 3   A <u>major scale</u>, with <u>F♯</u> as the tonic, played over two octaves. *(see p.24)*
Try writing out the notes of the scale on a stave. Remember — TTSTTTS.

Track 4   The <u>three</u> different types of <u>minor scale</u> with <u>D</u> as the tonic. *(see p.25)*
     a) The <u>natural minor</u> scale
     b) The <u>harmonic minor</u>
     c) The <u>melodic minor</u>

Track 5   The two different types of pentatonic scale. *(see p.27)*
     a) <u>Major pentatonic</u> scale starting on <u>C</u>
     b) <u>Minor pentatonic</u> scale starting on <u>A</u>
     These are relative scales, and because they're pentatonic all the notes are the same.

Track 6   A <u>whole tone</u> scale. *(see p.27)*
     It starts off like the major scale, but the 4th and 5th notes are further apart (<u>harmonically distant</u>) than in a major scale, so it sounds odd.

Track 7   A <u>chromatic</u> scale. *(see p.27)*
     This one starts on <u>G</u>, but all <u>chromatic</u> scales use all the notes, so they sound nearly the same.

Track 8   The <u>major</u> and <u>perfect</u> intervals. *(see p.29)*
     They're played at the same time so they're <u>harmonic</u>.

Track 9   The <u>minor</u> and <u>diminished intervals</u>. *(see p.29)*
     a) Minor 2nd
     b) Augmented 2nd / minor 3rd
     c) Augmented 4th / diminished 5th
     d) Augmented 5th / minor 6th
     e) Augmented 6th / minor 7th

Practice Questions

Now check you've got the hang of it all with these practice questions.

Practice Questions

Track 10 Listen to the four different types of scale. What are they?

a) ....

b) ....

c) ....

d) ....

You can play these tracks more than once — some of them are quite tricky.

Tracks 10-13

Track 11 What type of scale does this tune use?

....

Track 12 Listen to these harmonic intervals. Write down what each of them is called.

a) .... b) ....

c) .... d) ....

e) .... f) ....

g) .... h) ....

Track 13 Now name these melodic intervals.

a) .... b) ....

c) .... d) ....

e) .... f) ....

g) .... h) ....

Warm-up and Exam Questions

Time for another round of questions...

Warm-up Questions

1) How many notes would you find in a normal scale?

2) What does a key or key signature tell you about the music?

3) What do the scales of C major and A minor have in common?

4) Name the **three** types of minor scales.

5) Which mode is formed by playing the white notes from G to G?

6) Which scale uses only notes 1, 2, 3, 5 and 6 from the major scale?

7) Why is a chromatic scale unusual?

8) What type of interval is formed when two notes are played together at the same time?

9) Which is smaller, a minor 7th or a diminished 7th?

Exam Question

This exam-style question includes a couple of questions on intervals to test your knowledge.

Play the excerpt **three** times. Leave a short pause between each playing.

 Track 14

Track 14

a)   Here are the first three bars.

Exam Question

    i)   How many beats are there in a bar?

....

[1 mark]

    ii)   What is the interval between the notes highlighted in red at letter **a**?

....

[1 mark]

    iii)   What is the interval between the two lower notes in the
           left-hand chord indicated at letter **b**?

....

[1 mark]

b)   What key is this excerpt in?

....

[1 mark]

c)   What does the mark ⁻ above a note tell the performer to do?

....

[1 mark]

Chords — The Basics

A **chord** is two or more notes played together. Chords are great for writing **accompaniments**.

Only **Some** Instruments **Play Chords**

Don't play chords.

Do play chords.

1) A lot of instruments only play <u>one note at a time</u> — flutes, recorders, trumpets, clarinets, trombones... You can't play a chord with one note, so these instruments <u>don't</u> play chords.

2) You can <u>only</u> play chords on <u>instruments</u> that play <u>more than one</u> note at a time. <u>Keyboards</u> and guitars are both great for playing chords — you can easily play several notes together.

3) Other <u>stringed instruments</u> like violins and cellos can play chords, but not very easily, so chords are only played from time to time.

Some Chords Sound **Great**, Others Sound **Awful**

1) The notes of some chords <u>go together</u> really well — like apple pie and ice-cream.

When you have nice-sounding chords it's called <u>CONCORDANCE</u> or <u>CONSONANCE</u>.

2) Other chords have <u>clashing notes which disagree</u> — more like apple pie and pickled eggs.

When you have horrible-sounding chords it's called <u>DISCORDANCE</u> or <u>DISSONANCE</u>.

The **Best-Sounding** Chords are Called **Triads**

- You can play <u>any</u> set of notes and make a chord — but most of them sound <u>harsh</u>.
- An <u>easy, reliable</u> way of getting nice-sounding chords is to play <u>triads</u>.
- Triads are chords made up of three notes, with <u>set intervals</u> between them.
- Once you know the intervals, you can easily play <u>dozens</u> of decent chords.

How to make a triad...

1) On a piano, start with any white note — this is called the <u>root note</u>. You <u>build</u> the triad <u>from the root</u>.

2) Count the root as 'first' and the next white note to the <u>right</u>, as 'second'. The <u>third</u> note you reach is the <u>third</u> — the middle note of the triad.

3) Keep counting up and you get to the <u>fifth</u> — the final note of the triad.

4) The intervals between the notes are <u>thirds</u>.

5) If the root note's a <u>B</u>, then you end up with a <u>B triad</u>. If the root note's a <u>C</u>, you end up with a <u>C triad</u>.

6) You can build triads on black notes too, so long as the intervals between notes are <u>thirds</u>.

FIFTH
THIRD
ROOT

C E G

COMPOSING TIP

Good things come in threes...

The next six pages will be useful when it comes to writing your compositions. You'll need to think about which instruments can play chords, and which notes sound nice together.

Triads

There's more than one type of triad...

Triads Use Major and Minor Thirds

1) All triads have an interval of a third between each pair of notes.

2) The intervals can be major or minor thirds.

A major third is four semitones.

A minor third is three semitones.

3) Different combinations of major and minor thirds give different types of triad:

Major triads

- Major triads have a major third followed by a minor third.
- The major third goes between the root and the third.
- The minor third goes between the third and the fifth.

Minor triads

- Minor triads use a major and a minor third too, but in the opposite order.
- The minor third goes between the root and the third.
- The major third goes between the third and the fifth.

DIMINISHED TRIADS use two minor thirds.
AUGMENTED TRIADS use two major thirds.

These two kinds aren't nearly as common as major and minor triads.

You Can Add a Note to a Triad to Get a 7th Chord

1) 7th chords are triads with a fourth note added — the seventh note above the root.
2) The interval between the root and the 7th can be a major seventh or a minor seventh — see p.29.

These Symbols Stand for Chords

A special notation is used to represent the various chords. For a triad starting on a C:

C = C major

Caug or **C+** = augmented C chord

C7 = C major with added minor 7th

Cmaj7 = C major with added major 7th

Cm = C minor

Cdim or **C-** or **Co** = diminished C chord

Cm7 = C minor with added minor 7th

Cm maj7 = C minor with added major 7th

For chords other than C, just change the first letter to show the root note.

It's not as hard as it looks and it's VERY useful...

If you play the guitar or play in a band you need to learn these symbols right now. Even if you only ever play classical music they're still worth learning — they're really useful as shorthand.

Fitting Chords to a Melody

There are some basic rules about fitting chords to a melody:
No.1: All the notes in the chords have got to be in the **same key** as the notes in the melody.

The **Melody** and **Chords** Must be in the **Same Key**

1) A melody that's composed in a certain key sticks to that key.
2) The chords used to harmonise with the melody have got to be in the same key or it'll clash.
3) As a general rule each chord in a harmony should include the note it's accompanying, e.g. a C could be accompanied by a C chord (C, E, G), an F chord (F, A, C) or an A minor chord (A, C, E).

There's a Chord for **Every Note** in the **Scale**

You can make dozens of triads using the notes of major and minor scales as the roots. Every note of every chord, not just the root, has to belong to the scale. This is how C major looks if you turn it into chords:

The odd accidental or ornament in a different key is OK — see p.41.

Chord I	Chord II	Chord III	Chord IV	Chord V	Chord VI	Chord VII	Chord I
Tonic	Supertonic	Mediant	Subdominant	Dominant	Submediant	Leading Note	Tonic

- Chords I, IV and V are major triads. They sound bright and cheery.
  A 7th can be added to chord V to give a dominant 7th chord (written V^7).
- Chords II, III and VI are minor triads. They sound more gloomy.
- Chord VII is a diminished triad. It sounds different from the major and minor chords. Another name for Chord VII is the leading note chord — it sounds like it should lead on to another chord.
- Chords built on any major scale, not just C major, follow the same pattern.
- A series of chords is known as a harmonic progression (also called a chord progression or chord sequence).
- The speed at which the chords change is called the harmonic rhythm.

The **Primary Chords** are Most **Useful**

1) The three major chords, I, IV and V, are the most important in any key. They're called primary chords. Between them, the primary chords can harmonise with any note in the scale.
2) This is how it works in C major:

Minor Chords Make Harmony **More Interesting**

1) Primary chords can get a bit boring to listen to after a while — the harmonies are fairly simple.
2) Composers often mix in a few of the other chords — II, III, VI or VII — for a change.
3) Instead of just having endless major chords, you get a mixture of minor and diminished chords too.

Inversions

Inverting triads means **changing the order** of the notes. It make accompaniments more **varied**.

Triads with the **Root** at the **Bottom** are in **Root Position**

These triads are all in <u>root position</u> — the <u>root note</u> is at the bottom.

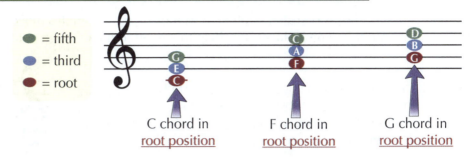

● = fifth
● = third
● = root

C chord in <u>root position</u>   F chord in <u>root position</u>   G chord in <u>root position</u>

First Inversion Triads have the **Third** at the **Bottom**

These chords are all in <u>first inversion</u>. The root note's moved up an octave, leaving the <u>third</u> at the bottom.

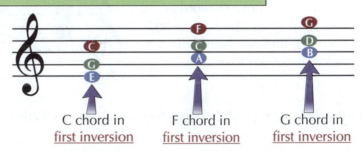

C chord in <u>first inversion</u>   F chord in <u>first inversion</u>   G chord in <u>first inversion</u>

Second Inversion Triads have the **Fifth** at the **Bottom**

Chords can be played in <u>second inversion</u> too.

From the first inversion, the third is raised an octave, leaving the <u>fifth</u> at the bottom.

C chord in <u>second inversion</u>   F chord in <u>second inversion</u>   G chord in <u>second inversion</u>

7th Chords Can Go into a **Third Inversion**

1) 7th chords can be played in root position, first inversion or second inversion — just like triads.

2) But there's also a <u>third inversion</u> — where the <u>7th</u> goes <u>below</u> the standard triad. They have a third inversion because they're <u>four-note</u> chords.

There's a **Symbol** for Each **Inversion**

This means a C chord with E at the bottom.

ROOT POSITION		5/3 chords	because there's a <u>fifth</u> and a <u>third</u> between the notes		Ia	C
FIRST INVERSION	...also known as...	6/3 chords	because there's a <u>sixth</u> and a <u>third</u> between the notes	...and in Roman numerals...	Ib	C/E
SECOND INVERSION		6/4 chords	because there's a <u>sixth</u> and a <u>fourth</u> between the notes		Ic	C/G
THIRD INVERSION		6/4/2 chords	because there's a <u>sixth</u>, a <u>fourth</u> and a <u>second</u> between the notes	...and in good old chord symbols...	Id	Cmaj7/B

These numbers are used in figured bass — see page 57.

Section Three — Keys, Scales and Chords

Inversions

So now you know what inversions **are**. Now get to grips with what to **do** with them too...

Inversions are Handy for **Moving Between Chords**

When you play chords one after another, it sounds <u>nicer</u> if the notes move <u>smoothly</u> from one chord to the next. Inversions help to smooth out any rough patches...

1) Moving from a <u>C chord in root position</u> to a <u>G chord in root position</u> means <u>all</u> the notes have to jump a <u>long way</u>. It sounds <u>clumsy</u> and not all that nice.

Try playing both sets of chords a few times, until you can hear the difference.

2) If you move from a C chord in root position to a <u>G chord</u> in <u>first inversion</u> instead, the transition is much, much smoother.

3) You can use <u>second</u> and <u>third inversions</u> too — whatever sounds best.

Unscramble the **Inversion** to Work Out the **Root Note**

This isn't exactly a life-saving skill. But it's <u>dead useful</u>...

If you come across an inverted chord you can <u>work out</u> which is the <u>root note</u>. Once you know that, and you know what <u>key</u> you're in, you can tell whether it's chord IV, VII, II or whatever.

1) Basically you have to turn the chord back into a <u>root position triad</u>.
2) Shuffle the order of the notes around until there's a <u>third interval</u> between each one.
3) When the notes are arranged in <u>thirds</u>, the root will <u>always</u> be at the <u>bottom</u>.

B to D is a THIRD, but D to G is a FOURTH.
You need to <u>move the G</u> to find the root chord.

G to B is a THIRD so the G goes here — <u>G</u>'s the <u>root note</u>.

4) There are no sharps or flats in the key signature, so the piece is in C major. G's the fifth note of C major, so this is <u>chord V</u>.

Unscramble inversions — go back to your roots...

There's a lot to take in when it comes to inversions. Don't go racing through this page — go over it one bit at a time, letting all the facts sink in. Playing the chords for yourself will help.

Different Ways of Playing Chords

So far, the chords in this section have all been written as three notes. It sounds dull if you do it all the time. To liven things up there are **chord figurations** — different ways of playing the chords.

Block Chords are the Most Basic

This is probably the easiest way to play chords.
The notes of each chord are played all together and then held until the next chord.

Rhythmic Chords Give You Harmony and Rhythm

1) Rhythmic chords are chords played to a funky rhythm.
2) You play all the notes of each chord at the same time, like you do for block chords.
3) You don't hold the notes though — you play them to a rhythm that repeats in each bar.
4) Rhythm guitar and keyboards often play rhythmic chords.

In Broken and Arpeggiated Chords the Notes are Separate

Accompanying chords don't have to have to be played at all once. You can play the notes separately.

1) Here's one way of doing it — it goes root, fifth, third, root.

2) This pattern was really popular around the time Mozart was alive (last half of the 1700s). It's called Alberti bass after the composer Domenico Alberti — it usually goes root, fifth, third, fifth.

3) The notes of a chord are sometimes played in order (e.g. root, third, fifth, root) going up or coming down. This is called an arpeggio (are-pedge-ee-o).

4) In an arpeggiated chord, you play the notes one at a time, but in quick succession (imagine strumming a harp). On a piano, you hold down each key as you build up the chord. They're usually written with a wiggly line, like this:

5) A walking bass usually moves in crotchets, often either in steps (see p.28) or arpeggios.
6) A drone is a long, held-on note, usually in the bass, that adds harmonic interest.
7) Pedal notes are a bit different — they're repeated notes, again usually in the bass part. However, the harmony on top of a pedal note changes (whereas a drone sets up the harmony for the whole piece).

Think about using an Alberti bass in your composition...

When you get chord symbols over the music you can play the chords any way you like.
Try all these ways of playing chords and think about using them in your compositions.

Examples and Practice

Read on for some more examples of the different kinds of chords.

Examples

Track 15 These are some of the most <u>common</u> chords — learn to recognise them.

a) <u>major</u> triad   b) <u>minor</u> triad

c) <u>diminished</u> triad   d) <u>augmented</u> triad

e) <u>major</u> triad with a <u>major</u> 7th   f) <u>major</u> triad with a <u>minor</u> 7th

g) <u>minor</u> triad with a <u>major</u> 7th   h) <u>minor</u> triad with a <u>minor</u> 7th

Track 16 A <u>sequence</u> of chords, showing different <u>inversions</u>:

What inversion a chord is depends on which note is on the bottom — it doesn't matter how the other notes of the triad are arranged on top.

In these first <u>three</u> chords, chords in the <u>first inversion</u> lead nicely on to <u>root chords</u> a <u>perfect 4th</u> up. The <u>semitone</u> steps in the bass make these progressions sound smooth and logical.

At the <u>end</u> of the sequence, listen out for the <u>third from last</u> note (<u>second inversion</u> of <u>chord I</u>), which leads into the <u>cadence</u> that ends the phrase (see p.42-43 for more on cadences).

How well do you know your chords... Find out by answering these practice questions.

Practice Questions

Track 17 Describe each of the eight chords on the track, using one of the following words:

You can play these tracks more than once.

major	minor	diminished	augmented

a) ....   b) ....   c) ....

d) ....   e) ....   f) ....

g) ....   h) ....

Track 18 For each of the following you'll hear a root note, and then an inversion. Which inversions are they?

a) ....   b) ....   c) ....

d) ....   e) ....   f) ....

g) ....   h) ....

Using Decorations to Vary the Harmony

If you want to **liven things up** in a harmony, you can add a sprinkle of **melodic decoration**.

Melodic Decoration **Adds Notes** to the Tune

1) <u>Decorative notes</u> are <u>short notes</u> that move between notes or create <u>fleeting clashes</u> (<u>dissonance</u>) with the accompanying chord. They make things sound <u>less bland</u>.

2) Decoration that belongs to the key of the melody (e.g. B in C major) is called <u>diatonic</u>.

3) Decoration that <u>doesn't</u> belong to the key (e.g. F♯ in C major) is called <u>chromatic</u>.

4) There are <u>four</u> main ways of adding melodic decoration.

1) **Auxiliary** Notes are **Higher** or **Lower** than the Notes **Either Side**

- An auxiliary note is either a <u>semitone</u> or <u>tone</u> <u>above</u> or <u>below</u> the notes either side.

- The two notes before and after the auxiliary are always the <u>same pitch</u>, and always belong to the accompanying chord.

2) **Passing** Notes **Link** the Notes **Before** and **After**

- A passing note <u>links</u> the notes before and after. They either belong to the same chord or link one chord with another.

- They're usually put on <u>weak beats</u>. When they <u>are</u> on the strong beat they're called '<u>accented passing notes</u>'.

3) **Appoggiaturas Clash** with the Chord

- An appoggiatura <u>clashes</u> with the accompanying chord. It's written as a <u>little note</u> tied to the note of the chord, and takes <u>half the value</u> of the note it's tied to.

- The note <u>before</u> it is usually quite a <u>leap</u> away (jumps between notes of more than a <u>2nd</u> are called <u>leaps</u>).

- The note after the appoggiatura is always <u>just above</u> or <u>below</u>. It's called the <u>resolution</u>. The <u>resolution</u> has to be from the <u>accompanying chord</u>.

- Appoggiaturas usually fall on a <u>strong beat</u>, so the resolution note falls on a <u>weaker beat</u>.

4) **Suspensions Clash** then Go Back to **Harmonising**

A suspension is a series of three notes called the <u>preparation</u>, <u>suspension</u> and <u>resolution</u>.

- The <u>preparation</u> note belongs to the accompanying chord. It's usually on a weak beat.

- The <u>suspension</u> is the <u>same pitch</u> as the preparation note. It's played at the same time as a <u>chord change</u>. It <u>doesn't go</u> with the new chord, so you get <u>dissonance</u>.

- The <u>resolution</u> note moves up or down (usually down) from the suspension to a note in the accompanying chord. This <u>resolves</u> the dissonance — everything sounds lovely again.

Phrases and Cadences

Notes in a melody fall into '**phrases**' just like the words in a story are made up of **sentences**.
A **cadence** is the movement from the second-to-last to the last chord of a **phrase** — it **finishes it off**.

A **Phrase** is Like a Musical '**Sentence**'

There should be clear <u>phrases</u> in any melody. A tune <u>without</u> phrases would
sound odd — just like a story with no sentences wouldn't make much sense.

1) Phrases are usually <u>two</u> or <u>four</u> bars long.

2) Phrases are sometimes marked with a <u>curved
line</u> called a <u>phrase mark</u>, that goes <u>above</u>
the stave. Not all music has phrase marks but
the phrases are <u>always</u> there. Don't confuse
phrase marks and slurs. A phrase mark
<u>doesn't</u> change how you play the notes.

Cadences Emphasise the End of a Phrase

1) A <u>cadence</u> is the <u>shift</u> between the <u>second-to-last chord</u> and the <u>last chord</u> in a phrase.

2) The <u>effect</u> you get from shifting between the two chords works like a <u>comma</u> or a <u>full stop</u>.
It <u>underlines</u> the end of the phrase and <u>gets you ready</u> for the next one.

These <u>last two chords</u> make the cadence.

There are **Four Main Types** of Cadence

These pairs of chords are <u>only</u> cadences when they come at the end of a phrase.
Anywhere else in a phrase, they're <u>just chords</u>.

Second Last Chord	Last Chord	Cadence
Chord V	Chord I	PERFECT
Chord IV	Chord I	PLAGAL
Chord I, II or IV	Chord V	IMPERFECT
Chord V	any except Chord I, (usually Chord VI)	INTERRUPTED

More on these on the next page…

Cadences

Learning the **names** of the different cadences is no use unless you also learn what they're **for**.

Perfect and Plagal Cadences Work Like Full Stops

1) A perfect cadence makes a piece of music feel finished or complete.
2) It goes from Chord V to Chord I — in C major that's a G chord to a C chord.
3) This is how a perfect cadence goes at the end of 'Twinkle, Twinkle, Little Star':

Here's the perfect cadence.

4) A plagal cadence sounds really different from a perfect cadence but it has a similar effect — it makes a piece of music sound finished.
5) A plagal cadence in C major is an F chord (IV) to a C chord (I). Play it and see what it sounds like. The plagal cadence gets used at the end of lots of hymns — it's sometimes called the 'Amen' cadence.

Imperfect and Interrupted Cadences are Like Commas

Imperfect and interrupted cadences are used to end phrases but not at the end of a piece. They work like commas — they feel like a resting point but not an ending.

An imperfect cadence most commonly goes from chord I, II or IV to V.
Here's one going from chord I to chord V at the end of the third line of 'Twinkle, Twinkle':

Here's the imperfect cadence.

In an interrupted cadence chord V can go to any chord except I, but it usually goes to chord VI. You expect it to go to chord I — so it sounds "interrupted". In C major an interrupted cadence may go from a G chord (V) to an Am chord (VI).

Some Minor pieces Finish with a Tierce de Picardie

1) If a piece of music is in a minor key, you'd expect it to finish with a minor chord.
2) However, some composers (especially Baroque composers) finish a minor piece with a major chord, by using a major third in the last chord. This is known as a Tierce de Picardie (or Picardy third).

This excerpt is from Scarlatti's Piano Sonata in G Minor (Cat's Fugue). Even though the piece is in G minor, it finishes with a G major chord.

REVISION TIP

You need to listen to cadences to understand them...

Cadences probably won't make much sense unless you try playing them. Play the cadences for yourself (or listen to Track 19 — see p.48) until you can hear the differences between them.

Modulation

Most of the notes in a piece of music come from one key — but to vary the melody or harmony you can **modulate** (change key). It can happen just once, or a few times. It's up to the composer.

The **Starting Key** is Called '**Home**'

1) The key a piece starts out in is called the home key or tonic key.
2) If the music's modulated it goes into a different key.
3) The change of key is usually only temporary. The key goes back to the home key after a while.
4) However much a piece modulates, it usually ends in the home key.

There are **Two** Ways to Modulate

1) Modulation by **Pivot Chord**

- A pivot chord is a chord that's in the home key and the key the music modulates to.
- Chord V (G, B, D) in C major is exactly the same as chord I in G major — so it can be used to pivot between C major and G major.
- Sometimes, the key signature changes to show the new key.
  More often, accidentals are written in the music where they're needed.

The home key here is C.
At the end of the first bar the accompaniment uses the chord G, B, D to pivot into G major:

Pivot chord

F♯ belongs to G major.

This is called a V/I pivot because it uses V from the home key and I from the key it modulates to.

Related keys...

1) It sounds best if you modulate to related keys.
2) The closest keys are (major) keys IV and V and the relative minor.
3) The next closest are the relative minors of keys IV and V.

| Relative minor of **IV**
D minor | | **IV**
F major | | Home key
I
C major | | **V**
G major | | Relative minor of **V**
E minor |

Relative minor
A minor

2) **Abrupt** Modulation

- In abrupt modulation there's no pivot chord, and no other preparation either. It just happens.
- Often the modulation is between two keys just one semitone apart, e.g. from C major to C♯ major.
- Pop songs often modulate up one semitone. It creates a sudden, dramatic effect — it's meant to give the music an excited, uplifting feeling.

You can choose related keys but you can't choose your family...

If you see accidentals it often means the music's modulated, but not always. The accidental could also be there because: 1) the music's written in a minor key — harmonic or melodic (see p.25); or 2) the composer fancied a spot of chromatic decoration (see p.41). That's composers for you...

Texture

Here's one last way composers vary the harmony — by changing the **texture**. Texture's an odd word to use about music — what it means is how the different parts (e.g. chords and melody) are **woven together**.

Texture is How the parts Fit Together

- An important part of music is how the <u>different parts</u> are <u>woven together</u>.
  This is known as <u>texture</u> — it describes how the <u>melody</u> and <u>accompaniment</u> parts <u>fit together</u>.
- <u>Monophonic</u>, <u>homophonic</u> and <u>polyphonic</u> are all different types of texture.
- Some textures are made up of the <u>same</u> melodic line that's passed round <u>different parts</u>.
  <u>Imitation</u> and <u>canons</u> are good examples of this.

Monophonic Music is the Simplest

1) In <u>monophonic</u> music there's <u>no harmony</u> — just one line of tune (e.g. a <u>solo</u> with <u>no accompaniment</u>).
2) Parts playing in <u>unison</u> or <u>doubling</u> each other (i.e. the same notes at the same time) are also monophonic.
3) Monophonic music has a <u>thin texture</u>.

Polyphonic Music Weaves Tunes Together

- <u>Polyphonic</u> music gives quite a complex effect because there's <u>more than one tune</u> being played at once.

- It's sometimes called <u>contrapuntal</u> music.
- Parts that move in <u>contrary motion</u> (one goes <u>up</u> and another goes <u>down</u>) are polyphonic.
- <u>Two-part music</u> (with two separate melodic lines) is also polyphonic.

In Homophonic Music, the Parts Move Together

1) If the lines of music move at more or less the <u>same time</u>, it's <u>homophonic</u> music.
2) <u>Parallel motion</u> (when parts move with the <u>same interval</u> between them, e.g. parallel 5ths) is also homophonic.
3) If the melody line is <u>independent</u> and plays a <u>different rhythm</u> to the accompaniment, this texture is known as <u>melody with accompaniment</u> (it's <u>different</u> to homophony).

In Heterophonic Music the Instruments Share the Tune

In heterophonic music there's <u>one tune</u>. <u>All</u> the instruments play it, but with <u>variations</u>, and often at <u>different times</u>.

Polyphonic, homophonic and heterophonic music all have quite a thick texture.

You might have to write about texture in the exam...

Make sure you know all the proper words to describe texture, and that you can tell the difference between the different types — examiners love asking about it so it'll come in handy...

Texture

When there's **one** part, the music's **pure** and **simple**, but put **more parts in** and it's much more **complex**.

Imitation — Repeat a Phrase With **Slight Changes**

1) In imitation a phrase is repeated with slight changes each time.

2) It works particularly well if one instrument or voice imitates another and then overlaps.

Canon — **Same Melody** Different Parts

1) In a canon, each part plays the same melody, but they come in separately and at regular intervals. The parts overlap.

2) A canon is also known as a round. There are some really well-known rounds, e.g. 'London's Burning'.

3) Canons are an example of contrapuntal (or polyphonic) music (see previous page).

4) Composers from the Baroque period (1600-1750) like Bach and Vivaldi used lots of canons.

This excerpt comes from 'Spring' from Vivaldi's Four Seasons. The solo violin and first violin often play in canon.

Another common Baroque texture is the continuo (or basso continuo) — see p.57.

Looping and Layering are Modern Techniques

1) In the 1960s and 70s, composers like Steve Reich started developing new techniques in their music.

2) They took recordings of sections of music, words, rhythms and other sounds and repeated them over and over again. These are called loops.

3) The loops were often created by cutting pieces of tape and sticking the ends together so they could be played over and over again — this is looping.

4) If there are lots of different loops being played at the same time it's called layering.

A layer of fruit, a layer of sponge, a layer of custard...

There are a few more words on this page that'll be useful if you need to write about musical texture in the listening exam — imitation, canon, looped and layered. Make sure you know what they mean.

Texture

Composers use **different textures** to **vary** their music. They can change the **number** of instruments and whether they play the **same notes** or in **harmony**. They can also **split** tunes between **different instruments**.

More Than One Part Can Play the Same Melody

1) If there's just <u>one part</u> playing with <u>no accompaniment</u>, there's just a <u>single melody line</u>.

2) If there's <u>more than one</u> instrument playing the <u>same melody</u> at the <u>same pitch</u>, they're playing in <u>unison</u>.

3) If there's <u>more than one</u> instrument playing the <u>same notes</u> but in <u>different ranges</u>, they're playing in <u>octaves</u>.

All of these are examples of monophonic textures.

Some Instruments Play Accompanying Parts

1) The instruments that <u>aren't</u> playing the tune play the <u>accompaniment</u>. Different <u>types</u> of accompaniment give different <u>textures</u>.

2) If the accompaniment is playing <u>chords</u> underneath the melody with the <u>same rhythm</u> as the melody but <u>different notes</u>, the texture is <u>homophonic</u>. It sounds <u>richer</u> than a single melody line, unison or octaves.

3) If there are <u>two choirs</u> singing at <u>different times</u>, the music is <u>antiphonal</u>. The two choirs will often sing <u>alternate phrases</u> — like <u>question and answer</u> or <u>call and response</u>. A lot of <u>early religious vocal music</u> was antiphonal. You can also get the same effect with two groups of <u>instruments</u>.

Group 1
Group 2

4) If there's <u>more than one</u> part playing <u>different melodies</u> at the <u>same time</u>, the music is <u>contrapuntal</u> (or <u>polyphonic</u>). Contrapuntal parts <u>fit together</u> harmonically.

The examples on this page use the melody from Handel's 'Water Music'.

REVISION TIP

Would you care to accompany me to the cinema...

There are quite a few tricky <u>textures</u> to learn on this page. Listen to the different types, and try and <u>recognise</u> what they sound like so that you can describe them if they come up in the <u>exam</u>.

Examples

Track 19 should help you get a better idea about cadences, and Track 20 gives you some different examples of modulation. Listen to them lots of times until you can recognise them straight away.

Examples

Track 19 You'll hear this bar played **four** times, followed by a different cadence each time.

Tracks 19-20

a) The perfect cadence sounds totally complete — perfect, in fact. You can't imagine it moving on to any other chord.

V   I
a   a

b) The plagal cadence is sometimes called the "amen cadence" — it sounds peaceful and reassuring.

IV   I
a   a

c) The imperfect cadence is the opposite of the perfect cadence. Instead of bringing things to a close, it seems to open up loads of possibilities.

I   V
c   a

d) The interrupted cadence starts off like a perfect cadence but ends with a more open, melancholy feel.

V   VI
a   a

Track 20 Listen to these **three** short excerpts. Each one is a different example of a modulation from one key to another. In each excerpt the pattern goes like this:

Note 1 Original key

Note 2 Original key

Note 3 Pivot chord (in the original key and the new key)

Note 4 New key

Practice Questions

Practise your hard-won knowledge of chords, modulation and texture with the questions on this page and the next. Listen to each track a few times to make sure you've heard it properly.

 Track 21 This question is about identifying cadences. You will hear eight phrases, a)-h), all starting like this:

Tracks 21-23

Write down whether the final cadence is perfect, plagal, imperfect or interrupted.

a) ....

b) ....

c) ....

d) ....

e) ....

f) ....

g) ....

h) ....

 Track 22 *For each of the following tracks, fill in the missing notes in the melody, then answer the questions.*

a)

b) The chord in the fourth bar has an A in the bass.
What inversion of chord I is this?

....

c) What type of cadence does the passage end with?

....

Track 23 a)

b) In this passage, the harmony tends to move in time with the melody.
What is the name of this type of musical texture?

....

c) What type of cadence does the passage end with?

....

d) Which note is sustained in the bass in the second-to-last bar?

....

Section Three — Keys, Scales and Chords

Practice Questions

Practice Questions

Tracks
24-26

b) In the first chord in bar 2, the left hand plays the major of chord II. Which note in this chord is not in the scale of the home key?

....

c) What type of cadence does the passage end with?

....

b) Circle each auxiliary note in the passage, and say whether each is diatonic or chromatic.

c) Which one of the following best describes the chord in bar 4? Ring your answer.

     1st inversion   **harmonic**   **relative minor**   **suspension**

b) What key does this passage start in?

....

c) What key does it finish in?

....

d) The B flat chord at the start of bar 3 comes before the dominant chord of the new key. Give the name of a chord in this position in a modulation.

....

e) Fill in the blanks in the following sentence with the appropriate Roman numerals:

The B flat chord is chord .... in the home key

and chord .... in the final key.

Warm-up and Exam Questions

Warm-up Questions

1) Name **two** instruments that are frequently used to play chords.

2) Which **three** chords in a major key produce major triads?

3) If the *root* of a chord is on the top, and the *third* of the chord is on the bottom, which inversion is the chord in?

4) Name **three** different ways of playing chords.

5) What do you call a melodic decoration that belongs to the same key as the main melody?

6) List **three** ways melodies can be decorated to help vary the harmony within a piece of music.

7) At what point in a piece of music would you expect to find an imperfect or interrupted cadence?

8) What's another name for the texture known as polyphonic?

Exam Question

Now practise your exam technique with the question below and over the page.

Track 27

Play the excerpt **four times** then answer the questions on the next page.

Leave a short pause for writing time before each playing.

Here is the complete score for the excerpt:

Exam Question

a) What instrument is playing this piece?

....

[1 mark]

b) How would you describe the way the left hand is playing at **1**?

....

[1 mark]

c) Which of the following best describes the cadence at **2**?
    Circle your choice from the options below.

    perfect   plagal   imperfect

[1 mark]

d) Which key is this excerpt in?

....

[1 mark]

e) Look at the key of the piece. How would you explain the sharpened note at **3**?

....

[1 mark]

f) What term is used to describe the dots above the notes at **4**?

....

[1 mark]

g) Which of these options best describes the texture of this music?
    Circle your choice.

    monophonic   melody with accompaniment   heterophonic

[1 mark]

Revision Summary for Section Three

You've reached the end of Section Three — it's time to find out what you've taken in.
- Try these questions and tick off each one when you get it right.
- When you've done all the questions for a topic and are completely happy with it, tick off the topic.

Major and Minor Scales (p.24-26) ☑

1) How many notes are there in a major scale? How many notes are there in a minor scale?
2) Write out the names of the notes of a scale in words, numbers and Roman numerals.
3) Write down the tone-semitone pattern for a major scale.
4) What does a key signature tell you?
5) How do you find the 'relative minor' of a major scale?
6) D major has two sharps — F and C. What's the key signature of the relative minor?
7) Write out A minor in each of the three types of minor scale and label the tone and semitone gaps.
8) How many major scales are there altogether?
9) How many minor scales are there altogether?
10) Write down all the major scales in order around the circle of fifths, starting with C major.

Modes, Other Scales and Intervals (p.27-29) ☑

11) Write out two common modes.
12) What's a pentatonic scale? What types of music often use pentatonic scales?
13) What are the notes in a G major pentatonic scale?
14) What's a chromatic scale? How many notes are there in a chromatic scale?
15) What's the difference between a melodic and a harmonic interval?
16) Give the name and number of each of these intervals: a) A to C   b) B to F   c) C to B   d) D to A
17) What's a tritone?

Chords, Triads and Inversions (p.34-39) ☑

18) What do you call chords with: a) clashing notes   b) notes that sound good together?
19) What are the two most common types of triad? Describe how you make each one.
20) What makes a 7th chord different from a triad?
21) Write down the letter symbols for these chords: a) A minor   b) D diminished triad
22) Draw the scale of G major on a stave, then build a triad on each note. (Don't forget the F sharps.)
23) Which three chords of any major or minor scale are known as the 'primary' chords?
24) Where do the root, third and fifth go in: a) a first inversion chord   b) a second inversion chord?
25) Name and describe four different chord figurations.

Decorations, Cadences, Modulation and Texture (p.41-47) ☑

26) What's the difference between a 'diatonic' decoration and a 'chromatic' decoration?
27) Explain the following terms: a) auxiliary note   b) passing note   c) appoggiatura
28) What is a musical phrase and what job does a cadence do in a phrase?
29) How many chords make up a cadence?
30) Write down the four different types of cadence and which chords you can use to make each one.
31) What do you call it when a piece in a minor key ends on a major chord?
32) What do people mean when they talk about the 'texture' of music?
33) Explain the difference between monophonic music, homophonic music and polyphonic music.

Common Melodic Devices

Melodic devices are methods that composers use to construct **melodies**.
You need a few good **technical** words to describe them — like **conjunct**, **disjunct**, **triadic** and **scalic**.

Melodies can be Conjunct or Disjunct

1) Conjunct (or stepwise) melodies move mainly by step — notes that are a tone or a semitone apart.

2) The melody doesn't jump around, so it sounds quite smooth.
   This example shows a conjunct melody:

This excerpt's from 'The Silver Swan' by Orlando Gibbons.

3) Disjunct melodies move using a lot of jumps — notes that are more than a major 2nd (a tone) apart.

4) The melody sounds quite spiky as it jumps around a lot.

5) Disjunct melodies are harder to sing or play than conjunct ones.
   This example shows a disjunct melody:

This one's from 'Nessun Dorma' by Puccini.

6) The distance between the lowest and highest notes in any melody is called the range (or compass).

Triadic Melodies Use the Notes of a Triad

1) Triads are chords made up of two intervals of a third on top of each other — so triadic melodies usually move between the notes of a triad. (There's more on triads on page 35.)

2) For example, a C major triad is made up of the notes C, E and G. There's a major third between C and E, a minor third between E and G and a perfect fifth between C and G. There's more on intervals on pages 28-29.

3) This example shows a triadic melody:

This excerpt is from the first movement of Haydn's Trumpet Concerto.

Scalic Melodies Use the Notes of a Scale

1) A scalic melody moves up and down using the notes of a scale.

2) Scalic melodies are similar to conjunct melodies, but they can only move to the next note in the scale. Conjunct melodies can have a few little jumps in them.

3) Like conjunct melodies, scalic melodies sound quite smooth. Here's an example of a scalic melody (it's also from the first movement of Haydn's Trumpet Concerto):

Some melodies contain all of these melodic devices...

These different types of melody are pretty easy to spot if you have the music in front of you, but it's a bit harder if you're listening to them. Listen out for them in all types of music and practise identifying them.

Common Melodic Devices

Call and response is used a lot in **blues**, **rock** and **pop**, as well as **African** and **Indian** music — so it's important that you know what it is. It's used in both **instrumental** and **vocal** music.

Call and Response is Like a Musical Conversation

1) Call and response is a bit like question and answer. It takes place either between two groups of musicians, or between a leader and the rest of the group.

2) One group (or the leader) plays or sings a short phrase. This is the call. It's then answered by the other group. This is the response.

3) The call ends in a way that makes you feel a response is coming — e.g. it might finish with an imperfect cadence (see page 43).

4) Call and response is very popular in pop and blues music. Often the lead singer will sing the call and the backing singers will sing the response.

In a 12-bar blues structure (see p.130), the usual pattern of a call and response would be A, A1, B:

A is the call (4 bars)
A1 is the call repeated with slight variations (4 bars)
B is the response (4 bars).

To make things more complicated, sections A and B can have a 2-bar call and response of their own:

Indian and African Music Use Call and Response

- In Indian music, call and response is usually used in instrumental music. One musician will play a phrase and it'll either be repeated or improvised upon by another musician.

- African music uses call and response in religious ceremonies and community events. The leader will sing first and the congregation will respond.

- Call and response is also used in African drumming music (see p.133). The master drummer plays a call and the rest of the drummers play an answering phrase.

Some Melodies Form an Arch Shape

1) If a melody finishes in the same way it started, then the tune has an arch shape.

2) The simplest example of this is ABA — where the first section is the same as the last section of the piece. This is extended in some pieces to ABCBA, or even ABCDCBA.

3) This gives a symmetrical melody because the sections are mirrored. It makes the whole piece feel more balanced.

Call and response is used in a lot of music...

... so make sure you can spot it if it comes up in the exam — remember to listen out for it in both instrumental and vocal music. Keep your ears pricked for arch-shaped melodies too.

Common Forms

Form or structure is the way a piece of music is organised as a whole. **Strophic** form, **through-composed** form and **da capo arias** are all **song structures**. **Cyclic** form is found in **large** works like **symphonies**.

In **Strophic Form** Each **Verse** has the **Same Tune**

1) In strophic form, the same section of music is repeated over and over again with virtually no changes.
2) Strophic form is used in Classical, folk, blues and pop music.
3) In strophic songs, the music for each verse is the same, but the lyrics change in every verse. Hymns are a good example of this.
4) Strophic form can be thought of like this: A, A1, A2, A3, etc. — the same section is repeated but with a small change (the lyrics).
5) The first part of Led Zeppelin's 'Stairway to Heaven' is in strophic form.

In **Through-Composed Form** Each **Verse** is **Different**

• Through-composed form is the opposite of strophic form — the music changes in every verse.
• Every verse of lyrics has different music to accompany it, so there's no repetition.
• Verses can have different melodies, different chords, or both.
• This form is popular in opera, as the changing music can be used to tell stories. Verses sung by different characters can be completely different.
• A lot of film music is through-composed — the music changes to reflect what's happening on-screen.

'Bohemian Rhapsody' by Queen (see p.115) is a through-composed pop song.

Baroque Composers Used **Ternary Form** in **Arias**

• An aria is a solo in an opera or oratorio (see p.86).
• Arias from the Baroque period (1600-1750) are often in ternary form (see p.81). Arias like this are called 'da capo arias'. Handel wrote lots of these.

After repeating Section A and Section B you come to the instruction da capo al fine. It means "go back to the beginning and play to where it says fine". The fine is at the end of Section A. That's where the piece finishes.

fine   da capo al fine

‖:SECTION A:‖ ‖:SECTION B:‖

Works in **Cyclic Form** Have a **Common Theme**

1) Pieces in cyclic form have common themes in all the movements. These themes link the movements together.
2) Big works like sonatas, symphonies and concertos are sometimes in cyclic form.
3) The linking themes vary in different ways, e.g. they might be played on different instruments, played faster or slower, or played in a different key in different movements. You'll still be able to recognise them though.
4) An example of a common theme in a piece in cyclic form is the four-note theme of Beethoven's Fifth Symphony. It appears in all the movements of the symphony.
5) Film music often has a theme — a bit of melody that keeps popping up throughout the film. The main theme from 'Star Wars®' by John Williams is really easy to recognise.

Don't mind me — I'm just passing through...

Make sure you're completely sorted with the definitions and proper names of all these forms.
Have a listen to the suggested pieces, and check you can spot the features of the forms they're written in.

Common Forms

Continuo and **ground bass** are both types of **bass part**. A **cadenza** is played by a **soloist**.

A **Continuo** is a **Bass Part**

1) A continuo (or basso continuo) is a continuous bass part. Most music written in the Baroque period has a continuo that the harmony of the whole piece is based on (see p.80).

2) The continuo can be played by more than one instrument, but at least one of the continuo group must be able to play chords (e.g. a harpsichord, organ, lute, harp, etc.). A cello, double bass or bassoon could also be used. The most common combination was a harpsichord and a cello.

3) Continuo parts were usually written using a type of notation called figured bass. Only the bass notes were written on the stave, but numbers underneath the notes told the performers which chords to play. The continuo players would then improvise using the notes of the chord.

4) If there weren't any numbers written, the chord would be a normal triad (the root, the third and the fifth). A 4 meant play a fourth instead of the third, and a 6 meant play a sixth instead of the fifth. A 7 meant that a 7th should be added to the chord.

5) The improvisation is called a realization — the performer would 'realize' a continuo part.

means

Some versions of Handel's Water Music still have the continuo written in figured bass.

Ground Bass Pieces Have **Repetition AND Variety**

1) A ground bass is a repeated bass part that's usually four or eight bars long. It can be played by the left hand on a harpsichord or piano, or by the cello and double bass in a chamber orchestra. A ground bass is a type of ostinato — a short pattern of notes repeated throughout a piece of music.

2) The tune is played over the ground bass part. First you hear the main tune, then a load of variations. The variations are played as one continuous piece — there are no gaps between them.

3) The ground bass part can be varied too. You change the starting note but keep the pattern the same.

First time round, the ground bass tune starts on C.

Later on you get the same tune starting on G.

4) The ground bass piece gets more and more complex as it goes on. It can be developed by adding extra, decorative notes to the melody, using more advanced harmonies and adding more instruments to give a richer texture.

A **Cadenza** is Where a **Soloist** can **Show Off**

• A cadenza is a bit of music that's played by a soloist, usually in the middle of a concerto (see p.91).

• Almost all concertos have a cadenza — it allows the soloist to show off their technique.

• Cadenzas started out as improvisations on the main themes of a piece, but now most of them are written out by the composer. However, different musicians will interpret the cadenza in their own way.

Right, that's this page done — better continuo onto the next one...

Listen to a couple of different musicians' performances of Haydn's Trumpet Concerto in E♭ major — the cadenzas will sound different in each one, even though the soloists are playing the same notes.

Popular Song Forms

It's not just **Classical** music that follows set **structures** — **pop songs** do as well.

Pop Songs Usually Have an **Intro**

Pop tunes almost always start with an <u>intro</u>. It does <u>two jobs</u>:

- It often uses the best bit from the rest of the song to <u>set the mood</u>.
- It grabs people's <u>attention</u> and makes them <u>sit up and listen</u>.

Most Pop Songs Have a **Verse-Chorus Structure**

<u>After</u> the intro, the structure of most pop songs goes <u>verse-chorus-verse-chorus</u>.

- All the verses usually have the <u>same tune</u>, but the <u>lyrics change</u> for each verse.
- The chorus has a <u>different tune</u> from the verses, usually quite a catchy one. The lyrics and tune of the chorus <u>don't change</u>.
- In a lot of songs the verse and chorus are both <u>8 or 16 bars long</u>.

'Be My Baby' by 60s girl group The Ronettes has a verse-chorus structure.

The old verse-chorus thing can get repetitive. To avoid this most songs have a <u>middle 8</u>, or <u>bridge</u>, that sounds different. It's an <u>8-bar section</u> in the <u>middle</u> of the song with <u>new chords</u>, <u>new lyrics</u> and a whole <u>new feel</u>.

The song ends with a <u>coda</u> or <u>outro</u> that's <u>different</u> to the verse and the chorus. You can use the coda for a <u>big finish</u> or to <u>fade out gradually</u>.

Pop Songs Can Have **Other Structures** Too

For example:

CALL AND RESPONSE

This has <u>two bits</u> to it. <u>Part 1</u> is the call — it asks a musical <u>question</u>. <u>Part 2</u>, the response, responds with an <u>answer</u> (p.55).

RIFF

A <u>riff</u> is a <u>short section</u> of music that's <u>repeated</u> over and over again (a bit like an <u>ostinato</u> — see p.83). Riffs can be used to build up a <u>whole song</u>. <u>Each part</u>, e.g. the drums or bass guitar, has its own riff. All the riffs <u>fit together</u> to make one section of the music. They often <u>change</u> for the <u>chorus</u>.

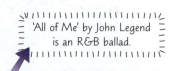
'All of Me' by John Legend is an R&B ballad.

BALLADS

These are songs that tell <u>stories</u>. Each verse usually has the <u>same rhythm</u> and <u>same tune</u>.

32-BAR SONG FORM

This breaks down into <u>four 8-bar sections</u>. Sections 1, 2 and 4 all have the <u>same melody</u>, but may have different lyrics. Section 3 has a <u>contrasting melody</u>, making an AABA structure. The 32 bars may be repeated. The song 'Somewhere Over the Rainbow' from the film 'The Wizard of Oz' has this form.

SUGGESTED LISTENING

Verse — chorus — verse — chorus — tea break — chorus...

Songs from <u>musicals</u> follow these structures too. Have a listen to '<u>Any Dream Will Do</u>' from '<u>Joseph and the Amazing Technicolour Dreamcoat</u>', '<u>Bui Doi</u>' from '<u>Miss Saigon</u>' and '<u>Somewhere That's Green</u>' from '<u>Little Shop of Horrors</u>', and look for the structures.

Warm-up and Exam Questions

1) Describe each of the following melody structures:

   Conjunct   **Disjunct**   **Triadic**   **Scalic**

2) What is through-composed form?

3) What is a ground bass, and what instruments often play these parts?

Exam Question

If there are bits you get stuck on in this question, reread the last few pages, then try again.

Play the excerpt **four** times, leaving a short pause between each playing.

Track 28

a) i) The key signature of the excerpt is shown below.
      What key is the excerpt in?

   ....

   [1 mark]

   ii) What is the interval between the notes shown on the right?
       Circle your answer.

   Diminished fifth   **Perfect fifth**   **Augmented fifth**

   [1 mark]

b) In the first half of the excerpt, the piano's lines are answered by
   the violin. What is this back-and-forth movement called?

   ....

   [1 mark]

c) Describe how the violin melody changes throughout the excerpt.

   ....

   ....

   ....

   ....

   [3 marks]

Exam Question

Play the excerpt **four** times, leaving a short pause between each playing.

Track 29

a) What musical period was this piece composed in?

....

[1 mark]

b) Name two instruments that play in the excerpt.

....

....

[2 marks]

c) The melody at the start of the excerpt is shown below.

i) Fill in the missing notes in bars 3 and 4.
The rhythm is given above the stave.

[7 marks]

ii) Which word best describes the melodic style in this excerpt?
Circle your choice from the options below.

Conjunct   **Disjunct**   **Triadic**

[1 mark]

d) What type of bass part is used in this piece?

....

[1 mark]

e) Give one instrument that plays the bass part.

....

[1 mark]

Revision Summary for Section Four

You're done and dusted with <u>Section Four</u> — do a quick stretch and get ready to <u>test your knowledge</u>.

- Try these questions and <u>tick off each one</u> when you <u>get it right</u>.
- When you've done <u>all the questions</u> for a topic and are <u>completely happy</u> with it, tick off the topic.

Common Melodic Devices (p.54-55) ☑

1) Explain what is meant by each of the following words that are used to describe melodies:
   - a) conjunct,
   - b) disjunct,
   - c) triadic, - 3 notes moving in step
   - d) scalic. - ☑
2) What is call and response? ☑
3) Name two types of music that use call and response. ☑
4) Explain what is meant by an arch-shaped melody. ☑

Common Forms (p.56-57) ☑

5) What's the difference between strophic and through-composed form? ☑
6) Give an example of a type of music that's often written in through-composed form, and explain why this form is used. ☑
7) What's a da capo aria? ☑
8) What is cyclic form? ☑
9) What is basso continuo? ☑
10) Explain how figured bass works. ☑
11) Describe the structure of a ground bass piece. ☑
12) What's a cadenza? ☑

Popular Song Forms (p.58) ☑

13) Why do pop songs have an introduction? ☑
14) Describe verse-chorus structure. ☑
15) What is a bridge? ☑
16) What is a riff? ☑
17) What is the structure of a song in 32-bar form? ☑
18) Name two structures (other than 32-bar form) often used in pop songs. ☑

Brass Instruments

You probably know a lot about **your** instrument. It's also a good idea to know about the instruments other people play so you can understand what they're up to. **Brass** first.

Brass Instruments are All Made of Metal

1) Brass instruments include horns, trumpets, cornets, trombones and tubas.

2) They're all basically a length of hollow metal tubing with a mouthpiece (the bit you blow into) at one end and a funnel shape (the bell) at the other.

3) The different shapes and sizes of these parts gives each brass instrument a different tone and character.

4) Brass instruments often play fanfares (short musical flourishes) in orchestral pieces. They're most commonly played on the trumpet, and can be accompanied by percussion. A fanfare might also be played as part of a ceremony.

trumpet   **French horn**

trombone   **tuba**

You Get a Noise by 'Buzzing' Your Lips

1) To make a sound on a brass instrument, you have to make the air vibrate down the tube.

2) You do it by 'buzzing' your lips into the mouthpiece. You squeeze your lips together, then blow through a tiny gap so you get a buzzing noise.

3) You have to squeeze your lips together tighter to get higher notes.

4) Notes can be slurred (played together smoothly) or tongued (you use your tongue to separate the notes).

Brass Instruments Use Slides and Valves to Change Pitch

1) Squeezing your lips only gets a limited range of notes. To get a decent range, brass instruments use slides (like on a trombone) or valves (like on a trumpet).

2) The slide on a trombone is the U-shaped tube that moves in and out of the main tube. Moving it out makes the tube longer so you get a lower note. Moving it in makes the tube shorter so you get a higher note.

3) Horns, trumpets and cornets use three buttons connected to valves. The valves open and close different sections of the tube to make it longer or shorter. Pressing down the buttons in different combinations gives you all the notes you need.

Brass Players use Mutes to Change the Tone

- A mute is a kind of bung that's put in the bell of a brass instrument. It's used to make the instrument play more quietly and change the tone. You wouldn't usually use one all the way through a piece — just for a short section.
- Different shapes and sizes of mute change the tone in different ways, e.g. the wah-wah mute gives the instrument a wah-wah sound.

 EXAM TIP

Brass instruments aren't always made of brass...

If you get brass in a listening test and need to say what instrument it is, remember that bigger instruments generally play lower notes and smaller instruments usually play higher notes.

Woodwind Instruments

Some people get woodwind and brass muddled up. If you're one of them, **learn the difference**.

Woodwind Instruments Used to be Made of Wood

Woodwind instruments got their name because they all use air — wind — to make a sound and once upon a time were all made of wood. Nowadays some are still made of wood. Others are made of plastic or metal. These are the main ones:

Woodwind Instruments Make Sound in Different Ways

To get a sound from a woodwind instrument, you have to make the air in its tube vibrate.
There are three different ways woodwind instruments do this:

1) Edge-tone instruments — flutes and piccolos. Air is blown across an oval-shaped hole. The edge of the hole splits the air. This makes it vibrate down the instrument and make the sound.

2) Single-reed instruments — clarinets and saxophones. Air is blown down a mouthpiece which has a reed (a thin slice of wood/reed/plastic) clamped to it. The reed vibrates, making the air in the instrument vibrate, and creating the sound.

3) Double-reed instruments — oboes and bassoons. The air passes between two reeds, tightly bound together and squeezed between the lips. The reeds vibrate and you get a sound.

Like brass instruments, woodwind instruments can be slurred or tongued as well.

Different Notes are Made by Opening and Closing Holes

*   Woodwind instruments are covered in keys, springs and levers (or just holes for some instruments). These operate little pads that close and open holes down the instrument.
*   Opening and closing holes effectively makes the instrument longer or shorter. The shorter the tube, the higher the note. The longer the tube, the lower the note.

I can't see the woodwind for the clarinets...

Flutes and saxophones are made of metal but they're still woodwind instruments. The general term 'wind instruments' refers to both woodwind and brass instruments together, as they both use air to make a noise.

Orchestral Strings

Orchestral strings are the **heart** of the orchestra — or so string players would have you believe.

Orchestral Strings are Very Alike

The <u>double bass</u>, <u>cello</u>, <u>viola</u> and <u>violin</u>
are all <u>made</u> and played in a <u>similar way</u>.
The main differences are the <u>size</u> and <u>pitch</u>.

The <u>bigger</u> the instrument is, the <u>lower</u> the sounds
it makes. So the double bass plays the lowest
notes and the violin plays the highest.

cello

double bass

violin

viola

bow (made of wood and hair). The hair is drawn across the strings.

Stringed Instruments can be **Bowed** or **Plucked**

When the <u>strings vibrate</u>, the air inside the instrument <u>vibrates</u> and
amplifies the <u>sound</u>. There are two ways to get the strings vibrating:

1) <u>Bowing</u> — drawing a bow across the string. *<u>Con arco</u>* (or just *<u>arco</u>*) means '<u>with bow</u>'.

2) <u>Plucking</u> the string with the tip of your finger. The posh word for this is *pizzicato*.

The **Strings** are 'Stopped' to Make **Different Notes**

1) You can get an "<u>open note</u>" just by plucking or bowing one of the four strings.

2) To get all the other notes, you have to change the <u>length</u> of the strings.
   You do this by <u>pressing down</u> with your finger. It's called <u>stopping</u>.

3) If you stop a string <u>close to the bridge</u>, the string's short and you get a <u>high</u> note.

4) If you stop a string <u>further away</u> from the bridge, the string's longer and you get a <u>lower</u> note.

5) <u>Double-stopping</u> is when <u>two</u> notes are played at the same time. Both strings are <u>pressed</u> (not open).

6) If you just <u>touch</u> a string <u>lightly</u> at certain points (instead of stopping), you
   can produce a series of <u>higher</u>, <u>fainter-sounding notes</u> called <u>harmonics</u>.

You Can Get **Very Varied** Effects with Stringed Instruments

- **Tremolo** The bow's moved <u>back and forth</u> really <u>quickly</u>. This makes the notes
  sort of trembly. It's a great effect for making music sound <u>spooky</u> and <u>dramatic</u>.

- **Col legno** The <u>wood</u> of the bow (instead of the hair) is tapped on the strings.
  This makes an <u>eerie</u>, <u>tapping</u> sound.

- **Con sordino** A <u>mute</u> is put over the <u>bridge</u> (the piece of wood that supports the
  strings). It makes the strings sound <u>distant</u> and <u>soft</u>. Mutes are made of <u>wood</u>, <u>rubber</u> or <u>metal</u>.

- **Vibrato** By <u>wobbling</u> the finger used to stop a string, a player varies the <u>pitch</u> slightly,
  creating a <u>rich tone</u>. This technique is also used on the <u>guitar</u> (see next page).

mute

strings

bridge

The **Harp** is Different...

1) The harp's <u>always plucked</u> — not bowed.

2) Most have <u>47</u> strings. Plucking each string in order on a
   concert harp is like playing up the <u>white notes</u> on a piano.

3) It has <u>seven pedals</u>. Pressing and releasing these lets you play <u>sharp</u> and <u>flat</u> notes.

4) You can play <u>one</u> note at a time, or play <u>chords</u> by plucking a few strings together.

EXAM TIP

Don't stop now, there are lots more instruments to come...
Make sure you learn the different string effects — you might need to identify them in the exam.

Guitars

Guitars are **everywhere**, so it's best to know a bit about how they work.

An **Acoustic Guitar** has a **Hollow Body**

The acoustic guitar makes a sound the same way as the orchestral strings — by vibrating air in its belly. Slightly different types are used by pop, folk and classical guitarists, but the basic design is similar.

HOLLOW BODY makes the string vibrations resonate, giving a louder sound.

acoustic guitar

STRINGS tuned to the notes E(low)-A-D-G-B-E(high). Low E is the string nearest your head as you're playing. Played with fingers or a plectrum.

FRETS (the little metal strips on the fingerboard/neck) help the player find the correct finger position for different notes.

There are three different kinds of acoustic guitar:

1) The classical or Spanish guitar has nylon strings (the thickest three are covered in fine wire).
2) The acoustic guitar has steel strings and is used mainly in pop and folk music.
3) The 12-stringed guitar is often used in folk music. There are two of each string, giving a 'thicker' sound which works well for accompanying singing.

Some guitar music is written in tablature (tab for short) — the numbers tell guitarists which frets to place their fingers at for each string.

```
E ———————————
B ———————————
G ———————————
D ———0—0———
A —2———2———
E ———————————
```

This means play the 2nd fret on the A string, then the open D string, then both at the same time.

Electric Guitars Use an **Amplifier** and a **Loudspeaker**

electric guitar

1) An electric guitar has six strings, just like an acoustic guitar, and is played in a similar way.
2) The main difference is that an electric guitar has a solid body. The sound's made louder electronically, using an amplifier and a loudspeaker.
3) A combo (short for combination) is an amplifier and loudspeaker 'all in one'.

The **Bass Guitar** has **Four Strings**

1) The bass guitar works like a guitar except it usually has four strings, not six.
2) They're tuned to the notes E-A-D-G (from lowest note to highest).
3) It's lower pitched than other guitars because it has thicker and longer strings.
4) Most bass guitars have frets, but there are some (imaginatively named fretless basses) that don't.

Like ordinary guitars, you can get electric or acoustic basses.

Guitar Strings are **Picked** or **Strummed**

- Plucking one string at a time is called picking. Classical and lead guitarists pick the notes of a melody. Bass guitarists almost always pick out the individual notes of a bass line. They hardly ever strum.
- Playing two or more strings at a time in a sweeping movement is called strumming. It's how chords are usually played. Pop and folk guitarists tend to play accompaniments rather than tunes, so they do more strumming than picking.
- A plectrum is a small, flat piece of plastic that guitarists can use to pluck or strum with.
- 'Hammer-on' (ho) and 'pull-off' (po) are techniques that allow a guitarist to play notes in quick succession — they create a smoother, more legato sound than picking.
- Another guitar technique is 'palm muting' (pm) — dampening the sound with your hand whilst plucking the strings. This can be done on bass guitars too.
- To produce a different sound on the bass guitar, you can strike the strings with your thumb (instead of plucking with your fingers), which gives a more percussive sound. This is known as slap bass.
- Guitarists can also press a tube (usually made of metal) called a slide or bottleneck against the strings. The player can move smoothly between notes by sliding this up or down the neck of the guitar.

Keyboard Instruments

The actual **keyboard** looks much the same on most keyboard instruments, but the wires and mysterious levers **inside** vary quite a bit. That means the **sounds** they make vary too.

Harpsichords, Virginals and Clavichords Came First

harpsichord

1) Harpsichords were invented long before pianos. They're still played today but they were <u>most popular</u> in the <u>Baroque</u> and <u>early Classical</u> periods.

2) Harpsichords have quite a <u>tinny</u>, <u>string</u> sound. When you press a key a string inside is <u>plucked</u> by a lever. You can't vary the <u>strength</u> of the pluck, so you <u>can't</u> vary the <u>dynamics</u>.

3) A <u>virginal</u> is a <u>miniature</u> table-top version of a harpsichord. In the <u>sixteenth century</u>, virginals were really popular in England.

4) The <u>clavichord</u> is another early keyboard instrument. Clavichords are small and have a <u>soft</u> sound. The strings are <u>struck</u> with hammers (called "blades"), not plucked, so you can <u>vary</u> the dynamics a <u>little bit</u>.

The Most Popular Keyboard Instrument Now is the Piano

- The piano was invented around <u>1700</u>. The <u>technology</u> is <u>more sophisticated</u> than it was in earlier keyboard instruments. When a key's pressed, a hammer hits the strings. The <u>harder</u> you hit the key, the <u>harder</u> the hammer hits the strings and the <u>louder</u> the note — there's a big range of <u>dynamics</u>.

- Pianos have a wide range of <u>notes</u> — up to <u>seven and a half octaves</u>.

- Pianos have <u>pedals</u> that let you change the sound in different ways.

The <u>soft</u> pedal on the left <u>mutes</u> the strings, making a softer sound.

The <u>sustain</u> pedal on the right <u>lifts</u> all the <u>dampers</u>. This lets the sound <u>ring on</u> until you release the pedal.

For more detail on the piano, have a look at page 100.

<u>Grand pianos</u> have a <u>middle pedal</u> too. This lets the player <u>choose</u> which notes to sustain. Modern pianos might have an extra mute pedal for <u>very quiet</u> practising.

Traditional Organs Use Pumped Air to Make Sound

1) The traditional organ (the <u>massive instrument</u> with hundreds of metal pipes that you see in churches and concert halls) is one of the most <u>complicated</u> instruments ever designed.

2) Sound is made by <u>blowing air</u> through sets of pipes called <u>ranks</u>. The air is pumped in by <u>hand</u>, <u>foot</u> or, on more recent organs, <u>electric pumps</u>.

3) The pipes are controlled by <u>keyboards</u> (called <u>manuals</u>) and lots of <u>pedals</u> which make a keyboard for the player's feet.

4) <u>Pressing</u> a key or pedal lets air pass through one of the pipes and play a note. <u>Longer</u> pipes make <u>lower</u> notes. <u>Shorter</u> pipes make <u>higher</u> notes.

5) Organs can play <u>different types of sound</u> by using differently designed pipes. Buttons called <u>stops</u> are used to select the different pipes. One stop might select pipes that make a <u>trumpet</u> sound, another might select a <u>flute</u> sound...

6) Modern <u>electronic organs</u> don't have pipes. Sound is produced <u>electronically</u> instead. These organs are much <u>smaller</u> and <u>cheaper</u> to build.

You've got to learn it all...
Listen to music played on each of these instruments so that you know how they all sound — harpsichords have a more <u>jangly</u> tone than pianos, and organs are fairly easy to spot as well.

Percussion

A percussion instrument is anything you have to **hit** or **shake** to get a sound out of it. There are **two types**: those that play tunes are called **tuned percussion**, and the ones you just hit are **untuned**.

Tuned Percussion Can Play Different Notes

XYLOPHONES have wooden bars. The sound is 'woody'.

GLOCKENSPIEL — Looks a bit like a xylophone but the bars are made of metal. Sounds tinkly and bell-like.

CELESTA — a bit like a glockenspiel except that you use a keyboard instead of whacking it with a hammer.

TUBULAR BELLS — Each of the hollow steel tubes plays a different note. Sounds a bit like church bells.

TIMPANI — also called kettledrums. The handles on the side or the foot pedal can be used to tighten or relax the skin, giving different notes.

VIBRAPHONE — This is like a giant glockenspiel. There are long tubes called resonators below the bars to make the notes louder and richer. Electric fans can make the notes pulsate, giving a warm and gentle sound.

There are Hundreds of Untuned Percussion Instruments

Untuned percussion includes any instrument that'll make a noise — but can't play a tune. These are the instruments that are used for pure rhythm. It's pretty much impossible to learn every untuned percussion instrument, but try and remember the names of these.

cymbals, bass drum, tambourine, maracas, triangle, castanets, sleigh bells, timbale, bongos, bodhrán, snare drum

Percussion instruments make different sounds depending on what you hit them with — e.g. hard wooden drumsticks, mallets, beaters (sticks with hard or soft round heads), brushes...

Remember — xylophones are wooden, glockenspiels are metal...

In a band, the drummer's job is to make a song sound like it's going somewhere and keep everyone in time. In an orchestra, percussion emphasises the rhythm of the piece and also adds special effects — you can imitate thunder with a drum roll on the timpani, or the crashing of waves with clashes of the cymbals.

The Voice

There are special names for male and female **voices** and **groups** of voices.

Female Singers are **Soprano, Alto** or **Mezzo-Soprano**

1) A singer with a particular type of voice is expected to be able to sing a certain <u>range</u> of notes.

2) The range of notes where a particular singer is most <u>comfortable</u> is called the <u>tessitura</u>. This term can also describe the <u>most commonly used</u> range of notes within a vocal or instrumental part of a piece.

3) A <u>high</u> female voice is called a <u>soprano</u>. The main female parts in operas are sung by sopranos.

4) A <u>lower</u> female voice is called an <u>alto</u>.

5) <u>Mezzo-sopranos</u> sit somewhere <u>in between</u> — they don't sing quite as <u>low</u> as an <u>alto</u> or as <u>high</u> as a <u>soprano</u>, but cover the <u>middle range</u>.

Male Voices are **Tenor** or **Bass**

1) <u>Higher</u> male voices are called <u>tenors</u>.

2) <u>Low</u> male voices are called <u>basses</u> (it's pronounced "bases").

3) <u>Baritones</u> sit somewhere <u>in between</u> — they don't sing quite as <u>low</u> as a <u>bass</u> or as <u>high</u> as a <u>tenor</u>, but cover the <u>middle range</u>.

4) Men who sing in the <u>female vocal range</u> are called <u>countertenors</u>.

5) Some tenors, baritones and basses can push their voices <u>higher</u> to sing some of the same notes as a <u>soprano</u>. This is called <u>falsetto</u> singing.

Children's Voices are Either **Treble** or **Alto**

- A <u>high child's</u> voice in the <u>same range</u> as a <u>soprano</u> is called a <u>treble</u>.
- A <u>low child's</u> voice is called an <u>alto</u>. They sing in exactly the <u>same range</u> as an adult alto.
- <u>Girls'</u> voices <u>don't change much</u> as they get older. <u>Boys'</u> voices <u>drop</u> to a <u>lower range</u> when they hit puberty.

When **Several Voices** Sing Each Part It's a **Choir**

1) A <u>choir</u> is a group of singers. Each part is performed by <u>more than one</u> singer.

2) A <u>mixed voice choir</u> has sopranos, altos, tenors and basses (<u>SATB</u> for short).

3) An <u>all-male choir</u> has trebles, altos, tenors and basses — a treble has the same range as a soprano, so it's basically SATB.

4) A <u>male voice choir</u> is slightly different — it tends to have two groups of <u>tenors</u>, as well as <u>baritones</u> and <u>basses</u> (<u>TTBB</u> for short), with no higher parts.

5) An <u>all-female choir</u> has <u>two groups of sopranos</u> and <u>two groups of altos</u> (<u>SSAA</u> for short).

6) When a choir sings <u>without</u> an instrumental <u>accompaniment</u>, this is known as '<u>a cappella</u>'.

7) Music written for a choir is called <u>choral music</u> — see page 85.

These are the names for smaller groups:
2 singers = a **duet**
3 singers = a **trio**
4 singers = a **quartet**
5 singers = a **quintet**
6 singers = a **sextet**

No excuses — get on and learn all the voices...

The different voices don't just sound different in pitch — they've got different characters too, e.g. sopranos usually sound very clear and glassy, and basses sound more rich and booming.

Wind, Brass and Jazz Bands

In your listening exam, you'll get marks for saying what type of **group** (or **ensemble**) is playing. **Wind**, **jazz** and **brass** bands can sound quite **similar**, so make sure you know the differences.

Wind Bands have Woodwind, Brass and Percussion

1) Wind bands are <u>largish groups</u>, made up of 'wind' instruments — woodwind and brass — and percussion instruments.

2) There's <u>no string section</u>. If there was it would be an orchestra...

3) <u>Military bands</u> are wind bands. They tend to play <u>marches</u> — pieces with a <u>regular rhythm</u> (usually $\frac{4}{4}$ or $\frac{2}{4}$ time) that can be marched to.

Brass Bands have Brass and Percussion

1) A brass band is a group of <u>brass</u> and <u>percussion</u> instruments.

2) A typical brass band would have <u>cornets</u>, <u>flugelhorns</u>, <u>tenor</u> and <u>baritone horns</u>, <u>tenor</u> and <u>bass trombones</u>, <u>euphoniums</u> and <u>tubas</u>.

3) The exact <u>percussion instruments</u> depend on the piece being played.

4) Brass bands have been popular in <u>England</u> for <u>years</u>.

5) <u>Contests</u> are organised through the year to find out which bands are 'best'. There's a <u>league system</u> similar to football. The divisions are called <u>sections</u>. There are <u>five sections</u> and bands are <u>promoted</u> and <u>demoted</u> each year depending on how they do at the <u>regional</u> and <u>national</u> contests.

Jazz Bands are Quite Varied

1) Jazz bands have <u>no fixed set of instruments</u>.

2) Small jazz groups are known as <u>combos</u>. A typical combo might include a <u>trumpet</u>, <u>trombone</u>, <u>clarinet</u>, <u>saxophone</u>, <u>piano</u>, <u>banjo</u>, <u>double bass</u> and <u>drum kit</u> — but there's no fixed rule. Combos play in small venues like <u>clubs</u> and <u>bars</u>.

3) Larger jazz bands are known as <u>big bands</u> or <u>swing bands</u>. Instruments are doubled and tripled up so you get a <u>much bigger sound</u>. Big bands were really popular in the <u>1930s</u> and <u>1940s</u>. They played live at <u>dance halls</u>.

4) A large jazz band with a string section is called a <u>jazz orchestra</u> (though some jazz orchestras don't have a string section — they're just big jazz bands).

Jazz Bands have a Rhythm Section and a Front Line

In a jazz band, players are either in the <u>rhythm section</u> or the <u>front line</u>.

- The <u>rhythm section</u> is the instruments responsible for <u>keeping the beat</u> and <u>adding the harmony parts</u>. The rhythm section's usually made up of the <u>drum kit</u> with a <u>double</u> or <u>electric bass</u>, <u>electric guitar</u> and <u>piano</u>.

- The instruments that <u>play the melody</u> are the <u>front line</u>. This is usually <u>clarinets</u>, <u>saxophones</u> and <u>trumpets</u>, but could also be guitar or violin.

Keep at it — there are more groups to come...

You need to know the differences between wind, brass and jazz bands — if you reckon you've got it sorted, test yourself by covering up the page and writing down the instruments that play in each type of band.

Chamber Music

Chamber music is music composed for **small groups** and it's pretty formal stuff.

Chamber Music was Originally 'Home Entertainment'

1) 'Chamber' is an old word for a room in a posh building like a palace or a mansion.

2) Rich people could afford to pay musicians to come and play in their 'chambers'. Musical families could play the music for themselves. The music written for these private performances is called chamber music.

3) Nowadays, you're more likely to hear chamber music in a concert hall or at home on a recording than live at someone's house. Let's face it — most people haven't got the cash to hire musicians for the evening, and they can download any music they want to listen to.

Chamber Music is Played by Small Groups

1) The rooms where musicians came to play were nice and big — but not enormous. Limited space meant that chamber music was written for a small number of musicians — between two and eight.

2) There's a name for each size of group:

> **Duet** = two players
> **Trio** = three players
> **Quartet** = four players
> **Quintet** = five players
> **Sextet** = six players
> **Septet** = seven players
> **Octet** = eight players

Have a look at the names for singing groups on p.68 — they're much the same.

These instruments make up a 'piano trio' — see below.

3) With so few people in chamber groups, you don't need a conductor. Instead, one of the players leads. The others have to watch and listen carefully, to make sure the timing, dynamics and interpretation are right.

4) Each part in the music is played by just one person.

Some Chamber Groups are Extra-Popular with Composers

Chamber music is written more often for some instrumental groups than others.
These are some of the most popular types of chamber group:

String trio	— violin, viola, cello
String quartet	— first violin, second violin, viola, cello
Piano trio	— piano, violin, cello (not three pianos)
Clarinet quintet	— clarinet, first violin, second violin, viola, cello (not five clarinets)
Wind quintet	— usually flute, oboe, clarinet, horn and bassoon

Chamber groups are small...

Learn the instruments that play in all the different chamber groups. Keep a special eye out for the piano trio and clarinet quintet — they're not what you'd expect. And finally, don't forget there's no conductor.

The Orchestra

If you go to a classical concert, more often than not there'll be an **orchestra** up there on stage. Loads and loads of classical music has been written for orchestras.

A **Modern Orchestra** has **Four** Sections

If you go and see a modern symphony orchestra, it'll have four sections of instruments — strings (p.64), woodwind (p.63), brass (p.62) and percussion (p.67). The strings, woodwind, brass and percussion always sit in the same places.

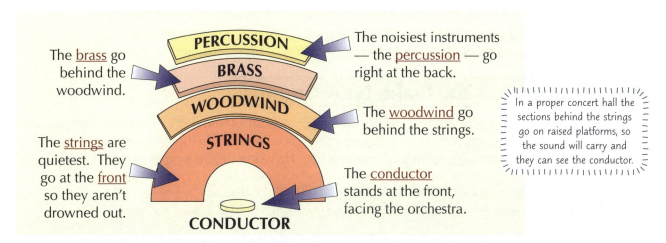

The brass go behind the woodwind.

The noisiest instruments — the percussion — go right at the back.

The woodwind go behind the strings.

The strings are quietest. They go at the front so they aren't drowned out.

The conductor stands at the front, facing the orchestra.

In a proper concert hall the sections behind the strings go on raised platforms, so the sound will carry and they can see the conductor.

The **Conductor** has a **Complete Overview**

1) The conductor has a score — a version of the piece with all the parts. The parts are arranged in a standard order, one on top of the other, so that it's easy to see what any part is doing at any time. Woodwind parts are written at the top, followed by brass, percussion, and strings at the bottom.

2) The conductor controls the tempo by beating time with their hands, or a baton — a pointy white stick that's easy to see. There's a different way of beating time for each time signature.

3) The conductor 'cues in' musicians — especially helpful for brass and percussion, who sometimes don't play anything for hundreds of bars, then suddenly have to play a really loud, important bit.

4) The conductor interprets the music. A conductor can decide whether to play one bit louder than another, whether to play a section in a moody or a magical way, and whether to make a piece sound very smooth or very edgy. They're a bit like a film director deciding the best way to tell a story.

An **Orchestra** is Any **Large Group with Strings**

Symphony orchestras (above) are the biggest type of orchestra. There are other smaller kinds too:

- String orchestra — an orchestra with stringed instruments only.
- Chamber orchestra — a mini-orchestra. It has a small string section, a wind and brass section with one or two of each instrument (but no tubas or trombones) and a small percussion section.

You have to do what the conductor tells you...

Copy out the diagram of the orchestra, but don't copy the labels. Close the book and see if you can fill in the different instrument sections in the right places. Then learn all about the conductor.

Music Technology

Modern **technological** and 'virtual' instruments allow a huge variety of sounds to be created.

MIDI lets you Connect Electronic Musical Instruments

1) MIDI was invented in 1983. It stands for Musical Instrument Digital Interface. It's a way of connecting different electronic instruments.

2) MIDI equipment is connected by MIDI cables.

3) MIDI data is digital information (i.e. in zeroes and ones). It's sent down the MIDI cables. MIDI instruments turn MIDI information into sound (or vice versa).

4) One important advantage of MIDI is that it allows musical equipment to be linked with computers, opening up a whole new world of music-making.

Synthesizers Let You Make New Sounds

Synthesizers come in different forms — some have keyboards and some don't. The most common ones today are virtual synthesizers, which are software-based (see below). The point of them is to let you create sounds, which often imitate musical instruments. There are different types of synthesizers:

1) Analogue synthesizers were mainly made in the 70s and early 80s. They've often got lots of knobs and sliders — you use these to change the sound.

2) Digital synthesizers started to be popular in the 80s. Most modern synthesizers are digital, though some of them try to mimic analogue synths. Digital synths usually have fewer knobs and sliders than analogue ones.

3) Software synths started to become popular in the late 90s. Software synths are computer programs (often linked to a sequencer — see below). They often have graphical sliders and knobs that you can move with a mouse. Some of them try to be like analogue and early digital synthesizers. They also try to recreate classic electric instruments like the Hammond organ.

Sequencers Let You Record, Edit and Replay Music

- Sequencer is the posh word for equipment that can record, edit (mess about with) and replay music stored as MIDI or audio information. A "sequenced composition" is a musical piece produced mainly from synthesized sounds using a sequencer.

- Modern sequencers are usually computer programs, which often include synthesizers and samplers.

- Most sequencers can record audio (real sounds) as well as the MIDI stuff, so you can create synthesized music and then record your own voice or instruments along with it. If you're unhappy with part of a recording, it's easy to replace that section with a re-take.

- Modern sequencers are multi-track recorders. This allows the various lines of music, such as those played by different instruments, to be recorded on separate tracks. The individual tracks can then be edited separately to achieve the perfect balance of sounds.

- One of the big advantages of a sequencer is that it shows your music as actual notation or as representative boxes — this makes it much easier to change and try out new ideas.

- Drum machines are special sequencers that play back rhythm patterns using built-in drum sounds.

This can all be a bit confusing...

Some of this stuff is quite technical — but don't panic. You don't need to have an in-depth understanding of how the different types of technology work — as long as you know what they do and what people use them for. You can even have a go at using them in your compositions.

Music Technology

Sampling is a very popular way of putting **different sounds** into your music.
Samples can be **fiddled with** and **looped** to make long repeated sections.

Samplers let you 'Pinch' Other People's Sounds

1) A <u>sampler</u> is a piece of equipment that can <u>record</u>, <u>process</u> (change) and <u>play back</u> bits of sound.

2) These sections of sound are called <u>samples</u>.

3) Samplers are often used to take a bit of a piece of music that's <u>already been recorded</u> to use in some new music.

4) You can sample anything from <u>instruments</u> to <u>birdsong</u> — even weird things like a <u>car horn</u>.

5) Today, samplers are most often used to <u>reproduce</u> the sound of <u>real instruments</u>, such as <u>strings</u> or <u>piano</u>. Most <u>pop music</u> is sampled.

6) <u>Pop stars</u> often use samples of <u>other people's</u> music in their own music — anything from <u>other pop songs</u> to bits from <u>Classical pieces</u>. For example:

- Stevie Wonder's '<u>Pastime Paradise</u>' (1976) has been sampled multiple times — most famously by Coolio in '<u>Gangsta's Paradise</u>' (1995), and also in songs by <u>Blue</u> (2004) and <u>Ella Henderson</u> (2024).
- <u>Take That</u> used a sample from <u>Verdi's</u> *Requiem* (see p.103) in '<u>Never Forget</u>' (1995).
- <u>Madonna</u> used <u>ABBA's</u> '<u>Gimme! Gimme! Gimme! (A Man After Midnight)</u>' in '<u>Hung Up</u>' (2005).
- <u>Ed Sheeran's</u> '<u>Galway Girl</u>' (2017) sampled the song '<u>Minute 5</u>' (2011) by the Irish folk band <u>Beoga</u>.

Samples Can be Added to Other Pieces

1) You don't have to create a piece made up <u>entirely</u> of samples — you can just add one or two, or use a whole range to create a <u>collage</u> of sound. The collage can then be put over the top of a repeating <u>drum and bass loop</u>.

2) <u>DJs</u> and <u>producers</u> often do this when they make a <u>dance remix</u> of a piece.

> <u>REMIX</u> is a term used for a <u>different version</u> of a piece of music.
> They're often used to turn <u>pop</u> or <u>rock</u> tunes into <u>dance</u> music
> — e.g. by <u>speeding them up</u> and giving them a <u>fast drum beat</u>.

3) Samples can be added to a piece by <u>over-dubbing</u> — adding tracks <u>over the top</u> of other tracks. You can record a drum track, then <u>overlay</u> the guitar part, then the vocal part, etc.

DJs Choose, Play and Alter Music

1) <u>DJs</u> (<u>disc jockeys</u>) <u>choose</u> which tracks (lines of music) to play, and <u>change</u> bits of them (e.g. by adding <u>samples</u>). They choose <u>compatible tracks</u> — ones that work <u>well</u> together, e.g. tracks in the <u>same key</u>.

2) DJs play music in <u>clubs</u> and on the <u>radio</u>.

3) At a <u>live performance</u> in a club, the DJ sometimes adds <u>extra sounds</u> using <u>samples</u>, <u>keyboards</u> or a <u>drum machine</u> to build the piece up. Some DJs also <u>rap</u> over the top of the music.

4) DJs use a <u>mixing desk</u> to <u>combine</u> different tracks and <u>add extra sounds</u> to the music, and a set of <u>decks</u> to play their music.

5) The <u>amplification</u> is important — DJs need to make sure the right parts <u>stand out</u>, and that all parts can be <u>heard</u>. The amplification can be changed in <u>live performances</u>.

There's even a dance remix of Beethoven's 5th Symphony...

Again, there's lots of <u>technical bits</u> on this page. You might choose to use some samples in your own compositions, but even if you don't, you need to know how <u>other people</u> (like DJs) might use them.

Timbre

When you're listening to music, you can pick out **individual instruments** because of their **unique sound** — e.g. a trumpet sounds nothing like a violin. This is all down to a little thing called **timbre**.

Every Instrument Has its Own **Timbre**

1) Timbre is the type of sound that different instruments make. It's also known as tone colour.

2) Musical notes (and all sounds) are made by vibrations. Different instruments produce vibrations in different ways. For example, on a string instrument, the bow is drawn across the string to make it vibrate. On a brass instrument the vibrations are produced when the player 'buzzes' their lips. The different vibrations make the timbres different.

3) The size and material of the instrument alter the timbre as well — e.g. a cello has a different timbre to a violin because it's bigger, and wooden flutes sound different from metal ones.

4) The same instrument can sound different depending on who's playing it. The tone (or quality) of the sound is affected by an individual's playing style and can be described as rich, full, strong, etc.

5) The overall nature of the sound produced by an instrument is called its sonority. Timbre and tone contribute to this, along with the dynamics and articulation of the music.

Instruments From the **Same Family** Have **Similar Timbres**

Even though each instrument has a unique timbre, it can still sometimes be hard to tell ones from the same family apart. Different families of instruments change the timbre in different ways:

STRING INSTRUMENTS

- String instruments (like the violin, viola, cello and double bass) have a warm sound. Notes are produced by making the strings vibrate, either using a bow or the fingers.
- All string instruments can be played *con arco* (with a bow), *pizzicato* (plucked), *con sordino* (muted) or *sul ponticello* (close to the bridge).
- Double stopping is when two strings are pressed at the same time, so two notes can be played at once.
- Tremolo sounds like trembling — the bow is moved back and forth very quickly.

PIANO

- When you press the keys, a hammer hits the strings inside the piano, making them vibrate.
- The timbre of the piano can be changed by using the soft or sustain pedals.

There's more on families of instruments and types of ensembles on pages 62-71.

WOODWIND INSTRUMENTS

- Wind instruments (e.g. flute, clarinet, oboe and bassoon) have a soft, mellow sound.
- Edge-tone instruments (e.g. flutes) make a softer, breathier sound than reed instruments (e.g. clarinets).
- Clarinets and oboes can alter their timbre by using a technique called 'bells up', where the player points the end of the instrument upwards. This produces a harsher sound.

BRASS INSTRUMENTS

- Brass instruments (like the trumpet, French horn, trombone and tuba) have a bright, metallic sound.
- Playing with a mute (*con sordino*) can change the timbre.

PERCUSSION INSTRUMENTS

- Percussion instruments (e.g. drums and xylophones) make a sound when they're struck.
- What you hit them with can change the timbre — e.g. whether you use sticks, brushes or your hands.

SINGERS

- Singers produce notes when their vocal cords vibrate.
- The speed that they vibrate changes the pitch and the timbre — e.g. bass voices sound very different to sopranos.
- Techniques like vibrato (making the note wobble) can give a richer sound.
- Falsetto singing produces a much thinner sound.

I'm picking up good vibrations...

You may be asked to describe the timbre of different instruments that crop up in your exam.

Timbre

Electronic effects can be used to **alter** the timbre of an instrument or voice.

There are Lots of Different **Electronic Effects**

1) There are loads of <u>different ways</u> to <u>change</u> the sound of an instrument.

2) These effects are often used with electric guitars — they're really popular with <u>rock bands</u>, especially during <u>guitar solos</u>. Guitarists use <u>pedals</u> (e.g. a <u>wah-wah</u> pedal) to alter the <u>tone</u> or <u>pitch</u>.

3) The effects can also be used to change the sound of recorded music during <u>mixing</u> or <u>post-processing</u>.

4) <u>Electronic effects</u> (also called <u>studio effects</u>) include:

- **DISTORTION** <u>distorts</u> the sound.
- **REVERB** adds an <u>echo</u> to the sound.
- **CHORUS** makes it sound as if there's <u>more than one</u> player or singer — <u>copies</u> of the original sound are <u>mixed together</u>, with slight changes in <u>timing</u> and <u>pitch</u>.
- **PHASER** creates a '<u>whooshing</u>' effect (a bit like the noise an <u>aeroplane</u> flying overhead makes).
- **FLANGER** similar to a <u>phaser</u>, but makes a more <u>intense</u> sound. The effect is created by <u>combining</u> the <u>original sound</u> with a <u>copy</u>, and <u>varying the delay</u> between them. It's used a lot in <u>sci-fi programmes</u>.
- **PITCH SHIFTING** used to <u>bend</u> the natural note or <u>add</u> another <u>harmony</u>.
- **OCTAVE EFFECTS** creates <u>octaves</u> above or below the note being played.

Synthesized Sounds have Different Timbres to Real Sounds

1) The <u>natural</u> sound of an instrument can be digitally reproduced to create a <u>synthesized sound</u>.

2) <u>Electronic keyboards</u> have different <u>settings</u>, so they can be made to sound like pretty much any instrument, from violins to percussion.

> One big <u>difference</u> between <u>real</u> and <u>synthesized sounds</u> is what happens to the <u>timbre</u> when the <u>volume</u> changes. When a <u>real</u> instrument is played <u>louder</u>, it has a <u>different timbre</u> to when it's played quietly. However, a <u>synthesized</u> sound has the <u>same timbre</u> at any volume — it's just the <u>loudness</u> that changes.

Sampling Uses Recordings of Real Instruments

1) The most effective way to <u>recreate</u> the sounds of real instruments is to use <u>sampling</u> (see p.73).

2) Sampling is where you <u>record</u> an instrument and use the recording (called a <u>sample</u>) in your music.

3) The samples can be <u>altered</u> to create different effects — there are lots of different <u>computer programs</u> that help you do this.

4) Samples can be <u>looped</u> (played over and over again), and other samples can be added <u>over the top</u>.

5) Most <u>electronic music</u> produced today uses looping, especially <u>drum patterns</u>.

6) It's <u>not</u> just instruments that can be sampled — you can take samples of anything you like, e.g. <u>traffic noises</u> or <u>doorbells</u>.

7) Lots of <u>pop songs</u> use samples — see if you can spot any in your favourite songs.

I'd like a sample of that cake please...

Have a listen to the 2005 hit '<u>Gold Digger</u>' by <u>Kanye West</u> — he uses a sample of '<u>I Got A Woman</u>' by <u>Ray Charles</u> (which was released more than 50 years earlier, in 1954).

Warm-up and Exam Questions

The questions on these pages are great for finding out what you know — don't ignore them.

Warm-up Questions

1) For each of the words below, name an instrument that links with the word:

   slide   single reed   double reed   pizzicato   wooden bars

2) Explain each of these words and phrases:

   tremolo   con sordino   tenor   falsetto

3) Name the **three** main types of guitar and briefly describe each of them.

4) In which period was the harpsichord the most popular keyboard instrument?

5) Explain the difference between a military band, a brass band and a jazz band.

6) List all the instruments that play in a piano trio and a clarinet quintet.

7) Define the following terms:

   MIDI   sampler   remix   sequencer

Exam Question

Brush up on your exam technique with this question.

This question is about two excerpts, Track 30 and Track 31.
First play Track 30 **three** times, leaving a short pause for writing time
between each playing.

Tracks
30-31

Track 30

a)   Name the solo woodwind instrument that plays at the beginning.

....
[1 mark]

b)   What is the other instrument that plays in the excerpt?

....
[1 mark]

Exam Question

c) Tick **one** box to indicate which shape best represents the opening of the melody played by the solo instrument.

Shape A ☐

Shape B ☐

Shape C ☐

[1 mark]

d) Describe the relationship of the two instruments heard here. Refer to the **texture** and any other interesting features.

....

....

[2 marks]

Two marks available means you need to make two points. Don't forget to write about texture.

Track 31

Now play Track 31 **three** times, leaving a short pause for writing time between each playing.

e) Name the two solo woodwind instruments which play the melody at the beginning of this excerpt.

....

....

[2 marks]

Make sure you write about the melody, not the accompaniment.

Turn over

Exam Question

f) Name the family of instruments playing throughout this excerpt.

    ....

    [1 mark]

g) Ring the word that describes the scale used throughout the excerpt.

    major   minor   chromatic

    [1 mark]

h) Tick one of the following to represent the backing melody played by the two
    wind instruments.

    A   ☐

    B   ☐

    C   ☐

    [1 mark]

i) Ring **one** feature that you can hear in this excerpt.

    accelerando   crescendo   ritardando

    [1 mark]

Revision Summary for Section Five

That's a wrap on Section Five — have a go at these questions to see what you remember.
- Try these questions and tick off each one when you get it right.
- When you've done all the questions for a topic and are completely happy with it, tick off the topic.

Brass, Woodwind and Orchestral Strings (p.62-64) ☑

1) Name three brass instruments.
2) How do you vary the pitch on a brass instrument?
3) Name three woodwind instruments.
4) What are the three different mouthpieces used on woodwind instruments called? How do they work?
5) What are all those little keys, springs and levers for on a woodwind instrument?
6) What's the smallest orchestral string instrument?
7) What's the biggest string instrument that you play with a bow?
8) How do you make different notes on a string instrument?
9) What makes a harp different from the other string instruments? Give three differences.
10) Where would you put a mute on a bowed string instrument and what effect would it have?

Guitars, Keyboards, Percussion and Voices (p.65-68) ☑

11) How many strings are there on: a) an acoustic guitar   b) an electric guitar   c) a bass guitar?
12) What do you call those metal bits on the fingerboard of a guitar? Do you get them on a bass?
13) What's the proper word for twanging a guitar string with a plectrum?
14) Name three different keyboard instruments.
15) What's the biggest type of keyboard instrument?
16) What's the most popular keyboard instrument?
17) How could you tell you were listening to a church organ and not a harpsichord?
18) Name three tuned percussion instruments and six untuned percussion instruments.
19) What's the highest type of singing voice? What's the lowest type of singing voice?
20) What do you call a boy's voice when it's got the same range as a soprano?

Ensembles and Groups (p.69-71) ☑

21) How can you tell the difference between a wind band and a brass band?
22) What are the two sections of a jazz orchestra called, and what are their jobs?
23) Why's chamber music called chamber music?
24) How many people are there in: a) a trio   b) a sextet   c) a quartet   d) an octet?
25) How many clarinets are there in a clarinet quintet?
26) Sketch a plan of a standard symphony orchestra. Label the different sections and the conductor.
27) What sections are there in a string orchestra, chamber orchestra and jazz orchestra?

Music Technology and Timbre (p.72-75) ☑

28) How is MIDI information stored?
29) What do sequencers do?
30) What are samples? How can they be used in tracks?
31) Explain how sound is produced on: a) a string instrument   b) a piano   c) a brass instrument?
32) Name four different electronic effects.

The Baroque Style

You need to know all about the **features** and **development** of **Western classical music** between **1650** and **1910**. Let's start with the musical style from the start of that period — **Baroque music**.

Baroque has a Recognisable Sound

The Baroque period was from about 1600-1750. Key composers include Bach, Handel, Vivaldi and Purcell. Baroque music's pretty easy to recognise. These are the main things to look out for:

1) The melodies are built up from short musical ideas (called motifs), so you get quite a bit of repetition.

2) The harmonies are simple, with a fairly narrow range of chords — mainly I and V.

3) The melody is packed with ornaments, added in to make it sound more interesting (see p.84).

4) The music often involves counterpoint — where two or more different lines of melody are played at the same time. This texture is described as contrapuntal (or polyphonic — see p.45).

5) The dynamics change suddenly. Each bit is either loud or soft — this is called terraced or stepped dynamics. You won't hear any gradual changes in volume (no crescendos or diminuendos). This is mainly due to the prominence of the harpsichord in Baroque music — harpsichords could either play loud or soft, but couldn't change gradually between the two.

6) Baroque music is tonal:

> • From about 1600, Western composers used major and minor keys to write tonal music — this replaced modal music (see p.27).
>
> • Composers used modulation to switch between keys (see p.44) — this created contrast in their music.
>
> • Compositions were often made up of sections in different keys, with modulation between them. New structures were developed for organising pieces of music with a number of sections, e.g. binary and ternary forms (see next page).

String and Keyboard Instruments Played Key Roles

1) String instruments were dominant in a Baroque orchestra (just like today) — violins, violas, cellos and double basses were all used. (If you see 'violone' in the score, it's played by a double bass today.)

2) Keyboard instruments such as the harpsichord and organ were also very important in Baroque music.

3) Woodwind instruments such as the flute, recorder, oboe and bassoon were also used.

4) The instruments available were much more limited than in the later musical periods. There were some early forms of brass instruments, such as trumpets and horns, but they didn't have any valves so could only play a limited range of notes.

5) Orchestras were generally small compared to modern orchestras. The size of an orchestra depended on the resources available, and the performance space. Music was often performed by chamber groups (see p.70) with a small number of musicians, but there were larger orchestras too.

Baroque Music Often Had a Basso Continuo

> 1) A basso continuo is a continuous bass part (see page 57). It's played throughout a piece, and is based on the chords of the piece.
> 2) It was often played on an organ or harpsichord, but could also feature additional instruments — e.g. cellos, double basses or bassoons.

 'Baroque Around the Clock' was a huge hit...
You have to spot key features of Baroque music in the exam so make sure you learn them.

Baroque Structures

Baroque composers used various **standard structures** to construct their music.

The **Concerto Grosso** was a **Popular Form** of **Orchestral Music**

- In a concerto grosso, a small group of soloists (called the concertino) is contrasted with the rest of the orchestra (the ripieno) and the basso continuo. The ripieno is usually a string orchestra. Handel wrote several concerto grossi (plural for grosso) — in his Concerto Grosso No. 5 (Op. 6), the concertino is made up of two violins and a cello, the ripieno is a string orchestra, and the continuo is played on the harpsichord. J.S. Bach's Brandenburg Concertos are concerto grossi.

- Baroque composers also wrote solo concertos. Here a single solo instrument is 'showcased', allowing its performer to demonstrate the instrument's capabilities, accompanied by an orchestra. Vivaldi's 'Four Seasons' is a solo concerto for the violin. It was this type of concerto that was further developed by composers such as Mozart and Haydn in the Classical period — see p.91.

Binary and **Ternary Forms** are Made Up of **Different Sections**

1) Binary means something like 'in two parts' — binary form has two sections.
2) Binary form is usually used for Baroque dances, e.g. bourrée, minuet, gavotte, sarabande and gigue.
3) Each section is repeated. You play Section A twice, and then Section B twice, so it goes AABB.
4) Section B contrasts with Section A — the two bits should sound different.
5) The contrast is often made by modulating to related keys. Pieces in a minor key usually modulate to the relative major, e.g. A minor to C major. Pieces in a major key usually modulate to the dominant key (V), e.g. C major to G major.

1) Ternary form has three sections. The general structure is ABA, but the sections are often repeated, producing structures such as AABBAA.
2) Section A ends in the home key, normally with a perfect cadence (see pages 42-43). This makes it sound like a complete piece in itself.
3) In Section B the music often modulates to a related key, like the dominant or relative minor, and then goes back to the home key before it ends.
4) The last section can be exactly the same as Section A, or a slightly varied version. If it is varied, you call it A1 instead of A.

In a ritornello, the same musical idea or theme is repeated at various points in the piece. A more formal structure of this type is a rondo, where a main theme (A) is repeated, separated by a number of different sections, creating forms such as ABACA (see p.93).

Some **Works** Have an **Introduction** Called a **Prelude**

1) In the Baroque period, a prelude was a short, relatively simple piece of music. It usually served as an introduction to a longer piece or to a number of pieces of music.
2) The first movement of a suite (a set of dances) is often a prelude.
3) A prelude was often used as an introduction to a more complex piece such as a fugue. Bach wrote a prelude and fugue in each of the 24 keys in 'The Well-Tempered Clavier' — a collection of solo pieces for keyboard instruments.
4) In the Romantic period (see p.99-100), the term came to be used to describe a short, stand-alone piece.

This page is just a prelude to yet more fascinating structures...

You need to be able to spot these various structures, so make sure you learn all their features. If you're struggling to identify the different sections, listen out for a change of key — it'll probably be a new section.

Baroque Structures

Variations are pieces which start with **one pattern** or tune, and then **change it** in different ways. There are **two** main structures for variations. They're called '**theme and variation**' and '**ground bass**'.

Theme and Variation Form Varies the Melody

- In <u>theme and variation form</u>, the theme's usually a memorable <u>melody</u>.
- The theme is played <u>first</u>. There's a short <u>pause</u> before the <u>first variation</u> is played, then another pause before the next variation. Each variation is a <u>self-contained</u> piece of music. There can be <u>as many</u> or <u>as few</u> variations as the composer wants.
- Each variation should be a <u>recognisable</u> version of the main theme, but <u>different</u> from all the others.

'The Harmonious Blacksmith' by Handel is in theme and variation form.

You can vary a melody in loads of simple ways:

1) Start off with a <u>basic theme</u>...

2) <u>Add notes</u> to make the melody more complex.

3) <u>Remove</u> notes to <u>simplify</u> the melody.

4) Change the <u>metre</u> — e.g. from 2 beats in a bar to 3.

5) Add a <u>countermelody</u> — an extra melody over the top of the theme.

6) You can also change the <u>tempo</u>, change the <u>key</u> (from major to minor or vice versa), change some or all of the <u>chords</u> or add a different type of <u>accompaniment</u> instead of block chords.

A <u>fantasia</u> is a composition with an <u>improvised</u> feel — the composer uses their <u>imagination</u> and <u>skill</u> to compose a piece that <u>doesn't</u> follow a <u>set structure</u>. Fantasias often involve <u>variations</u> on a <u>theme</u>.

Ground Bass Form Varies Ideas Over a Fixed Bass Part

<u>Ground bass</u> is a <u>continuous</u> set of variations — there are <u>no pauses</u>. The main theme (called the <u>ground</u>) is a <u>bass line</u> which <u>repeats</u> throughout the piece — it is also known as <u>basso ostinato</u>. <u>Varying melodies</u> and <u>harmonies</u> which become gradually <u>more complex</u> are played <u>over</u> the ground. There are two types of Baroque dance that are in ground bass form — the <u>chaconne</u> and <u>passacaglia</u>. They're quite <u>slow</u> and <u>stately</u>.

Freshly ground bass — it goes all powdery...

Make sure you've learnt all the ins and outs of these structures. The examples of variations on this page are fairly simple, but they can become quite complex and require a lot of skill and practice to play well.

Baroque Melody Patterns

Composers often create a melody by starting with a **key phrase**, then **adapting** it using different **techniques**.

Melodic Inversion — Turning the Tune **Upside Down**

With <u>melodic inversion</u> you keep the <u>same intervals</u> between the notes, but they go in the <u>opposite direction</u>, i.e. down instead of up, and up instead of down. Basically you turn the tune on its head.

The first melody goes up a major third from C to E, then up a minor third to G.

In the inversion the melody goes down a major third to A♭, then down a minor third from A♭ to F.

Retrograde — Playing the Tune **Backwards**

Playing the notes <u>in reverse order</u> but with the same rhythm is called <u>retrograde</u>. This is the retrograde version of the first melody (above).

If you switch the notes so they're in reverse order <u>and</u> inverted, you get a <u>retrograde inversion</u>. This is the retrograde inversion of the first melody.

Sequencing — Repeat a **Pattern**, Vary the **Pitch**

1) Repeat the <u>pattern</u> of a phrase but start on a <u>different note</u>, higher or lower. This is called a <u>sequence</u>.

2) <u>Ascending</u> sequences go up in pitch. <u>Descending</u> sequences go down.

Imitation — Repeat a Phrase With **Slight Changes**

1) In <u>imitation</u>, a phrase is repeated with <u>slight changes</u> each time.

2) It works really well if one instrument or voice imitates <u>another</u> and then <u>overlaps</u>.

original phrase

original phrase, one octave higher

imitation with modulation

overlap starts in relative minor

Ostinato — Keep **One Pattern** the **Same**, Change the Rest

1) An ostinato is a pattern that's played <u>over and over</u> again.

2) The rest of the piece <u>changes around it</u>.

3) An ostinato is usually in the <u>bass</u> line, but it can be in other parts too.

4) <u>Ground bass form</u> (p.82) features ostinato <u>phrases</u> in the bass line — the repeated phrases can be quite <u>long</u>.

Here's the repeating pattern.

Ornaments in Baroque Music

Ornaments are **short extra notes** that liven up the main melody — Baroque composers used them a lot in their music. There are a few **different types** of ornament...

A **Trill** is Lots of **Tiny Quick Notes**

1) In <u>Baroque</u> music, the trill starts one note <u>above</u> the written note then goes quickly <u>back and forth</u> between the <u>written note</u> and the note you <u>started</u> on.
2) Sometimes a trill ends with a <u>turn</u> (see below).
3) If the note above the written note <u>doesn't</u> belong to the <u>key signature</u>, there'll be a <u>sharp</u>, <u>flat</u> or <u>natural</u> sign above the trill symbol.
4) A trill is slightly different in <u>Classical</u> music — it starts <u>on</u> the written note and goes <u>up</u> to the note above.

This is how you play a trill in Baroque music...

The trill lasts the same length of time as the written note.

An **Appoggiatura** is an **Extra Note** in a **Chord**

1) The appoggiatura starts on a note that <u>clashes</u> with the chord, then moves to a note that <u>belongs</u> in the chord (this is called the <u>resolution</u>).
2) The two notes are usually just one <u>tone</u> or <u>semitone</u> apart.
3) It normally takes <u>half the time value</u> of the note it 'leans' on.

Squeezing in a **Tiny Note** is Called **Acciaccatura**

"Acciaccatura" means <u>crushing in</u>. An acciaccatura is a note that's squeezed in before the main note and played <u>as fast as possible</u>.

Mordents and **Turns** are **Set Patterns** of Notes

MORDENTS

Mordents <u>start off</u> like trills.
The difference is they <u>end</u> on the written note, which is played a bit <u>longer</u> than the trilled notes. There are loads of different mordents but these two are the most common.

TURNS

Start on the note <u>above</u> the written note, then play the <u>written note</u>, followed by the note <u>below</u> the written note. End back on the <u>written note</u>.

For an <u>inverted turn</u> play the note <u>below</u> the written note, the written note, the note above that and finally the written note.

 I've done my bit — now it's your turn...
COMPOSING TIP
Take a look at p.41 for more on decoration. You might even want to add some of these ornaments to your compositions to make them more exciting (don't go overboard though).

Choral Music

Choirs have been around for ages. They vary in size from just a **few** singers to **hundreds**, and perform anywhere from **school halls** and **churches** to **concert halls**, **theatres** and **cathedrals**.

Choral Music has Been Around for Over 600 Years

1) The first choral pieces were sung in churches in the 14th century. Before that, monks used to sing plainsong (a unison chant).
2) Most choral music in Renaissance and Baroque times was sacred (church music). Some was sung a cappella (without accompaniment) and some was accompanied by an instrument, such as an organ.
3) Masses were sung in Catholic churches. They were part of the church service. A requiem was a mass for the dead. There's more about masses and requiems on p.103.
4) Oratorios are Bible stories set to music (see next page). Masses, requiems and oratorios are all sacred music. They're made up of choir sections and solo sections.
5) Secular (non-religious) choral music is mainly made up of choruses in operas (see next page). Operas often tell love stories and are performed on stage. The chorus emphasises important bits.

Choirs Were Originally All Male

There's more on the different types of voice on p.68.

1) Baroque choirs were fairly small — they'd sometimes have just one singer on each part. All parts were sung by men (women were banned from singing in church).
2) Most choir music was written for 4 different voices: treble (a boy soprano), countertenor or alto (a high-pitched voice known as falsetto), tenor (a high male voice) and bass (a low male voice).
3) By the Victorian era, choirs were huge — they'd often have over 100 members (it was a popular Victorian hobby). The Huddersfield Choral Society was started in 1836 and still exists today.
4) Some choirs are mixed-sex, with music arranged for SATB voices: soprano (a high female voice), alto (a lower female voice), tenor (a high male voice) and bass (a low male voice).
5) All-female choirs are usually SSAA (2 soprano parts and 2 alto parts) or SSA (2 soprano parts and 1 alto part). Male voice choirs are often TTBB (2 tenor parts, 1 baritone part and 1 bass part).

Choral Singing is Still Popular Today

• 20th and 21st century choirs are generally smaller than the large Victorian choirs — they'll often have around 80 members though. Some can have as many as 130 members.
• Lots of 20th century choral works are written for chamber choir and chamber orchestra. These are just small versions of choirs and orchestras (they're called 'chamber' because they used to perform in rooms or chambers, rather than a concert hall). Chamber choirs normally have 20-25 members.
• Chamber choir pieces may have been a reaction against 19th century composers, who often composed pieces for massive choirs.

Choirs Have Soloists Too

There are sometimes solo sections in choral works — the soloist might be accompanied by the rest of the choir, or just sing on their own, with or without orchestral accompaniment. The main solo voices are:

• Soprano, alto, tenor or bass (as described above).
• Mezzo-sopranos (a female voice that's lower than a soprano but higher than an alto), baritones (a male voice that's lower than a tenor but higher than a bass) or contralto (the lowest female voice that has a similar range to a countertenor).

Requiems, oratorios — there's Masses of stuff on this page...

J.S. Bach and Handel wrote a lot of choral music in the Baroque period — both sacred and secular. There's a whole page on Handel's oratorios and anthems on p.87 (but Bach doesn't get a page — sorry Bach).

Operas and Oratorios

Operas and oratorios are large vocal works, both made up of solo and chorus sections.

Operas are Like Plays Set to Music

1) An opera is a story set to music with singing and acting. Most operas are divided up into three parts (or 'Acts'). Operas are secular (non-religious).

2) The main characters are played by solo singers and are supported by a chorus and an orchestra.

3) The story is acted out — usually with lavish sets, costumes and special effects.

4) In some operas every single word is sung (this is known as sung-through) — in others there's a bit of talking from time to time.

5) Some operas have really serious, tragic themes. Others are more light-hearted and comic. These are the names for the main types:

6) The words of an opera are called the 'libretto'. This is often written by a 'librettist' working alongside the composer.

Grand opera	serious, set entirely to music (sung-through)
Opera seria	formal, serious opera, often mythological themes
Opera buffa	comic opera with lighter, more everyday themes
Opéra comique	like opera buffa but with some spoken dialogue
Operetta	shorter than a proper opera, lighter themes

In Opera There are Three Types of Song

ARIA

- An aria is a solo vocal piece, backed by the orchestra.

- Arias are used to show the thoughts and emotions of the main characters.

- The arias have the memorable, exciting tunes. They're challenging for the performers and let them show their vocal tone and agility.

In England and France, arias are sometimes known as 'airs'.

RECITATIVE

- A recitative is a song for a soloist that tells the story and moves it along. The rhythm of the words tends to imitate the rhythm of normal speech.

- A recitativo secco is a recitative that's unaccompanied or backed by simple chords.

- A recitativo stromentato or accompagnato is a recitative with orchestral backing. The accompaniment is used to increase the dramatic tension of the words.

CHORUS — A bit where the whole chorus (or choir) sings together. Choruses are usually written for SATB choirs (see previous page), but in Baroque operas the soprano parts would be sung by trebles (boy sopranos).

Oratorios are Religious Versions of Operas

1) Oratorios often tell Bible stories, or tales with a religious or moral theme — they're a type of sacred music.

2) They're not usually acted out with scenery and costumes (unlike operas).

3) They normally have an instrumental accompaniment.

4) Oratorios have arias, recitatives and choruses just like operas.

COMPOSER	LIVED	FAMOUS ORATORIO
Carissimi	1605-1674	Jephte
Handel	1685-1759	Messiah
Haydn	1732-1809	The Creation
Berlioz	1803-1869	L'Enfance du Christ
Mendelssohn	1809-1847	Elijah
Elgar	1857-1934	The Dream of Gerontius
Tippett	1905-1998	A Child of Our Time

5) The table above gives some composers and their most famous oratorios. Have a listen to them and try to spot the different types of song, as well as listening out for the different musical styles.

Handel

Handel was one of the most important composers in the Baroque period.

Handel was a **German Composer**

1) <u>George Frideric Handel</u> was born in <u>Germany</u> in <u>1685</u>. From about <u>1710</u>, he lived in <u>England</u>. He died in <u>London</u> in <u>1759</u> and is buried in <u>Westminster Abbey</u>.

2) He was popular with <u>Queen Anne</u>, <u>George I</u> and <u>George II</u> — he composed '<u>Zadok the Priest</u>' for the <u>coronation</u> of George II (see below), and it's been played at every coronation since then. He also wrote music for the <u>Calvinist</u> church in Germany and the <u>Church of England</u>.

3) Handel wrote loads of music, including lots of <u>oratorios</u> and <u>operas</u> (see p.86). As well as <u>choral music</u>, he also wrote many <u>orchestral</u> pieces — one of the most famous is the '<u>Water Music</u>'.

Messiah is a Famous **Oratorio** by Handel

He also wrote lots of other oratorios — including Solomon, Israel in Egypt and Judas Maccabaeus (which has the famous 'See the Conquering Hero').

1) <u>Messiah</u> tells the story of <u>Jesus' life</u>.

2) It's written for <u>SATB soloists</u>, <u>SATB choir</u> and a <u>full orchestra</u>. At the time Handel wrote it, all the parts would have been sung by <u>men</u>.

3) Handel wrote it for a <u>small choir</u>, but it has since been performed by choirs with <u>hundreds</u> of singers.

4) Much of the Messiah is <u>melismatic</u> (a <u>single syllable</u> of text is sung over a <u>succession</u> of notes). In the chorus '<u>For Unto Us a Child is Born</u>', the <u>soprano</u> part has a run of <u>57 notes</u> for the word '<u>born</u>'.

The opposite of melismatic is syllabic, where every syllable is sung to a single note.

Tenor
Crook - ed

5) Handel also uses <u>word-painting</u> — where the music <u>matches</u> the words. E.g. the word '<u>crooked</u>' is <u>split</u> over four notes each time it is sung, making it <u>sound</u> crooked.

6) The most famous bit of the Messiah is probably the '<u>Hallelujah Chorus</u>', but there are lots of other <u>choruses</u>, <u>recitatives</u> and <u>arias</u> (as well as some <u>duets</u> and <u>instrumental</u> sections).

Handel Wrote the **Coronation Anthems** for **George II**

1) Handel wrote four <u>anthems</u> (<u>choral pieces</u> performed in <u>Protestant churches</u>) for the <u>coronation</u> of <u>George II</u> and <u>Queen Caroline</u> in <u>October 1727</u>.

2) The anthems are '<u>Zadok the Priest</u>', '<u>Let Thy Hand Be Strengthened</u>', '<u>The King Shall Rejoice</u>' and '<u>My Heart is Inditing</u>'. Each one is divided into different <u>sections</u>. The <u>lyrics</u> are taken from the <u>Bible</u>.

3) As they were written for a <u>grand occasion</u>, the anthems need a <u>large choir</u> and <u>massive orchestra</u> to perform them, which emphasised the <u>importance</u> of the event.

4) Although the <u>strings</u> are used for most of the <u>accompaniment</u>, Handel frequently uses <u>trumpet fanfares</u> in the most <u>triumphant</u> sections (e.g. when the choir sings '<u>rejoic'd</u>' in 'Zadok the Priest'), which adds to the <u>ceremonial</u> feel. He also uses <u>oboes</u>, <u>bassoons</u>, <u>timpani</u> and <u>organ</u> (which plays a <u>basso continuo</u> in some sections).

5) Much of the music is in a <u>major key</u> as it was written for a <u>celebration</u>, but there are a couple of sections in a <u>minor key</u> for the more <u>solemn</u> aspects of the coronation.

6) Handel uses a variety of <u>textures</u> to different effects. For example, the repeated line '<u>God Save the King</u>' in 'Zadok the Priest' is sung <u>homophonically</u> in <u>rich chords</u> to give it more <u>impact</u>. In contrast, the '<u>Alleluja</u>' section of 'Let Thy Hand Be Strengthened' is <u>polyphonic</u>, with parts weaving in and out of each other in <u>imitation</u> to give it a <u>bright</u>, <u>celebratory feel</u>. There's also <u>parallel harmony</u> (see p.45), with parts moving together in <u>thirds</u> (e.g. in the 'Glory and Worship' section of 'The King Shall Rejoice').

SUGGESTED LISTENING

Hallelujah — it's the end of the page...

Have a listen to 'Zadok the Priest' — it's in D major and sounds very triumphant. The last section ends with a plagal cadence (a plagal cadence is chord IV then chord I — see p.43).

From Baroque to Classical

Classical music came from Baroque, so it's **similar but not the same**...

Tastes Moved Towards a Simpler Sound

Classical
1750–1820

1) The <u>Classical</u> period of music was from around <u>1750 to 1820</u>. <u>Mozart</u>, <u>Haydn</u> and <u>Beethoven</u> were key composers during this time.

2) The style of music <u>didn't just change overnight</u> — the Classical style <u>developed</u> from the Baroque style as <u>tastes changed</u> and <u>instruments</u> became more <u>versatile</u>.

3) Towards the <u>end</u> of the Baroque era, many composers <u>moved away</u> from the <u>polyphonic</u> sound (see p.45) that had been a key feature of the period. They began to write more <u>homophonic music</u> with a <u>clear melody line</u> and <u>fewer ornaments</u> (see p.84).

4) This development can be seen in the compositions of J.S. Bach's sons, <u>C.P.E. Bach</u> and <u>J.C. Bach</u>. They were influenced by <u>new styles</u> as well as their <u>father's compositions</u>, and they composed much more <u>homophonic</u> music than their father.

5) There was also a move towards more <u>subtle dynamics</u>. Composers began to use <u>crescendos</u> and <u>diminuendos</u> rather than sudden changes in volume — this was partly due to the invention of the <u>piano</u> (see below).

Forms and Structures Developed Too

1) Baroque forms and structures <u>changed over time</u>, and grew into popular Classical <u>structures</u>:

- The <u>solo concerto</u> became <u>more popular</u> than the <u>concerto grosso</u> (see p.81) — it became an <u>important form</u> in the <u>Classical period</u>.

- The <u>Baroque trio sonata</u> consisted of a number of movements played by <u>three instruments</u> plus a <u>harpsichord continuo</u>. This developed into the <u>Classical sonata</u>, a form consisting of three or four movements, usually composed for a <u>solo instrument</u> (see p.91).

- In the <u>Baroque</u> period, operas often began with an '<u>Italian overture</u>' — an <u>orchestral</u> piece consisting of <u>three sections</u> — a <u>fast</u> section followed by a <u>slow</u> section, followed by another <u>fast</u> section. These pieces were often performed <u>independently</u> of the opera. The <u>Classical symphony</u> (see p.92) developed from this (although Classical symphonies tended to have <u>four</u> movements).

2) Other forms that were popular in the Baroque period continued to be used — <u>binary form</u>, <u>ternary form</u> and <u>theme and variation form</u> (see p.81-82) were still <u>important</u> in the <u>Classical era</u>. <u>New structures</u> such as <u>sonata form</u> (p.92) were also developed.

The Invention of the Piano had a Big Impact

- The <u>piano</u> was invented in about <u>1700</u>. It became more popular than the harpsichord because it was able to create a much <u>greater variety</u> of tones — the notes could be played in a <u>legato</u> or <u>staccato</u> style and the <u>dynamics</u> could be <u>varied</u> depending on how hard the keys were pressed. The full name of the piano is actually '<u>pianoforte</u>', which means '<u>soft-loud</u>'.

- <u>C.P.E. Bach</u> and <u>J.C. Bach</u> both composed for the <u>piano</u> and were <u>influential</u> in increasing its <u>popularity</u>. The piano became <u>very widely used</u> in Classical music.

- <u>Other instruments</u> (such as the <u>clarinet</u>) were <u>developed</u>, and this led to important changes in the structure of the <u>orchestra</u> — see the next page.

Souvenir shops suffered terribly as the use of ornaments declined...

Remember, Classical music developed from Baroque music, so many of the features you've come across in Baroque music still make an appearance. But there's lots of new stuff to get to grips with too...

The Classical Orchestra

Orchestras **got bigger** during the Classical period as new instruments were developed.
The **set-up** of an orchestra (i.e. what instruments were included) became more **standardised**.

Orchestral Music was Written for **Wealthy Audiences**

1) At the start of the Classical period, composers worked for royalty and aristocrats.
   They were paid to write music for official events, church services and plain old entertainment.
   Composers had to write music that their patrons (employers) would approve of.

2) Later in the Classical period, society changed. Middle-class people had more money and
   wanted entertainment. Public concert halls were built, where people could go to listen to music.

3) Famous Classical composers like Haydn and Mozart worked for patrons,
   but they also put on concerts in the new concert halls.

4) By the 1800s, composers could earn quite a bit of money from ticket sales
   at concert halls. This gave them more freedom — they could write for the
   tastes of concert-goers instead of just pleasing their patrons.

Orchestras **Grew** During the **Classical Period**

1) At the start of the Classical period, composers wrote for smallish orchestras — mainly strings,
   with horns, flutes and oboes. There'd be two horns and one or two woodwind.

2) Later on, the woodwind section grew — clarinets were developed during the Classical period and
   were included in the orchestra. Mozart was the first composer to use the clarinet in a symphony.

3) Brass instruments were used more widely. Horns were developed so
   they could produce more notes and play in a greater variety of keys.

4) The percussion section grew too — timpani became a
   standard fixture, and some orchestras used bass drums,
   snare drums, triangles and cymbals as well.

5) In some early Classical music, there'd be a harpsichord (see p.66),
   but after a while composers stopped using it. The harpsichord was
   there to fill in the harmonies, but it wasn't really needed once the
   extra woodwind had been added.

6) This is a fairly typical layout for a later Classical orchestra:

PERCUSSION		
FRENCH HORNS		TRUMPETS
FLUTES		CLARINETS
	OBOES	BASSOONS
SECOND VIOLINS	VIOLAS	DOUBLE BASSES
FIRST VIOLINS		CELLOS

Classical Orchestras Mostly Use **String Instruments**

1) The most important section in a Classical orchestra is the strings.
   They're the dominant sound in most Classical music.
   The violins generally play most of the melodies.

2) The wind instruments play extra notes to fill out the harmony.
   When they do get the tune, they mostly double the string parts.

3) You do hear the occasional wind solo. Orchestral pieces called concertos (see p.91)
   feature one or two solo instruments accompanied by an orchestra.

4) In later Classical music, the woodwind section started to have a more independent role.
   They'd sometimes play the melody alone, and there'd be more solos.
   The strings were still really important though.

You need to know what instruments were used in the Classical era...

Orchestras grew in size because composers in the Classical period began to include more parts
for different instruments. This gave rise to a greater variety of music later in the Classical period.

The Classical Style

A whole page about the features of Classical music... enjoy.

Classical Melodies Have a **Clear, Simple Structure**

Classical music sounds <u>clearer</u> and <u>simpler</u> than music from other periods. This is partly because the melodies are structured in a very straightforward way, with <u>short</u>, <u>balanced</u> 2- or 4-bar phrases.

Here's an excerpt from Haydn's *Clock Symphony* (see p.94):

And here's the opening of Mozart's *Piano Sonata No. 16 in C major* with two-bar phrases:

Classical **Textures** are Mainly **Melody** and **Chords**

1) Most Classical music has just <u>one melody</u> with <u>accompanying chords</u>. This makes the tune really stand out (see page 45).

2) These accompanying chords can be played in <u>different ways</u>:

3) <u>Polyphony</u> (where <u>several tunes</u> weave in and out of each other) is used too, but not as often.

Classical Music Uses **Major** and **Minor Keys**

• Classical music is always in either a major or minor key — the <u>tonality</u> is major or minor.
• <u>Bright</u>, <u>cheery</u> bits are in major keys and <u>gloomy</u>, <u>sad</u> bits are in minor keys.
• Classical harmony is what's known as <u>diatonic</u> — nearly <u>all</u> the notes belong to the <u>main key</u>.

The **Beat** is Obvious and **Easy to Follow**

• The <u>metre</u> in Classical music is very regular. You can happily <u>tap your foot</u> in time to the music.
• The <u>tempo</u> stays <u>constant</u> — the speed of the beat stays pretty much the same all the way through, <u>without</u> massively <u>speeding up</u> or <u>slowing down</u>.

Classical style — a wig, tailcoat and breeches...

This is important stuff, so make sure you're happy with the key features of the Classical period. Make a list of them all, then learn it. Keep going over it to check you know them off by heart.

Classical Structures

Concertos, sonatas and symphonies were very popular in the Classical period.
Take your time and make sure that you're familiar with each one of these structures.

Concertos are Played by a Soloist and Orchestra

1) A concerto is a piece for a soloist and orchestra. The soloist has most of the melody, and can really show off. The orchestra does get the melody too — they're not just an accompaniment.

2) A concerto usually has three movements — quick, slow and quick.

3) They often have a bit called a cadenza (p.57), where the orchestra stops and the soloist can show everyone how brilliant they are. A cadenza is sometimes improvised — it's often just indicated by a pause above the music.

4) Piano and violin concertos were the most popular in the Classical period, but some concertos were written for other solo instruments too. Composers used concertos to showcase the new instruments (like the clarinet and the keyed trumpet) and show off their capabilities.

5) Famous examples of Classical concertos include Haydn's Trumpet Concerto in E♭ major (listen out for the cadenza in the first movement) and Mozart's Horn Concerto No. 4 in E♭ major.

A Symphony is Played by a Full Orchestra

1) A symphony is a massive piece. They can last more than an hour and have real impact because they use the full orchestra.

2) Symphonies usually have four movements (but some have three, and they can have more than four). The contrast between the movements is important.

3) At least one of the movements is in sonata form (see next page) — usually the first, and sometimes the last.

4) Examples include Haydn's Surprise Symphony and Beethoven's Eroica Symphony.

Overtures and Suites were also Written for Orchestras

• An overture is a one-movement piece for orchestra.

• Overtures are written as introductions to larger works like operas and ballets.

• They use ideas, moods and musical themes from the main work to prepare the audience. For an example, have a listen to Mozart's overture to his opera *The Magic Flute*.

• Classical orchestral suites are another offshoot of ballets and operas.

• In music from this period, a 'suite' is an orchestral arrangement of the music used to accompany the action on stage. It would be put together as a separate piece of music and played at concerts.

Sonatas are for One or Two Instruments

1) Sonatas are mostly written for one instrument, but there are some sonatas for two instruments and a few for two different instruments, with each one playing a different part.

2) A sonata usually has three or four movements, with breaks in between them.

3) A sonata has a similar structure to a symphony — it has one or more movements in sonata form (see next page).

4) Piano sonatas were very popular in the Classical era — Haydn alone wrote 62. Have a listen to Mozart's Piano Sonata in C Major, Haydn's Piano Sonata in C Major and Beethoven's Sonata Pathétique.

Classical Structures

The **movements** of compositions were usually written in **standard forms** and arranged in a certain order. **Symphonies**, **sonatas** and **concertos** all follow a **similar pattern** — now there's a stroke of luck...

Symphonies, Sonatas and Concertos have a Standard Structure

1) The four movements of a symphony have the forms shown in the table below.

2) Sonatas with four movements also follow this structure. If the sonata only has three movements, the minuet (third movement in the table) is left out.

3) Concertos usually have three movements — they have the first, second and fourth movements from the table.

FIRST MOVEMENT	sonata form	brisk and purposeful
SECOND MOVEMENT	ternary or variation form	slower and songlike
THIRD MOVEMENT	minuet or scherzo	fairly fast and dance-like
FOURTH MOVEMENT	rondo, variation or sonata form	fast and cheerful

See page 81 for ternary form and page 82 for variation form. The other forms are explained over the next couple of pages.

Sonata Form has Three Main Sections

The movements of a sonata or symphony are themselves made up of a number of different sections. Sonata form has the following sections:

Exposition	Development	Recapitulation
Themes are "exposed" — heard for the first time.	Themes go through a number of interesting twists and turns.	Themes are "recapped" — played again.

1) The exposition has a number of contrasting themes. It ends in a different (but related) key to the one it started in.

2) The development keeps the piece interesting. It takes extracts from the exposition themes, explores variations on them, and presents them in different keys — the development often modulates through a number of keys. Completely new material might be introduced too.

3) The recapitulation pulls it all together again — the exposition themes are repeated, generally in the same order as in the exposition. They're usually changed a bit — the composer might add ornaments (see p.84) or shorten them. Some themes are heard in a different key — a theme that was in the relative key in the exposition usually moves to the tonic key in the recapitulation.

4) Composers sometimes use bridge sections between the themes and links between the main sections. They usually add a coda to finish off the piece neatly as well.

Fear not, there are more forms to come...

Make sure you've got sonata form clear in your head — it comes up in sonatas, symphonies and concertos. And don't get confused... sonata form is the structure of the first movement of a sonata, not the whole thing.

Classical Structures

Here's some more detail on the **forms** that make up the **movements** of a **concerto**, **sonata** or **symphony**.

Minuets and Scherzos are in Ternary Form

1) In a sonata or symphony, 'minuet' is short for 'minuet and trio' and scherzo is short for 'scherzo and trio'. The third movement of a four-movement work is either a minuet or a scherzo.

2) A minuet is a French dance with three beats in a bar.

3) The trio is another minuet in a contrasting but related key — often the dominant or relative minor. It's often written for three instruments (which is why it's called a trio).

4) The minuet is played first, followed by the trio section, and then the minuet is played again — this gives the movement ternary form (see p.81).

5) The individual minuet and trio sections often have their own ternary form. A common structure for a minuet and trio is shown below.

6) A scherzo and trio is very similar, but a scherzo is faster and more light-hearted than a minuet — scherzo means 'joke' in Italian. Beethoven was one of the first composers to use a scherzo like this.

Rondo Form Can Have Any Number of Sections

1) The final movement of a concerto, sonata or symphony is often a rondo.

2) Rondo means going round. A rondo starts with a main idea in Section A, moves into a new section, goes round again to A, moves into another new section, goes round again to A, etc., etc. The new section after each Section A always contrasts with A.

3) Section A is known as the main theme or refrain. The contrasting sections are called episodes.

4) The main theme is always in the home key. Each episode tends to modulate to a related key for contrast.

Musical Signposts Tell You What's Coming Next

1) You've seen that the movements of a work are themselves made up of a number of sections. The most obvious clue that a new section is starting in Classical music is a change of key.

2) Classical composers were also keen on dropping hints that a new section was about to start. These hints are known as musical signposts. They're not all that easy to spot at first, but with a bit of practice you should get the hang of it:

- Bridge passages lead smoothly into the new theme and also help prepare the new key.
- Cadences (p.42-43) clearly mark the end of a phrase or section, and they come at the end of a piece too. When they do, the chords used in the cadence are repeated several times, to let the audience know it's all over.

ABACADAEAFAGAHA — my rondo got a bit out of hand...

These structures might come in handy for your compositions (OK, writing a full symphony might be a bit over the top, but rondo form or minuet and trio form are a bit more manageable).

94

Orchestral Music of Haydn

Haydn was one of the most important composers of the Classical period.

Haydn was an Austrian Classical Composer

1) Franz Joseph Haydn (known just as Joseph Haydn) was born in Austria in 1732. He died in 1809.
2) He composed over 100 symphonies and many other works, including a number of concertos, string quartets, piano trios, oratorios and operas.
3) For most of his career, Haydn was employed as the Kapellmeister (musical director) for the noble Esterházy family — he composed, conducted and performed music for Prince Esterházy, who was his patron. Haydn worked for four different princes during his employment.

Haydn Wrote 12 Symphonies to be Performed in London

1) Over the course of his many symphonies, Haydn helped develop the structure and form used in Classical symphonies (and beyond). Along with Mozart, Haydn was one of the first composers to introduce sonata form (see p.92) as a standard structure in symphonies.
2) His symphonies display a sense of balance through his use of dynamics, phrasing, sequences and harmony. He was also known for his intelligence and wit in his compositions.
3) During the early 1790s, Haydn travelled to London twice. He wrote six symphonies for each visit — Nos. 93-104 (these 12 symphonies are known as the London symphonies).
4) These symphonies were written for a later Classical orchestra (see p.89). There'd be a string section (first and second violins, violas, cellos and double basses) and usually 2 each of woodwind (flutes, oboes and bassoons — and clarinets in the later symphonies), brass (trumpets and horns) and timpani.
5) Some of the London symphonies have names which describe a particular feature of the music:

- Symphony No. 101 in D Major is known as the Clock Symphony. It gets its name from a 'ticking' pattern in the second movement. The ticking is usually played pizzicato (plucked) on the strings and staccato on the woodwind.
- Haydn's sense of humour is demonstrated in the second movement of his 'Surprise' symphony (No. 94) with a sudden loud chord in the middle of a quiet section.
- Symphony No. 103 in E♭ Major is known as the Drumroll Symphony because the first movement opens with a long dramatic drumroll on the timpani.

He Also Wrote Concertos for Lots of Different Instruments

Haydn wrote many concertos, for a range of instruments — including violin, cello, double bass, horn, flute and oboe. He only wrote one concerto for trumpet, but this is one of his best-known concertos.

- Haydn's Trumpet Concerto in E♭ Major was written for his friend Anton Weidinger, who'd just invented a 'keyed trumpet', which was capable of playing many more notes than the earlier 'natural trumpet'. *The keyed trumpet was a precursor to today's valved trumpet.*
- Haydn used the concerto to show off the versatility of the new instrument — the first three notes of the trumpet's main melody were something it wouldn't have been capable of playing before. This immediately told the original audience that they were hearing something new and exciting.
- The concerto has three movements — the first (Allegro) is in sonata form, the second (Andante) is a slower, more lyrical movement in ternary (ABA) form, and the third (Allegro) is in rondo form.

What a surprise — you need to learn about Haydn...

Listen to the movements of the three London symphonies mentioned above, and try to spot the different features that give each one its name. Watch out for the surprise — it made me jump.

Orchestral Music of Mozart

Mozart is still considered to be one of the greatest composers that ever lived.

Mozart was an **Austrian Composer**

1) Wolfgang Amadeus Mozart was born in Salzburg, Austria in 1756 and died in Vienna in 1791. He was taught performance and composition by his father, Leopold Mozart, who was also a composer.

2) Wolfgang showed his musical talent at a very young age — he composed his first piece of music when he was just 5 years old. By the time he was 10, he had toured Europe, performed for kings and queens and written his first symphonies.

3) He went on to write over 600 pieces of music, including operas, masses, symphonies and concertos. He also wrote smaller works, like chamber music and string quartets.

He Wrote Lots of **Symphonies...**

See p.91 for more on symphonies.

1) Mozart wrote over 40 symphonies in his short life. Along with Haydn, Mozart was one of the first composers to introduce sonata form (see p.92) as a standard structure in symphonies.

2) He wrote most of his symphonies before he was 27, then took a break from them — he could make more money from composing concertos, and get a better reputation from writing operas. He returned to symphonies later on — Symphony No. 40 was written in 1788:

- Symphony No. 40 is one of only two of Mozart's symphonies in a minor key (the other is No. 25 — they're both in G minor).

- It was written for a fairly small orchestra — there's no percussion at all, and the only brass instruments are the French horns. The original version didn't have clarinets (as they'd only just been invented), but Mozart wrote a later version that included them.

- Like most symphonies, No. 40 has four movements. What's unusual is that he uses sonata form in three of the four movements (instead of just the first movement). The first movement has no introduction — the first theme starts at the end of the first bar.

- Another unusual feature of this symphony is that it finishes on a minor chord.

3) Mozart's works reflect the changing structure of the symphony — most of his early ones have three movements (as was typical of the time), with a quick-slow-quick structure (see p.91). Many of his later symphonies have four movements, with a minuet and trio coming after the slow second movement.

... and Many **Concertos** Too

See p.91 for more on concertos.

1) Mozart wrote concertos for a variety of instruments. Most (nearly 30) were for piano, but he also wrote a number of violin and horn concertos, as well as some for bassoon, flute, oboe and clarinet.

2) The concertos generally followed the three-movement quick-slow-quick structure, with the first movement in sonata form. However, as was typical in many Classical concertos, he tended to use a double exposition section. The orchestra would play first (usually without the soloist), and introduce the main themes. The soloist would then restate these themes (accompanied by the orchestra) — but often with some variation or new ideas.

3) As with all Classical concertos, Mozart's concertos gave the soloist an opportunity to show off. The soloist didn't always have a starring role throughout though — in his Clarinet Concerto in A Major, at one point the clarinet accompanies the orchestra with an Alberti bass (see p.39).

4) Mozart also wrote overtures to his operas (see p.91). These are often played as free-standing orchestral pieces (i.e. not just before the opera). Examples include *The Marriage of Figaro* and *The Magic Flute*.

Mozart's full name was Johannes Chrysostomus Wolfgangus Theophilus Mozart...

Remember — a symphony is a piece for a full orchestra and a concerto is for a soloist and orchestra.

Beethoven — Symphony No. 1, Movement 1

Beethoven was a very influential composer whose career bridged the Classical and Romantic periods. You'll be studying the first movement of his Symphony No. 1 in C major.

Beethoven was a German Composer

1) Ludwig van Beethoven was born in Germany in 1770 and died in Vienna in 1827.

2) He was a very significant composer in Western classical music — his music is famous for its drama, intensity and emotion. Beethoven was important in developing musical styles — he moved from the stricter forms and harmonies of the Classical period to the freer forms and richer harmonies of the Romantic era (see pages 99-100).

3) He wrote lots of orchestral music (including symphonies and concertos — see p.91), as well as sonatas and string quartets.

4) His hearing deteriorated over the course of his life, resulting in almost complete deafness for his last ten years. However, he continued to compose, and produced some of his most famous pieces despite this (e.g. Symphony No. 9 premiered in 1824).

5) Beethoven wrote nine symphonies, and many of them have names (e.g. Symphony No. 3 is the *Eroica* symphony, No. 6 is the *Pastoral* symphony and No. 9 is the *Choral* symphony).

6) Symphony No. 1 was first performed in 1800 in Vienna and published in 1801. It is one of his earlier works and was dedicated to Baron Gottfried van Swieten, who was a wealthy patron (see p.89) of composers including Beethoven, Haydn and Mozart.

Symphony No. 1 was written for a Classical Orchestra

1) Symphony No. 1 was written for strings, double woodwind, brass and percussion.

- Strings: first and second violins, violas, cellos and double basses
- Double woodwind: 2 each of flutes, clarinets in C, oboes and bassoons
- Brass: 2 trumpets in C and 2 French horns in C
- Percussion: 2 timpani tuned to C [I] and G [V]

2) Although some of the instruments at the time were transposing instruments, the clarinets, trumpets and horns in Symphony No. 1 are all in C. This means that the notes they play all sound the same as they are written.

Transposing instruments sound differently from how they are written. For example, when a clarinet in A plays a note written as C, it actually sounds as an A.

3) Beethoven began to give the woodwind instruments a much more important role. He included two clarinets, which were not standard in earlier symphonies (for example, only four of Mozart's 41 symphonies have clarinets). The woodwind also became more independent from the strings and were given more of the melody.

4) In his later symphonies, he started to expand the orchestra and include more instruments such as piccolo, contrabassoon and trombone. This meant that the whole orchestra had a larger pitch range and allowed him to explore a range of timbres and dynamic contrasts — his ninth symphony even featured a full choir.

It Follows the Typical Classical Four-Movement Form

See p.92-93 for more on structure, and p.44 for more on modulations.

- The first movement is in the tonic key (or home key) of C major and is in a lively sonata form with a slow introduction. This is your study piece — there's more about it on the next couple of pages.
- The second movement is the slow movement. It's in F major (the subdominant, IV).
- The third movement is labelled as a minuet and trio, although it's really more of a scherzo because it's faster than a typical minuet. It's back in the tonic key of C major.
- The fourth movement is fast and is also in sonata form with a slow introduction. It's also in C major.

I'm going to call my symphony Trevor...

Have a listen to Symphonies No. 3 and 6. 'Eroica' means 'heroic', so listen for the horn fanfares in movement 3. In No. 6, listen out for 'birds' in movement 2 and 'thunder' in movement 4.

Beethoven — Symphony No. 1, Movement 1

Movement 1 is in **Sonata Form**

The movement is in <u>C major</u>, with different sections <u>modulating</u> to different keys. Beethoven's harmony is <u>diatonic</u> (using notes belonging to the key), with <u>clear cadences</u> to reinforce the tonality.

Section		Bars	Key(s)
Introduction		1-12	Tonally ambiguous
Exposition (whole section is repeated)	1st Subject	13-32	C major (tonic)
	Transition	33-52	Modulations
	2nd Subject	52-87	G major (dominant)
	Codetta	88-109	G major
Development		110-177	Modulations
Recapitulation	1st Subject	178-188	C major
	Transition	189-205	Modulations
	2nd Subject	206-240	C major
	Codetta	241-259	C major
Coda		259-298	C major

There are transition sections where the music modulates...

...and codettas that reinforce the key.

There are also other brief modulations within some sections, e.g. to D minor at bar 19.

C major has <u>related keys</u>...

Subdominant (IV) — Dominant (V)

F	**C**	G
Dm	Am	Em

Relative minors

The **Slow Introduction** Creates **Uncertainty**

1) The introduction is labelled *Adagio molto* — very slow. It's in $\frac{4}{4}$.

2) The tonality is <u>ambiguous</u> — the piece starts with a <u>perfect cadence</u> in <u>F major</u>, followed by an <u>interrupted cadence</u>. We hear the <u>subdominant</u>, <u>dominant</u> and <u>relative minor</u> of C major, but C major is not <u>established</u> until the first subject.

3) All parts move at the same time in the opening in a <u>homophonic</u> texture. There's an <u>unusual sonority</u> where <u>pizzicato</u> strings are combined with long <u>woodwind chords</u>.

4) Beethoven adds sudden <u>dynamic contrasts</u>, ***fp***s and <u>crescendos</u> to increase the <u>drama</u>.

Two **Contrasting Subjects** Appear in the **Exposition**

1) The exposition is marked *Allegro con brio* in $\frac{2}{2}$ (¢) and finally confirms the <u>tonic key</u> of <u>C major</u>.

2) The melody of the <u>first subject</u> is played by the <u>first violins</u> and <u>accompanied by chords</u> in the lower strings, creating a <u>melody with accompaniment</u> texture. Unusually, the subject's phrasing is <u>irregular</u> — it's based on two <u>6-bar phrases</u>, whereas Classical phrases would usually be <u>4 or 8 bars</u>.

This subject is generally ascending, disjunct and staccato.

Start of next phrase in D minor

3) This 6-bar phrase then moves up a tone to <u>D minor</u>, which introduces <u>chromatic notes</u>. Beethoven uses the <u>motifs</u> introduced here in slightly <u>altered</u> forms throughout the <u>rest of the subject</u>.

4) A <u>transition</u> passage (or <u>bridge</u> passage) is heard between the subjects. It's based on the <u>triadic</u> and <u>semiquaver</u> motifs from the first subject in <u>octaves</u>, followed by <u>quaver sequences</u> played in octaves.

5) In <u>contrast</u> to the first subject, the <u>second subject</u> is played by <u>woodwind</u>, is <u>slurred</u> and <u>legato</u>, and features <u>conjunct descending quavers</u>. The phrasing is <u>regular</u> and <u>balanced</u>, with two <u>8-bar phrases</u>.

6) Its first four bars are a <u>dialogue</u> between the oboe and flute, which are a <u>perfect fourth</u> apart and play an <u>ascending sequence</u>. Violins then play a <u>developed version</u> of this dialogue with the flute and oboe.

This dialogue is an example of call and response.

7) The <u>codetta</u> starts with material from the first subject, this time in <u>G major</u>. From bar 100, there is a <u>closing idea</u> — a <u>descending melody</u> in the violins and flutes, and a series of <u>perfect cadences</u> in G.

Beethoven — Symphony No. 1, Movement 1

The Development **Modulates** to a **Wide Range of Keys**

1) The music of the development is more <u>chromatic</u> and <u>dissonant</u>. It features <u>diminished chords</u> (p.36) and there are exciting <u>sforzandos</u>, <u>fortissimos</u> and <u>crescendos</u>. <u>Repeated semiquavers</u> also add <u>drama</u>.

2) Exposition material is <u>combined</u> and <u>developed</u>. For example, bars 110-122 use the first subject in an <u>ascending sequence</u>, accompanied by <u>syncopated chords</u> from the second subject (first heard in bar 57).

3) After starting with an unexpected shift to <u>A major</u>, Beethoven <u>modulates</u> to related and unrelated keys:

- A <u>circle of fifths</u> (with some swaps to minor keys) is used to modulate from <u>A major</u> to <u>E♭ major</u>.
- E♭ is the most <u>distant</u> key from A major, and once Beethoven has reached it, he modulates back to A (this time A minor) via an <u>ascending harmonic sequence</u>.
- Bars 174-177 shift to <u>G7</u> (<u>dominant 7th of C</u>), leading into the C major <u>recapitulation</u>.

Circle of 5ths · Ascending sequence · *ff*, dramatic alternation between Am and E (dominant of Am)

Bar	110	114	118	122	126	130	144	148	152	156	158	160	174	178
Key	A	D	G	Cm	Fm	B♭	E♭	Fm	Gm	Dm	Am	E / Am	G7	C

Shift back to major · Thinner texture · Interrupts sequence · Woodwind in octaves play dominant 7th

Exposition Material is **Repeated** and **Altered** in the Recapitulation

- The recapitulation is a <u>repeat</u> of the exposition with <u>alterations</u>. Beethoven changes the exposition's <u>modulations</u>, <u>texture</u> and <u>instrumentation</u>, and creates a <u>new transition</u> section.
- The new transition uses the <u>falling semiquaver motif</u> from the first subject.
- Instead of being in G major, the second subject <u>stays in C major</u> — this is <u>typical</u> of sonata form.

  - The coda is based on <u>motifs</u> from the <u>first subject</u>. At the start of the coda, Beethoven emphasises <u>F major</u>, <u>A minor</u> and <u>G major</u> — the same keys heard in the <u>introduction</u>.
  - He finishes the coda using <u>pedal notes</u> and a <u>timpani roll</u> to emphasise the <u>tonic</u> of C major, and ends the movement with <u>tutti</u> crotchet C major chords.

Beethoven uses a Range of **Musical Devices**

1) There is a section of <u>canon</u> (see p.46) between the <u>first</u> and <u>second violins</u> in bars 136-139.

2) <u>Pedal notes</u> are often used to <u>reinforce</u> the keys — for example, at the beginning of the <u>exposition</u> (bars 13-16), the double basses and cellos play a <u>pedal on C</u> to confirm the tonic key as <u>C major</u>.

3) Other <u>musical devices</u> appear throughout:

- <u>Antiphony</u> (see p.47) — e.g. bars 45-49.
- String techniques (see p.64) like <u>pizzicato</u>, <u>arco</u> and <u>double</u>, <u>triple</u> and <u>quadruple stopping</u>.

Lower strings · Woodwind · Lower strings · Woodwind

- <u>Ornamentation</u> (p.84) such as <u>trills</u> (e.g. bar 24), <u>appoggiaturas</u> (bar 6) and <u>acciaccaturas</u> (bar 81).
- Harmonic and melodic <u>sequences</u> (see p.83) — e.g. bars 191-195.

Violins · Other strings · Violins · Other strings · Violins

My new Beethoven has a grill and can be turned up to 250 °C...

Get to know sonata form, as it's really important in this movement. Have a go at identifying where each section starts and ends. Listen out for different musical devices as well, and you're on the road to success.

The Romantic Period

The Romantic period was about how **passionate emotions** can be **expressed** through **art** and **music**.

The **Romantic Period** was in the **19th Century**

- The Romantic period was from about 1820-1910 (though there's always a bit of an overlap between different musical periods).
- Writers, artists and composers at this time were portraying contrasting emotions and ideas, such as love and hate, happiness and grief, and life and death.
- They were inspired by the natural world too, and were fascinated by supernatural ideas.
- Composers wrote programme music — music based on a poem or painting, or that tells a story.
- Tchaikovsky, Wagner and Chopin were all Romantic composers. Some of Beethoven's later pieces also fitted into the Romantic period.

Romantic Music is More **Dramatic** Than Classical

1) Romantic music used a wide range of dynamics. Sudden changes made the music very dramatic — it could go from *ppp* to *fff* and back again within a bar. Sforzandos and accents added to the drama.

2) To make the music more expressive, composers gave extra instructions — as well as tempo markings, they would include instructions like *dolce* (sweetly), *amoroso* (lovingly) or *agitato* (agitated).

3) There were more tempo changes — a piece might change speeds lots of times within the same section. Musicians in this period used *rubato* as well — it means 'robbed time' and it's when performers speed up a little in one phrase and slow down in another to make up for it. It gives them the freedom to be more expressive.

4) Composers added extra notes to chords to make the harmonies more interesting — they used 7ths, 9ths, 11ths and 13ths (9ths, 11ths and 13ths are just 2nds, 4ths and 6ths but an octave higher). They helped create dissonance (clashing notes), which let them show emotions like pain and misery.

5) There was a lot of virtuoso playing — composers wrote technically difficult music to give performers the chance to show off. It was very exciting to watch and listen to. Rachmaninov and Liszt wrote solo piano music that had to be written on four staves as there were so many notes to play.

6) Lots of Romantic composers were very proud of the countries they came from — they used folk tunes and dance rhythms from their homelands to show their national pride. Tchaikovsky used the French and Russian national anthems in his 1812 Overture.

The Orchestra **Developed** in the **Romantic Period**

1) Orchestras got much bigger — extra instruments were added.

2) The piccolo, bass clarinet and contrabassoon (which plays an octave lower than the bassoon) were added to the woodwind section.

3) Percussion sections grew to include xylophones, glockenspiels, drums, cymbals, bells and triangles as standard. Celestes (keyboard instruments that sound like glockenspiels) and harps were used too.

4) Brass instruments now had valves so were able to play more notes. Trombones and tubas were added.

5) The changes allowed composers to write music with a larger range of texture, timbre and dynamics.

6) The development of the piano (see next page) meant that it became a much more popular and important instrument. Lots of piano music was written in the Romantic period.

If music be the food of love — play on...

Make sure you know all the key features of Romantic music — you might well need to spot them in the exam. You'll need to listen out for dynamic contrasts, variations in tempo and interesting harmonies.

The Romantic Period

The **piano** was definitely one of the most **important** instruments in the **Romantic period**.

The **Piano Developed** in the **Romantic Period**

The piano's been around since the 18th century, but the developments in the 19th century made it really popular with Romantic composers.

SIZE: the piano changed shape a bit and got bigger (and louder). This meant it had a bigger dynamic range.

KEYS: the number of keys (and notes) increased to just over 7 octaves. Composers now had a larger range in pitch to compose for.

PEDALS: both pedals (the sustain pedal that holds notes on and the soft pedal) became more effective. Some modern pianos have three pedals — the third pedal allows some notes to be held on while others are not.

STRINGS: the strings inside were both thicker and longer, making a fuller tone. They were also pulled tighter, so they were more tense.

FRAME: the frame used to be made of wood, but was now made of metal (to cope with the new strings). This made it easier to transport them.

HAMMERS: the hammers were given a felt covering (instead of a leather one). This made the tone softer and more rounded.

Melodies Were the **Focus** of Piano Pieces

1) In Romantic piano pieces, the melody was the most important part. Melodies were often marked *cantabile* — to be played in a singing style.

2) There were lots of virtuosic sections and cadenzas (see p.57) to give the pianist chance to show off.

3) The music had a large range of dynamics, articulation and tone. Pianists had to use the pedals a lot to get the right sounds.

4) The accompaniment was often broken chords (see p.39), but unlike many Classical pieces, the broken chords would be spread across several octaves.

Concertos, Sonatas and **Preludes** Were Written for the **Piano**

1) The piano was popular as the solo instrument in concertos — the pianist was able to really show off in the cadenza. Rachmaninov wrote famous piano concertos.

2) Lots of sonatas (see p.91) were written for the piano — Chopin (see next page), Liszt, Mendelssohn and Schumann (see p.102) all composed piano sonatas.

3) Preludes were originally the bit of music that came before the main piece. During the Romantic period, they became popular as stand-alone pieces. Debussy, Liszt, Rachmaninov and Chopin all wrote preludes for the piano.

I'll have soup as a prelude to my dinner...

Pianos were popular because they were so versatile — with a range of over seven octaves, composers had fewer limitations when they were composing. The newly-developed piano could play a range of dynamics, and the pedals could be used to change the tone of the instrument too. Perfect for Romantics.

Piano Music of Chopin

As you saw on the previous page, the piano was very popular in the Romantic period. Some composers (like Chopin) just couldn't get enough of it.

Chopin was a **Polish Composer**

1) Frédéric Chopin was born in Poland in 1810 — lots of his music uses Polish folk tunes and dance rhythms. He died in Paris in 1849.

2) He made a name for himself in Vienna before moving to Paris.

3) As well as composing, he also performed and taught music.

4) He composed a lot of piano music, and had a reputation as a 'tragic' Romantic composer, because he was ill a lot, and died young.

Chopin Mainly Wrote **Piano Music**

This doesn't cover every single type of Chopin's piano compositions — he wrote loads of others too.

1) The vast majority of Chopin's compositions were solo piano pieces — even his main orchestral works were piano concertos. He also wrote a number of songs for voice and piano.

2) His music was characterised by its expressive melodies and unique treatment of the piano. He came up with new ways of fingering (such as playing the black keys with the thumb) and made extensive use of the pedals to explore the full potential of the piano.

3) Chopin wrote many piano solos based on dances — including mazurkas, polonaises (both types of Polish dance) and waltzes, as well as a few others, such as a bolero and a tarantella.

4) He composed four piano impromptus — compositions with no strict form and an improvised feel that were popular with Romantic composers.

5) Chopin wrote twenty-seven piano études (studies) that developed the style from a set of exercises to concert pieces that had an imaginative melody while still being technically demanding. Most have been given nicknames (e.g. 'Revolutionary' or 'Waterfall'), though Chopin didn't use these names.

6) A nocturne is a piece meant to represent the night. Chopin wrote twenty-one nocturnes, developing a style established earlier in the Romantic period. Key features of the nocturnes include a melody in the right-hand part above broken chords (see p.39) in the left, a generally sad feel and a slow tempo.

Chopin Wrote a **Prelude** in **Every Key**

He also wrote three other preludes that don't form part of this set.

1) Chopin wrote a set of twenty-four preludes — one in each major and minor key. The order of the preludes alternates between major and minor keys and follows the circle of fifths (see p.26) — No. 1 is in C major, No. 2 is in A minor, No. 3 is in G major, etc. Each prelude is fairly short (the longest is only 90 bars), so they're often performed as a set — but each works as a stand-alone piece.

2) Like the études, many of the preludes have been given nicknames that represent features of the piece — e.g. the 'Raindrop' prelude (see below). Each prelude has different characteristics (e.g. particular rhythms or distinctive bass parts). They cover a wide range of tempos, from *lento* to *presto*.

3) The preludes demonstrate many key features of Romantic music. For example:

- Prelude No. 15 in D♭ Major is known as the 'Raindrop' prelude because of repeated quavers played throughout the piece, in either the right hand (an inverted pedal) or left-hand part (a pedal note — see p.39). The 'raindrops' are occasionally doubled in octaves.

- The piece is marked *sostenuto* ('sustained'), which means it should have a slow, held-back tempo. Chopin uses augmentation (see p.18) to make parts of the prelude feel slow and heavy.

- Chopin also includes many other musical directions — such as *sotto voce* ('in an undertone'), *smorzando* ('dying away'), a range of dynamics and marks to show when to press the pedals.

- The piece is in ternary form (ABA) — section A is in D♭ major, and section B is in C♯ minor (D♭ and C♯ are enharmonic equivalents — see p.11), but both sections explore different keys as well.

Piano Music of Schumann

Schumann mainly wrote piano music and music for voice and piano —
but he did branch out into other genres, including symphonies and an opera.

Schumann was a German Composer

1) Robert Schumann was born in 1810 and died in 1856. He spent most of his life in Germany.

2) He gave up a degree in law with the aim of becoming a concert pianist, but an injury to his hand meant he had to abandon that dream. Instead, he focused on composition.

3) Most of his early work was piano music, but later in his career he composed other works, such as symphonies, Lieder (see below) and an opera.

4) He married Clara Wieck, the daughter of his piano teacher — she was also a talented pianist and composer. Many of Schumann's pieces were written for, or inspired by, his wife.

5) Schumann was an important composer in the Romantic period — he was highly regarded for his ability to combine poetry and music.

Schumann's Piano Pieces Have Descriptive Titles

1) Many of Schumann's piano pieces are examples of programme music (see p.99). Their titles describe what the music represents — examples include *Papillons* ('Butterflies'), *Nachtstücke* ('Night Pieces'), *Waldszenen* ('Forest Scenes') and *Kinderszenen* ('Scenes from Childhood').

> *Kinderszenen* is made up of thirteen pieces, most of which are fairly short (some of them last for less than a minute). Each piece has a name (such as 'Blindman's Buff' and 'The Poet Speaks'). Some of the pieces are light and playful, while others are more gentle and reflective. Nine are in major keys and the other four are in minor keys. The first and last are in the same key (G major), which provides a sense of unity for the whole set.

2) *Carnaval* is a solo piano piece composed in 1834-35 — it depicts a masked ball at a carnival. It has twenty-two movements — most of which represent characters at the carnival (e.g. a pierrot and a harlequin) or friends of Schumann (including Clara and Chopin).

3) He also wrote a number of variations (see p.82). He based his variations on themes written by composers he admired, such as Beethoven, Paganini and his wife Clara.

Other composers of Lieder include Schubert, Beethoven and Brahms.

Schumann Wrote Lots of Lieder

A Lied (pronounced 'leed') is a song for one singer and a piano (the plural of Lied is Lieder). Lieder were really popular in the Romantic period, especially with German composers.

- Lieder are usually based on German poems. They tell stories — they're often very dramatic.
- The piano part in a Lied is more than just a background accompaniment. It helps with the story-telling and sets the mood.
- Lieder are usually either through-composed or have a strophic structure (see p.56). They often have motifs — little bits of repeated music that represent an idea, character or place.
- A collection of Lieder could be put together in a song cycle (a set of songs with the same theme).

Schumann wrote many of his Lieder in 1840 (the year he married Clara), including two of his famous song cycles, *Frauenliebe und -leben* and *Dichterliebe*. The first (which means 'woman's love and life') is a set of eight Lieder, based on poems by Adelbert von Chamisso. The second (meaning 'a poet's love') is a set of sixteen, based on poems by Heinrich Heine. This cycle has themes of love, nature and fairy tales.

Robert Schumann — Lieder of the pack...

When you're listening to piano music by Chopin and Schumann, see if you can pick out the features of the piece that are typical of the Romantic period (see p.99-100 for a reminder).

Requiems

After many pages of orchestral or piano music, I'm going to finish this section with a return to choral music.

A **Mass** is a Type of **Sacred Music**

The term 'mass' can be used in the Church of England too.

1) A mass is a Roman Catholic church service. Parts of it are often set to music, and sung by a choir and soloists. These parts include:

2) The words of a mass were traditionally in Latin.

3) Masses were originally written to be used in church, but they're now often performed in concerts too.

4) Famous settings of the mass include J.S. Bach's Mass in B Minor and Beethoven's Mass in C Major. There are also modern masses, such as The Armed Man: A Mass for Peace by Karl Jenkins.

- *Kyrie* ('Lord have mercy...')
- *Gloria* ('Glory be to God...')
- *Credo* ('I believe in one God...')
- *Sanctus* ('Holy, holy, holy...')
- *Benedictus* ('Blessed is He...')
- *Agnus Dei* ('O Lamb of God...')

A **Requiem** is a **Mass** for the **Dead**

1) A mass for the dead is called a requiem. Requiems use some parts of the normal mass (such as the *Kyrie*, *Sanctus* and *Agnus Dei*), but miss out the happier sections (e.g. the *Gloria* and the *Credo*).

2) These sections are replaced by more solemn bits. These include the *Introit*, which begins 'Requiem aeternam' ('Grant them eternal rest'), the *Dies Irae* (which means 'Day of Wrath') and the *Pie Jesu* (which is taken from the last couple of lines of the *Dies Irae* and means 'Merciful Jesus').

Requiems were **Popular** with **Romantic Composers**

1) Although there had been earlier requiems (such as the well-known Requiem Mass in D Minor by Mozart), it was during the Romantic period that requiems became popular as a form of large-scale composition for performance in concert rather than a church service.

2) The text of the requiem is very dramatic and emotional (especially the *Dies Irae*), so it's easy to see why Romantic composers chose to set it to music.

3) Requiems are usually in a minor key to match the grave nature of the lyrics. Romantic requiems were often written for a large choir and massive orchestra to add drama and tension to the music.

Verdi's Requiem was written in 1873-74 in memory of the writer Alessandro Manzoni. It was sung by four soloists (soprano, mezzo-soprano, tenor and bass) and a full choir. The singers are accompanied by a huge orchestra — including 2 flutes, a piccolo, 4 bassoons and a large brass section with a whopping 8 trumpets. There's also a prominent percussion section, which has timpani, a bass drum and crash cymbals. This made it very dramatic — the *Dies Irae* in particular, which starts with loud orchestral chords (with bass drum off-beats) and a wide range of pitch from the choir. The trumpet fanfare after the *Dies Irae* starts with one trumpet and builds up to all eight before the choir enters, creating a rich polyphonic texture. There are gentler sections to provide contrast (such as the *Agnus Dei*), where the soloists sing above a light orchestral accompaniment.

In contrast to Verdi's operatic style, Fauré's Requiem (which he started in 1887 and revised several times before the final version was completed in 1900) is gentle and serene. The vocal parts are for a choir and just two soloists (a soprano and a baritone). The orchestra is joined by an organ. Instead of the exciting *Dies Irae*, Fauré includes a tranquil *Pie Jesu*, sung by the soprano soloist with a quiet orchestral accompaniment. Some sections are in a major key and sound calm and peaceful, though there are more emotional sections with rich harmonies and dramatic crescendos.

Be prepared for a dies irae if you don't revise...

There are later requiems too — a famous 20th century example is the War Requiem by Benjamin Britten (see p.153), which uses Latin words from the Requiem Mass and war poems by Wilfred Owen.

Warm-up and Exam Questions

Before you have a go at the exam questions, give these warm-up questions a whirl — they'll get your brain in gear and give you a fighting chance when you get onto the harder ones.

Warm-up Questions

1) Describe how dynamics were used in the Baroque period.

2) In a concerto grosso, what is: a)   the concertino?   b)   the ripieno?

3) Describe ground bass form.

4) What is a sequence?

5) What is an appoggiatura?

6) What were the four different types of voice in a Baroque choir?

7) What is an aria?

8) Who wrote 'Messiah'?

9) Name an instrument that was included in the Classical orchestra but was not used in orchestras of the Baroque period.

10) What is the standard structure of a Classical concerto?

11) What form does the first movement of Beethoven's Symphony No. 1 use? Name each section of this form.

12) How does the tempo change in Beethoven's Symphony No. 1?

13) Which instruments play the melody at the start of the first subject of Beethoven's Symphony No. 1?

14) Name two other Classical composers.

15) Give the approximate dates of the Romantic period.

16) What does *sotto voce* mean?

17) What is a Lied?

18) Name one section of a requiem that doesn't appear in a mass.

Exam Questions

Have a go at these exam-style questions.

Track 32 is an excerpt from the first movement of Beethoven's Symphony No. 1 in C major.

Play the excerpt four times, leaving a short pause between each playing.

Remember, you can find all the tracks for the listening questions at cgpbooks.co.uk/tempo.

Track 32

Track 32

a)   In this excerpt, the first and second subjects are introduced.
     What section of the movement is this from?

....

[1 mark]

Exam Questions

b) Identify one percussion instrument used in this excerpt.

....
[1 mark]

c) Identify two features of the excerpt that indicate it was composed in the Classical period.

1) ....

....

2) ....

....
[2 marks]

d) About halfway through the excerpt, the music moves from the first subject into the transition passage. Describe how Beethoven creates a sense of excitement here.

....

....

....

....
[2 marks]

e) Which of the following best describes the texture at the end of the excerpt?
Circle your answer.

   monophonic   **polyphonic**   **antiphonal**   **heterophonic**
[1 mark]

f) Describe two contrasts between the first and second subject.

1) ....

....

....

2) ....

....

....
[4 marks]

Exam Questions

Track 33 is an excerpt from 'Dies Irae' by Verdi.
Play the excerpt **four** times. Leave a short pause between each playing.

Track 33

a) i) What larger work does this movement come from?

....

[1 mark]

ii) What does 'Dies Irae' mean? Circle your answer.

Lord have mercy   **Eternal rest**   **Day of wrath**   **Merciful Jesus**

[1 mark]

b) Tick one box for each statement below to indicate whether it is true or false.

	True	False
The excerpt opens with homophonic chords.	☐	☐
The bass drum plays on the off-beats.	☐	☐
The choir sing in unison.	☐	☐
The strings play ascending runs between the choral sections.	☐	☐

[4 marks]

c) Describe the texture of this excerpt.

....

....

....

....

....

[3 marks]

d)   This piece is marked *allegro agitato*. Explain what this means.

....

....

[1 mark]

e)   i) During which period of Western classical music history was this piece composed?

....

[1 mark]

ii) Identify the features of this piece that are typical of that period and explain why they were used. You might want to comment on musical elements such as instrumentation, dynamics and harmony, as well as any other elements you think appropriate.

....

....

....

....

....

....

....

....

....

....

....

[8 marks]

Revision Summary for Section Six

That's the end of Section Six — test yourself to see how much you've picked up.
- Try these questions and tick off each one when you get it right.
- When you've done all the questions for a topic and are completely happy with it, tick off the topic.

The Baroque Period (p.80-84) ☑
1) Give the approximate dates of the Baroque period. ☑
2) What is a basso continuo and what instruments would normally play it? ☑
3) What is a concerto grosso? ☑
4) Which Baroque structure can be described as ABA? ☑
5) What was the function of a prelude in the Baroque period? ☑
6) In theme and variation form, what is the theme? ☑
7) What is the main difference between theme and variation form and ground bass form? ☑
8) Explain what each of these terms means: a) melodic inversion   b) retrograde   c) ostinato. ☑
9) Name three different ornaments used by Baroque composers and explain what they are. ☑

Choral Music (p.85-87) ☑
10) What is a falsetto voice? ☑
11) What are the four different voices in an SATB choir? ☑
12) What is a baritone voice? ☑
13) Name the three types of song in an opera. ☑
14) What is an oratorio? ☑
15) Give a brief definition of word-painting. ☑
16) Name two of Handel's coronation anthems. ☑

The Classical Period (p.88-98) ☑
17) Give the approximate dates of the Classical period. ☑
18) Why did the piano become increasingly popular in the Classical period? ☑
19) What was the most important section in a Classical orchestra? ☑
20) What is a symphony? ☑
21) What is the structure of a symphony with 4 movements? ☑
22) Briefly describe rondo form. ☑
23) Name two of Haydn's 'London symphonies'. ☑
24) Which form is used in three movements of Mozart's Symphony No. 40? ☑
25) In Beethoven's Symphony No. 1, what key are the transposing instruments (clarinets, trumpets and horns) in? ☑
26) What is the key of the second subject in the exposition of Beethoven's Symphony No. 1? ☑
27) Name two musical devices used by Beethoven in his Symphony No. 1. ☑
28) What is meant by 'chromaticism'? ☑

The Romantic Period (p.99-103) ☑
29) Name three techniques that Romantic composers used to show drama and emotion in their work. ☑
30) What instrument was most of Chopin's music written for? ☑
31) Describe Schumann's Carnaval. ☑
32) What is a song cycle? ☑
33) What is a requiem? ☑
34) What instruments and voices are needed to perform Verdi's Requiem? ☑

Voices in Pop

This section starts by looking at some general things that are relevant to most pop music — first up, vocals.

The **Lead Singer** Sings the **Main Melody**

The lead singer (or vocalist) sings the main melody of a song. They're the soloist, and if they're part of a band, they're often the most famous member (e.g. Freddie Mercury in Queen (see p.115), Jon Bon Jovi in Bon Jovi and Axl Rose in Guns N' Roses). If you get a pop song in the Listening Exam, say something about the lead vocalist's style. It's even worth mentioning obvious stuff like whether the singer's male or female.

Backing Singers Sing the **Harmonies**

The backing vocalists are the ones who sing the harmonies. These are the main ways backing singers do their thing:

> Listen out for the backing vocals in 'Surfin' USA' by The Beach Boys.

IN HARMONY	IN UNISON	DESCANT	CALL AND RESPONSE
all singing different notes	all singing the same notes	singing a higher part in time with the main tune	repeating whatever the lead vocalist sings or answering the lead with another tune

Singers Can Do All Sorts of **Fancy Stuff**

There are different ways to sing. Make sure you can describe exactly what you're hearing. Listen out for:

> Vocal parts can be syllabic (one note per syllable) or melismatic (multiple notes per syllable).

1) **A CAPPELLA** — singing with no instrumental backing.
2) **VIBRATO** — when singers quiver up and down slightly in pitch. It makes the voice sound warmer and more expressive.
3) **FALSETTO** — when men (or occasionally women) make their voices go really high. Sam Smith, The Bee Gees and Michael Jackson are all famous for their falsetto voices.
4) **PORTAMENTO** — when a singer slides from one note to another.
5) **SCAT** — improvising using syllables like 'doo' and 'dat'. Scat comes from jazz music.
6) **RIFFING** — when singers decorate and add bits to the tune. They often go up and down a scale before coming to rest on one note. Riffing usually comes at the end of a phrase, between sections or to finish the song. Whitney Houston, Mariah Carey and Celine Dion are famous for riffing.
7) **BELTING** — when a singer sings notes from their higher register at a louder volume than normal. It's often used for the emotional climax in musical theatre songs (see p.119-120).
8) **RAPPING** — when rhyming lyrics are spoken or chanted to a rhythmic beat.
9) **BEATBOXING** — using the voice to make percussive sounds, imitating a drum kit or DJ equipment.

Electronic Effects Can Be Added to Vocal Parts

> There's more on these effects on p.72-73 and p.75.

Another way to make the vocals on a pop song sound interesting is to add electronic effects.

- **REVERB** (short for reverberation) adds an echo to a sound.
- **MULTI-TRACKING** (or layering) is when each part is recorded on its own track, and all the tracks are played back together. It means one singer can record all the parts in a song — for example, in some Queen songs, Freddie Mercury sings the solo part and the backing vocals at the same time.
- **SAMPLING** is when you use a short recording (a sample) of someone else's voice in your song.
- A **VOCODER** (a type of synthesizer) electronically alters a voice recording and creates weird effects. Similar technology is used with auto-tuning — adjusting notes on a recording so that they're in tune.

He swore he could hit the high notes, but that was falsetto...

Next time you're listening to pop music, pay close attention to the techniques the singers use.

Instruments of Pop

Pop songs can use any instruments at all — but there are some common instruments that are often used.

Most Pop Songs Use **Electric Guitars**

The **Lead Guitar** Plays **Tunes**, the **Rhythm Guitar** Plays **Chords**

The lead guitar plays the melody, as well as improvised solos in the instrumental sections (Brian May from Queen and Slash from Guns N' Roses are famous for their guitar solos). The lead guitar also adds in fancy bits all the way through to decorate the tune.

The rhythm guitar fills in the harmony all the way through. They either strum the chords or pick out broken (arpeggiated) chords (see p.39) and often play rhythmic riffs (see p.58). Some artists (e.g. Bob Dylan and Ed Sheeran) play rhythms on acoustic guitars instead.

The **Bass Guitar** Plays the **Bass Lines**

See p.65 for more about guitars.

The bass guitar plays the lowest notes. The bass guitarist picks out individual notes (not chords) to form the bass line. As well as picking, bass guitarists sometimes play glissandos by sliding their finger up and down the string (this is easier on a fretless bass).

Electric Guitars Can Play **Effects**

By plugging an electric guitar into an effects box or using different pedals you can get all sorts of effects:

- **DISTORTION** — a grungy, dirty sound.
- **FUZZ** — fuzzy-sounding distortion.
- **CHORUS** — makes it sound like more than one instrument is playing.
- **FLANGER** and **PHASER** — create a 'whooshing' noise.
- **WAH WAH** — makes the guitar go, er... "wah wah".
- **COMPRESSION** — evens out variations in volume.
- **PANNING** — sends different sounds through different speakers. If you've got two guitarists trading solos, one could be panned left and one right to separate the sounds.

You can also produce reverb (echo) on a guitar as well. There's more about guitar effects on p.75.

The **Drums** Add the **Rhythm**

1) The drummer sets the tempo and plays rhythms to fit the style of the song (like the rhythm guitar).
2) The main instruments of a drum kit are snare drum, bass drum, hi-hat, tom-toms and cymbals. There are different playing techniques — e.g. for a rim shot, you hit both the rim and head of the snare drum.
3) Drum pads and drum machines can replace acoustic drums, or sometimes play alongside them.

The **Piano** or **Keyboard** Provides **Melody** and **Harmony**

The piano or keyboard can play the melody (and instrumental solos) or chords to fill out the harmony. Not all pop songs will have a piano, but some only have a piano accompaniment (e.g. Bob Dylan's 'Make You Feel My Love' and Adele's 'Someone Like You'). These songs tend to be gentler than other pop songs.

Synthesizers Can Do Lots of Jobs

There's more about synthesizers on p.72.

Synthesizers (synths) can play any part — they can make the sound of virtually any instrument you want, e.g. a full string section or brass section (although some bands have live strings or brass). They can play rhythmic chords, solos or hooks (short, catchy, memorable bits).

Rock 'n' Roll

Rock 'n' roll is sometimes used to mean rock music in general — but here we're talking about the particular style of music that developed in the USA in the 1950s and '60s and spread across the world.

Rock 'n' Roll Came from the United States in the 1950s

1) Rock 'n' roll developed in the southern states of America in the late 1940s and early 1950s. African Americans moved to urban areas, which meant that black and white people were living closer together than ever before. Their styles of music mixed and evolved, creating new genres of music.

2) Rock 'n' roll was a mix of rhythm 'n' blues (which itself came from blues — see p.129-130) and country and western music, but also had influences of gospel, folk and jazz. Typical songs were a faster version of the 12-bar blues with the distinctive twang of country and western singing.

3) It might seem pretty tame today, but rock 'n' roll caused a massive uproar in the 1950s. Teenagers loved it, but their parents' generation hated it — they thought it was tasteless and immoral, and some even went as far as to say it was evil. Teenagers could afford to buy their own records though, so rock 'n' roll was extremely successful, and made superstars out of its biggest artists (e.g. Elvis Presley). It was used in films and TV programmes, which made it even more popular.

Cleveland DJ Alan Freed made the term 'rock 'n' roll' popular.

4) Rock 'n' roll continued to develop throughout the '50s and '60s, leading to rock music itself from the mid 1960s (see p.112-113).

Rock 'n' Roll Songs Were Lively With a Strong Beat

1) Rock 'n' roll songs were generally up-tempo, with a clear beat (most of them were in $\frac{4}{4}$). This made them ideal for dancing — dances in high school gyms were popular (like in *Grease*), and popular TV shows featured teenagers dancing to current hits.

2) The general line-up for a rock 'n' roll band was a lead singer, electric guitars, a bass guitar, a drum kit and sometimes a piano. In earlier bands, the piano played more of a lead role and some had a saxophone as well. A double bass was used before the bass guitar became more common.

3) The lyrics appealed to teenagers because they were about teenage issues, such as love, school, cars and summer holidays. Key lines were repeated throughout the song, which made them memorable.

4) The structure of the songs was fairly simple — most were either strophic (all verses had the same tune — see p.56) or had a verse-chorus structure (see p.58). Some had an AABA structure (four sections, three with the same melody and one that contrasts). A lot of hits featured at least one instrumental section, where a soloist (usually the lead guitarist) would improvise.

5) The verses and choruses themselves were often based on a 12-bar blues. There was a lot of call and response between the lead singer and the band, and most songs had a catchy hook.

Early Rock 'n' Roll Stars Included Bill Haley and Elvis Presley

- One of the first rock 'n' roll hits was 'Rock Around the Clock' by Bill Haley & His Comets.
- Elvis Presley was a huge star — his early hits included 'Hound Dog', 'Heartbreak Hotel' and 'Jailhouse Rock'. Elvis also acted and sang in films, which made him even more popular. He was adored by teenage girls — at his concerts, his gyrating hips caused a commotion.
- Bill Haley, Elvis Presley, Jerry Lee Lewis (who sang 'Great Balls of Fire') and Buddy Holly ('That'll Be The Day') were all rockabilly singers (a sub-genre of rock 'n' roll).
- Britain produced some rock 'n' roll stars as well, who were heavily influenced by American rock 'n' roll. The Beatles started out in rock 'n' roll (there's more about them on p.114).

Rock 'n' roll was more controversial than pineapple on pizza...

In a nutshell, rock 'n' roll took the African American rhythm 'n' blues and made it accessible to young people of all backgrounds. Rock 'n' roll was more than just a type of music — it was an entire culture.

Rock Music

Rock music is **developing** all the time — but you need to know about rock music from the '**60s** and '**70s**.

Rock Music Developed in the 1960s

1) During the 1960s, rock 'n' roll evolved into more guitar-dominated music known simply as rock.

2) Like the 12-bar blues (see p.130), rock songs tend to be based around the chords I, IV and V (and sometimes VI). Songs are often in $\frac{4}{4}$ with a steady drum rhythm and follow a verse-chorus structure.

3) Rock music often uses power chords (chords made up of the tonic and fifth).

4) Many rock bands were formed in the 1960s — though most continued into the following decades.

- The Rolling Stones had hits in the '60s including '(I Can't Get No) Satisfaction' and 'Get Off Of My Cloud'.
- Led Zeppelin's most famous song, 'Stairway to Heaven' (see p.114), was released in 1971, but the band was formed in the late '60s.
- Other rock bands from the '60s and '70s include The Beatles (see p.114), The Kinks (who had a hit in the UK and the USA with 'You Really Got Me'), The Who (who sang 'My Generation' and 'Pinball Wizard'), The Doors (who had US No.1 singles with 'Light My Fire' and 'Hello, I Love You') and Fleetwood Mac (whose songs include 'Dreams' and 'Go Your Own Way').

The Instrumentation Varies

1) A rock band was originally made up of a lead electric guitar, a rhythm electric guitar, a lead singer, a bass guitar and a drummer.

2) As rock developed, more instruments were added. In some songs, bands might use a string section (with violins and cellos), a brass section (trumpets and trombones) or a wind section (flutes, clarinets, saxophones and oboes). They also brought in pianos or keyboards and synthesizers.

3) Musicians used the effects on electric guitars to produce new sounds — like distortion, feedback (the noise you get when a guitar or microphone is too close to a speaker) and reverberation (echo).

Developments in technology have played an important part in rock music.

4) Rock bands use lots of other techniques to get unusual sounds — Led Zeppelin often used a pounding beat turned up really loud as their main rhythm. They sometimes used violin bows on their guitar strings to get a sustained note.

Rock Songs Are a Way of Expressing Yourself

1) Lots of rock bands write their own lyrics to songs (as well as the music). They use things like religious themes, political causes and personal experiences of love, and some tell stories.

2) Led Zeppelin, David Bowie and Bob Dylan all use the influences of folk music — they've written whole albums in a folky style (often described as folk rock).

3) Costumes were used to help the music along — David Bowie's jumpsuits and make-up (such as his famous lightning bolt make-up) really helped to set the scene for the characters that appeared in Bowie's songs (e.g. Major Tom and Ziggy Stardust).

Don't forget the best rock instrument — the air guitar...

Listen to 'Stairway to Heaven' from Led Zeppelin's *IV*. The structure is different to a 'typical' rock song, but still has plenty of the rock features covered on this page — see if you can pick some out.

Rock Music

Don't worry, you don't need to know masses of detail about the different types of rock music below. Make sure you're happy with their common features though, such as the importance of the guitar.

There Are Lots of **Types** of Rock

Over time, rock has branched out into lots of different sub-genres. Here are some of the most popular:

HARD ROCK
- Loud and aggressive, dominated by a distorted electric guitar — solos and power chords were key features.
- Bands include Led Zeppelin and The Who.

HEAVY METAL
- Harder and more distorted than hard rock, with even longer guitar solos.
- Bands include Black Sabbath and Iron Maiden.

GLAM ROCK
- Theatrical and glitzy.
- Easier to listen to than hard rock, with a more rock 'n' roll feel and catchy hooks.
- Performers dressed up in spangly catsuits and wore lots of make-up.
- Artists include David Bowie and Kiss.

PUNK ROCK
- Harsh and angry music from the '70s — it's all about anarchy and rebellion. Lyrics were often shouted.
- Bands include The Sex Pistols, Blondie and Joan Jett and the Blackhearts.

PROGRESSIVE (PROG) ROCK
- Songs were experimental and complicated, and albums often had a theme.
- Features long instrumentals, electronic effects and mythological or nonsensical lyrics.
- Bands include Yes and Pink Floyd.

PSYCHEDELIC ROCK
- From the '60s artistic movement psychedelia — it tried to recreate the surreal images and sounds experienced with hallucinogenic drugs like LSD.
- The music used lots of guitar effects and unusual electronic instruments and effects. It took inspiration from other cultures (including Eastern music). Lyrics were weird and dreamlike.
- Bands include The Beatles and The Doors.

Classic Rock Songs are Known as **Anthems**

1) Because of the powerful nature of the music and lyrics, a lot of rock songs can be described as anthems. They usually have memorable, singable (or shoutable) choruses. Here are a few examples:

- 'Born to Be Wild' by Steppenwolf was released in 1968 — it was one of the first songs to be described as 'heavy metal' (see above), and even uses the words 'heavy metal thunder'. It has distorted electric guitars and the repeated title hook is simple and memorable.
- 'We Will Rock You' by Queen was released in 1977. The only accompaniment to the vocals is the instantly-recognizable 'stamp stamp clap' rhythm that continues throughout the song (go on, you know you want to). The chorus is just one repeated line, almost like a chant. An electric guitar comes in right at the end and plays a solo.

Rock anthems were perfect for arena performances.

2) Arena rock (or stadium rock) came about in the middle of the 1970s — developments in technology meant that rock bands could be amplified more. This allowed them to perform in larger spaces, such as arenas and stadiums (hence the name).

3) Technology also meant that special effects (such as pyrotechnics and light shows) could be used. Arena performances were about the effects and experience as much as the music.

My heavy metal band has a lead singer and a mercury guitarist...

'We Will Rock You' features in the 2001 film *A Knight's Tale*, where it's played at a jousting tournament. Perhaps not the most historically-accurate choice of song, but you can't beat a classic rock anthem.

Rock Music

I couldn't end these pages about rock music without talking more about a little band called **The Beatles**...

The Beatles Were Very Influential

- The members of the band were John Lennon, Paul McCartney, George Harrison and Ringo Starr. They were all from Liverpool.

  Their producer George Martin was often known as 'the fifth Beatle'.

- Their standard line-up was Lennon on rhythm guitar, McCartney on bass guitar, Harrison on lead guitar and Starr on drums, although there was some variation. All four members provided vocals, and Lennon and McCartney were the main songwriters. In later songs, they used a variety of other instruments, including the piano and sitar.

- Their early songs (such as 'I Saw Her Standing There' and 'She Loves You') were influenced by Elvis Presley, Chuck Berry and other rock 'n' roll stars.

- Although they're usually classed as a rock band, their style changed so much over the years that it's almost impossible to put them into one category. As well as rock 'n' roll, they used musical ideas from rhythm 'n' blues, folk, classical music and non-Western cultures (such as Indian music). They also used pioneering recording techniques such as sampling.

- These different styles can be heard on their albums — for example, *Please Please Me* is rock 'n' roll, whereas *Help* has more of a rock sound.

- They had loads of hits — some of their most famous songs include 'Yesterday', 'Hey Jude', 'All You Need is Love', 'A Hard Day's Night' and 'I Want to Hold Your Hand'.

  In the mid '60s, the Beatles inspired a lot of excitement in the USA, which was known as 'Beatlemania'.

Sgt. Pepper's Lonely Hearts Club Band is a Concept Album

1) The Beatles' 1967 psychedelic rock album *Sgt. Pepper's Lonely Hearts Club Band* was one of the first rock concept albums — an album with a theme that links all the tracks. The idea was that the album was a live performance by Sgt. Pepper's Lonely Hearts Club Band, so should be played in one go, with the tracks in the order that they appeared. This idea was reinforced by features such as noises of an orchestra tuning up before the start of the first track and audience applause during the song.

2) The name of the album is the name of the fictional band that The Beatles used as their alter ego — pretending to be someone else gave them the chance to experiment with different styles of music.

3) The songs on the album use a wide variety of instruments — including a 40-piece orchestra who play a long, dissonant crescendo in the middle of 'A Day In The Life', a French horn quartet on the title track and classical Indian instruments on 'Within You Without You'.

In the '70s, Songs Became Longer and Albums Had Themes

- 'Stairway to Heaven' (1971) by Led Zeppelin lasts for a whopping 8 minutes. It has different sections — the first is gentle, with a recorder and acoustic guitar accompaniment. The next section is a little faster, with electric guitars, and is followed by a long electric guitar solo. The final section is fast, hard rock (see page 113).
- The 1976 album *2112* by Rush is a concept album. It opens with a 20-minute song (also called '2112') made up of seven sections that tell a sci-fi story — this is an example of a rock opera.
- Pink Floyd's 1973 album *The Dark Side of the Moon* is another example of a concept album.
- Queen's 'Bohemian Rhapsody' (1975) is another classic example of this — see next page.

Did some gardening yesterday — it was beetle-mania...

The Beatles broke up in 1970 and the members went their separate ways, continuing to record and perform their own projects. However, the music they created together has had a lasting impact on the world of pop.

Queen

The Queen study pieces use lots of vocal and technological effects (see p.75 and p.109-110).

Queen are a British Rock Band

1) Queen formed in 1970. Their style mixes glam rock, heavy metal and pop rock, but it's also experimental.

2) The band originally had four members: Freddie Mercury (lead vocals, piano, backing vocals), Brian May (lead guitar, backing vocals), Roger Taylor (drums, backing vocals) and John Deacon (bass guitar).

3) They're hugely successful — they have sold millions of albums, had many Number 1 singles and performed in massive arenas.

Freddie Mercury passed away in 1991, but Brian May and Roger Taylor still perform with guest singers.

4) Two of the study pieces ('Bohemian Rhapsody' and 'Love of My Life') are from the album *A Night at the Opera* (1975). The album mixes operatic drama with lots of styles, including heavy metal, progressive rock, ballads and folk. 'Seven Seas of Rhye' featured on *Queen II* (1974), which has a more hard rock and progressive rock feel.

'Bohemian Rhapsody' Combines Several Distinctive Sections

1) 'Bohemian Rhapsody' is perhaps Queen's most famous song. At around 6 minutes long, it has an unusual structure. It's through-composed (see p.56) with six very different sections, and no chorus.

2) The song features standard rock band instrumentation (lead vocal, electric guitar, bass guitar, drum kit), alongside piano, backing vocals, timpani, mark tree (a set of chimes), and lots of effects (see below).

3) The song's especially notable for the technological effects used — there's lots of multi-tracking with voice and guitar overdubs, as well as panning, flanged cymbals, guitar distortion, double-tracking and reverb. In the introduction and operatic section, the vocal panning creates a sense of spatial disorientation.

Over 200 tracks were used in the multi-tracking.

4) The texture is mainly melody with accompaniment, with sections of homophony, antiphony and octaves. Much of the harmony mixes diatonic chords and chords with added notes (e.g. 6ths, 7ths or 9ths).

Intro	Ballad	Guitar solo	Operatic Section	Rock Section	Outro
B♭ major	B♭ major	E♭ major	A major, E♭ major	E♭ major	E♭ major, F major

Intro
- Slow, with homophonic a cappella vocals in 4-part harmony, before piano accompaniment enters.
- The vocals are mainly syllabic, featuring portamentos, conjunct legato motion and an overdubbed lead. Crescendos and chromaticism sound dreamlike, with a wind effect on flanged cymbals.

Ballad
- Solo voice sings two verses to set up the narrative, with bass and arpeggiated piano accompaniment. Other parts enter gradually, including vocal harmonies and an overdubbed vocal countermelody.
- Mercury's vocals feature falsetto and melismas, and there is some word-painting (a mark tree for a shivering effect, and panned overdubbing for wind). Crescendos highlight the lyrics to add drama.

Solo
- The overdubbed electric guitar solo is played by Brian May. His techniques include vibrato, glissandos and pitch bends. Conjunct scalic motion is mixed with arpeggios across a wide pitch range.
- It's rhythmically complex, featuring semiquavers, triplet semiquavers, sextuplets, and dotted rhythms.

Operatic
- The section imitates an operatic SATB-style chorus and is mainly syllabic, with more regular rhythms to create a 'classical' sound. It starts with staccato A major chords and a homophonic texture. Fast harmonic changes, some parts in octaves and chromatic motion increase the drama.
- Call and response between overdubbed solo voices and chordal backing vocals creates antiphony, emphasised with panning. There's dramatic falsetto — Roger Taylor sings a high B♭ at the climax.

Rock
- Power chords and loud dynamics add intensity to the double-tracked vocals (the same track recorded and played back) and defiant lyrics, along with cymbal crashes. There is a notable shift to 12/8.
- Bass and distorted electric guitar play a riff in octaves that starts with a descending minor 6th.

Outro
- Piano arpeggios with homophonic backing vocals and left-hand octaves accompany panned guitar.
- The solo voice sings similar lyrics to the intro and ballad, linking the start and end of the song. After a sudden shift to F major, vocals sing *p* on the final line.

Queen

'Love of My Life' is a Pop Ballad

1) 'Love of My Life' has the <u>slow tempo</u>, soulful <u>lyrics about love</u>, <u>piano accompaniment</u> and <u>legato vocals</u> of a <u>pop ballad</u>. It uses <u>voice</u>, overdubbed <u>backing vocals</u>, <u>piano</u>, <u>harp</u>, <u>electric guitar</u> and <u>bass guitar</u>.

2) The song has <u>two verses</u> and other sections which include a <u>guitar solo</u>. It starts and ends in <u>F major</u>. While the metre is mainly $\frac{4}{4}$, there are some <u>time changes</u> in the <u>verses</u> ($\frac{3}{4}$ and $\frac{6}{4}$) and <u>bridge</u> ($\frac{2}{4}$).

Section	Intro	Verse 1	Verse 2	Bridge	Interlude	Guitar solo	Coda
Key(s)	F major	C major (dominant) F major	C major F major	B♭ major	D minor (relative minor) G minor	F major C major B♭ major	D minor F major

3) Freddie Mercury's lyrics use the song's name as a <u>title hook</u>. Expressive devices like <u>crescendos</u> are used (e.g. backing vocals in verse 2) and there's some <u>word-painting</u> to emphasise the song's strong emotions (e.g. an <u>appoggiatura</u> over an <u>A minor</u> chord portrays a feeling of hurt). <u>Reverb</u> adds vocal emphasis.

4) Certain devices give the song a <u>classical</u> sound:

5) The harmony is largely <u>diatonic</u>, but it also uses <u>seventh chords</u> and <u>suspended (sus) chords</u>.

6) A recurring <u>rhythmic motif</u> features on the title lyrics and elsewhere. The rhythm consists mainly of <u>crotchets</u> and <u>quavers</u> (with some <u>syncopation</u>) and the guitar solo has <u>dotted</u>, <u>semiquaver</u> and <u>demisemiquaver rhythms</u>.

- <u>Classical harp</u> played by Brian May.
- Piano <u>broken chords</u> with <u>pedal notes</u>.
- <u>Sequential</u> melodies.
- <u>Ornamentation</u> such as trills.
- <u>Counterpoint</u> (piano / piano-guitar).
- <u>Perfect cadences</u> at the end of the intro and verses. A <u>plagal cadence</u> at the end.

7) There's a <u>melody with accompaniment</u> texture, with some sections of <u>homophony</u>.

'Seven Seas of Rhye' uses Hard Rock

1) This song has lyrics about <u>fantasy</u> and <u>power</u>. It's in $\frac{4}{4}$ with some bars of $\frac{2}{4}$, and uses aspects of <u>hard rock</u>:

- A <u>fast tempo</u>.
- Fortissimo <u>power chords</u>.
- Some <u>high vocals</u> with <u>falsetto</u>.
- Loud <u>bass drum</u>, snare and cymbal <u>backbeats</u>.
- <u>Fortissimo</u> bass and lead guitars with some <u>distortion</u>.

The texture is mainly melody with accompaniment.

2) There are lots of <u>distorted electric guitars</u> (two rhythm, three panned lead, one bass), <u>drum kit</u>, <u>piano</u>, <u>lead vocals</u>, <u>backing vocals</u>, <u>tambourine</u> and <u>stylophone</u>. The lead vocals feature <u>reverb</u> and <u>panning</u> — it's often <u>double-tracked</u> and <u>overdubbed</u> against <u>multi-tracked</u> backing vocals.

3) The song has <u>three verses</u>, with a <u>title hook</u> at the end of each verse instead of a <u>chorus</u>.

	Intro	Verses 1 and 2	Bridge 1	Solo	Bridge 2	Verse 3	Instrumental	Outro
Sonority	Piano riff, distorted electric guitars, drum fill	Solo voice enters, with electric guitar countermelodies in verse 2	Tambourine with backing vocals	Lead and rhythm guitars, ending with echoes	Vocals in close harmony with louder bass	Vocals in harmony	Piano riff, ending with guitars	Cross fade of music hall song, use of stylophone

4) The key is <u>D major</u>, with modulations to <u>B♭ major</u> for the guitar solo and <u>G major</u> for bridge 2. A <u>D pedal</u> is heard in the closing instrumental. Much of the vocal melody is <u>diatonic</u>, and Bridge 1 has <u>blue notes</u>.

5) A <u>syncopated semiquaver</u> piano <u>riff</u> in <u>octaves</u> appears throughout, with accents <u>every three</u> semiquavers (instead of the usual four). The riff acts as a <u>link</u> after verses 1 and 2. The bassline uses a repeated <u>dotted rhythm</u> motif, with <u>dotted rhythms</u> and <u>syncopation</u> also appearing in the voice.

6) The closing extract is a <u>music hall</u> song ('I Do Like to Be Beside the Seaside'), <u>mixing genres</u> in a <u>surreal</u> way that's more like <u>progressive rock</u>.

The harmony is mainly diatonic with a slow harmonic rhythm (p.36), but there are also some seventh chords and added note chords.

I'm not really a hard rock person, I'm more into chalk and limestone...

Queen sound distinctive — think about how they achieve this with mixed rock genres and Mercury's vocals.

Pop Music — 1990s-Today

The next two pages are going to look at **pop music** from **1990 onwards** — both bands and solo artists.

Girl Bands and Boy Bands Were Popular in the 1990s

1) As the name suggests, <u>boy bands</u> are groups with <u>all male</u> members and <u>girl bands</u> are <u>all female</u>. There are usually <u>four</u> or <u>five</u> members in the group, and they're generally quite <u>young</u> — i.e. in their <u>late teens</u> or <u>early twenties</u>. The bands tend to focus on <u>singing</u> (rather than playing instruments).

2) Although there have been boy and girl bands around for <u>years</u> (e.g. <u>the Jackson 5</u> formed in the <u>1960s</u>), they became really <u>popular</u> in the <u>1990s</u>. <u>British</u> and <u>Irish</u> groups included <u>Boyzone</u>, <u>Westlife</u>, <u>Take That</u>, the <u>Spice Girls</u> and <u>All Saints</u>, while the <u>USA</u> had the <u>Backstreet Boys</u>, *NSYNC and <u>Destiny's Child</u>.

3) These bands particularly appealed to <u>teenage girls</u>, who <u>fell in love</u> with the <u>boy bands</u>, and <u>wanted to be like</u> the <u>girl bands</u>. The <u>songs</u> were written for this <u>target audience</u> — they ranged from <u>ballads</u> (songs that tell <u>stories</u>, often <u>slow</u> and <u>emotional</u>, where the <u>voice</u> is the main feature) to <u>up-tempo dance numbers</u> (which the bands would dance to themselves). Songs were often about <u>love</u>.

Britpop Came About in the Mid '90s

1) <u>Britpop</u> was a reaction to American <u>grunge music</u> (a fusion of <u>punk rock</u> and <u>heavy metal</u> — like the music of <u>Nirvana</u>), which was popular in the early '90s. Britpop was influenced by <u>British bands</u> from the <u>'60s</u>, <u>'70s</u> and <u>'80s</u> — such as <u>The Beatles</u> (see p.114), the <u>Sex Pistols</u>, and <u>The Smiths</u>. It had elements of <u>glam rock</u>, <u>punk rock</u> (see p.113) and <u>indie rock</u>.

2) Key Britpop bands include <u>Pulp</u>, <u>Blur</u>, <u>Oasis</u> and <u>Suede</u> — there was a <u>rivalry</u> between Blur and Oasis. Blur's album *Parklife* and *Definitely Maybe* by Oasis were important early Britpop <u>albums</u>.

3) Britpop music tended to be quite <u>up-tempo</u> and was played by a <u>typical rock band</u> (see p.112), with a focus on the <u>guitar</u> (rather than synthesized instruments). The <u>lyrics</u> were important — they were often quite <u>witty</u> and about <u>everyday things</u>, and the singers' <u>British accents</u> were noticeable.

4) Later bands described as <u>post-Britpop</u> include <u>Coldplay</u>, <u>Radiohead</u> and the <u>Stereophonics</u>.

A Solo Artist's Voice and Personality are Key Features

1) <u>Solo artists</u> have been popular throughout the <u>'90s</u> and <u>'00s</u>, but today's charts in particular are dominated by solo artists. Many solo artists have <u>instantly recognisable</u> vocal features.

   - <u>Michael Jackson</u> was well known for his <u>high</u> (sometimes <u>falsetto</u>) singing voice. He also used '<u>vocal hiccups</u>' (a short intake of breath) and <u>vowel sounds</u> (such as "ah" and "hee hee").
   - <u>Whitney Houston</u> had an impressive <u>vocal range</u> and was capable of producing <u>big sounds</u>. She was famous for her use of <u>melisma</u> and <u>riffing</u> (see p.109).
   - <u>Adele's</u> rich, soulful voice is capable of producing a <u>range</u> of <u>timbres</u>, from a <u>gentle</u>, <u>raspy</u> sound (like at the start of '<u>Turning Tables</u>') to a <u>big</u>, <u>powerful</u> sound (like the chorus of '<u>Skyfall</u>').
   - <u>Charli XCX</u> sings with a distinctive <u>Essex accent</u> and uses <u>autotuning</u> for effect. <u>George Ezra</u>, <u>Amy Winehouse</u>, <u>Robbie Williams</u> and <u>Paloma Faith</u> also have voices that are easy to recognise.

2) <u>Image</u> is important to all pop musicians, but solo artists really need their <u>personalities</u> to come across. Personality can help <u>sell</u> a song — <u>charismatic</u> solo artists can <u>engage</u> with an audience on a more <u>personal level</u> than a band. This can be particularly effective in <u>live performances</u>.

<u>Stormzy</u> became the first black British solo artist to headline at <u>Glastonbury</u> in <u>2019</u>. His performance of '<u>Blinded by Your Grace, Pt. 2</u>' was packed with <u>feeling</u>. He had the audience <u>sing along</u> and later <u>stopped singing</u> to watch the crowd and listen to the <u>backing gospel choir</u>. The performance expressed his <u>faith</u> and his <u>appreciation</u> of the moment, creating an <u>emotional connection</u> with the audience.

If only personality was enough to make up for my horrible singing...

More recent boy/girl bands include One Direction, BTS, Fifth Harmony, Little Mix and Blackpink.

Pop Music — 1990s-Today

There have been so many different pop artists from the 1990s onwards — this page covers a few examples.

The **Accompaniment** and **Structure** Varies

Pop artists use different accompaniments and structures depending on the style and purpose of the song.

1990s
- 'Black or White' by Michael Jackson (released in 1991) has a typical rock band accompaniment (see p.112). The song has a number of different sections, including an intro featuring Jackson's distinctive falsetto 'ow's, verses that end with a mini chorus, a half-chanted section, a rap section and an outro, with guitar interludes in between.
- Bryan Adams' 1991 hit '(Everything I Do) I Do It For You' starts with a simple piano accompaniment, before the rest of the rock band comes in, building up the texture. There's a guitar solo in the middle.
- Westlife's 1999 hit 'Flying Without Wings' is a typical pop ballad. It's fairly slow, and opens with a solo voice before a gentle guitar comes in. The accompaniment builds up, adding a drum kit, strings, piano and backing vocals as the song reaches its emotional climax.

2000s
- 'Can't Get You Out Of My Head' by Kylie Minogue (released in 2001) has two memorable hooks — the repeated la la la and the first line of the chorus. The song doesn't follow a standard structure — choruses and sections with long, held-on notes are broken up by la la la sections. The song uses synthesized instruments and has a strong drumbeat, which makes it ideal to dance to in a nightclub.
- Britney Spears' hit 'Toxic' (2003) also uses synthesized instruments, distorted guitars and wailing strings to create a futuristic sound. It has a strong, driving beat.
- Rihanna's 2007 single 'Umbrella' mixes pop with hip-hop and R&B. It starts with rap verse by Jay-Z, then follows a standard verse-chorus structure, with a hook (repeated 'ella's and 'eh's) after each chorus. The accompaniment is based around a hi-hat drumbeat and synthesizers.

2010s
- 'Someone Like You' by Adele (released in 2011) has a simple accompaniment of a piano playing broken chords (see p.39). The song has a rough verse-chorus structure, but with some variations — the verses are different lengths, and one repeated verse has a different melody. There is a bridge with backing vocals sung by Adele herself (see below).
- For his 2014 single 'Sing', Ed Sheeran accompanies himself on the acoustic guitar, but the song also has electric guitars, percussion and backing vocals. There are several different sections to the song — including falsetto sections, repeated 'oh's and a half-sung, half-rap verse.

2020s
- 'Dance the Night', sung by Dua Lipa (released in 2023), combines disco, a funk bassline and contemporary synth-pop. The song is a glamorous dance track, which matches its use in the film _Barbie_™. It features a recurring synth string motif which imitates the main vocal hook.
- Taylor Swift's 2024 song 'Who's Afraid of Little Old Me?' is an example of chamber pop (rock music with orchestral instruments such as strings). It also has dark lyrics, typical of Southern Gothic music.

> Taylor Swift's career started in the 2000s with country pop — she's moved through lots of different styles since then, including folk and synth-pop.

Artists Use **Technology** to Create **Vocal Effects**

As well as synthesized instruments, many pop artists use technology and vocal effects to add variety. E.g.
- 'Can't Get You Out Of My Head' was recorded using MIDI technology (see p.72).
- 'Someone Like You' uses overdubbing in the bridge section. A separate track of Adele singing in harmony with the melody is recorded and then mixed in.
- 'Telephone' by Lady Gaga (featuring Beyoncé) uses different vocal effects such as delay, reverb and pitch bends, as well as samples (see p.73) of a telephone ringing and a telephone operator speaking.

EXAM TIP

Pop music doesn't fit neatly into one box...

It's hard to make generalisations about pop music as it's so varied. You might be asked about the vocals, the accompaniment, technology or style — try and pick out the key features.

Musicals

Musical theatre is a lighter, more modern version of **opera**. It's been **developing** since the 19th century. You need to know about **Broadway musicals** from the 1950s-1990s.

Musicals Have **Songs**, **Dialogue** and **Dances**

1) Musicals came from <u>less serious</u> versions of <u>opera</u>, like <u>opéra comique</u> and <u>operetta</u> (see p.86). Towards the <u>end</u> of the <u>19th century</u>, <u>Gilbert and Sullivan</u> wrote lots of popular <u>comic operas</u>.

2) The type of musicals that are around <u>today</u> started in the <u>1920s</u>, and <u>developed</u> throughout the rest of the <u>20th</u> and into the <u>21st century</u>. They started out on <u>Broadway</u>, a famous theatre street in <u>New York</u>. Some started in <u>London's West End</u>.

3) Musicals use <u>singing</u>, <u>dancing</u> and <u>talking</u> to tell stories.

4) They usually have an <u>orchestra</u> to accompany the singers and play <u>incidental (background) music</u>.

5) Some musicals that started out on the <u>stage</u> have been made into really popular musical <u>films</u> — like *Grease*, *West Side Story* and *Sweeney Todd*. Sometimes, a film is <u>adapted</u> into a musical performed on <u>stage</u> — like *Spamalot* (based on Monty Python and the Holy Grail) and *Billy Elliot*.

6) Some musicals are based on <u>novels</u> — like *Les Misérables*, *Oliver!* and *Jekyll & Hyde*.

Musical Styles are Always **Changing**

Musicals are generally written in the style of the <u>popular music</u> that's around at the time — so musicals from <u>different times</u> sound very different. <u>Earlier</u> musicals were influenced by <u>jazz</u> and <u>swing music</u> (see p.131-132), while lots of musicals from the <u>1970s onwards</u> used <u>rock music</u> (see p.112-113). Have a listen to some of these musicals to hear the different styles they use:

1920s-1950s	*COLE PORTER*: Paris, Anything Goes, Kiss Me, Kate, Silk Stockings
1940s-1950s	*RODGERS & HAMMERSTEIN*: Oklahoma!, South Pacific, The King and I, The Sound of Music
1950s-2010s	*STEPHEN SONDHEIM*: Follies, Sweeney Todd and lyrics for West Side Story
1960s-1990s	*KANDER & EBB*: Cabaret, Chicago, Kiss of the Spider Woman
1970s-2010s	*ANDREW LLOYD WEBBER*: Joseph and the Amazing Technicolour Dreamcoat, Jesus Christ Superstar, Evita, Cats, Phantom of the Opera, School of Rock
1970s-2000s	*SCHÖNBERG & BOUBLIL*: Les Misérables, Miss Saigon

Some Musicals Contain **Pop Songs**

- Songs from musicals sometimes hit the <u>charts</u>. In the UK, musicals by <u>Andrew Lloyd Webber</u> and <u>Tim Rice</u> have spawned a few chart hits, such as 'Don't Cry For Me Argentina' from *Evita*, 'Memory' from *Cats* and 'No Matter What' from *Whistle Down the Wind* (sung by Boyzone).

- Sometimes chart hits find their way into musicals — *Mamma Mia!* was written around a collection of <u>ABBA</u> hits. The <u>plots</u> of these musicals often have <u>nothing</u> to do with the band, but use their songs to tell a <u>story</u>. Others <u>tell the story</u> of the <u>band</u> or <u>singer</u> (e.g. *Buddy — The Buddy Holly Story*).

Musicals Can Be About **Any Topic**

1) Some musicals deal with very <u>serious</u> subject matter — *Miss Saigon* is set during and after the <u>Vietnam War</u>, and *Cabaret* is set in <u>Nazi Germany</u>. These musicals are often <u>tragic</u> and <u>emotional</u>.

2) Other musicals are based on <u>Shakespeare's plays</u> — *West Side Story* is based on *Romeo and Juliet*, but set in <u>1950s New York</u>. The two <u>rival gangs</u> are the <u>Jets</u> (Americans) and the <u>Sharks</u> (Puerto Rican immigrants). The music has lots of <u>jazz elements</u>, a number of <u>dance scenes</u> and looked at <u>social problems</u> in America, which made it quite <u>different</u> to other musicals at the time.

3) Some musicals have quite <u>bizarre</u> plots, such as *Little Shop of Horrors* (which is about a <u>man-eating plant</u>) and *Starlight Express* (which is about a <u>train set</u>, with the cast on <u>rollerskates</u>).

Musicals

Here's how to create that Broadway sound...

Most Musical Songs are **Easy on the Ear**

Musicals are meant to be <u>entertaining</u> and <u>easy to listen to</u>. This is how they do it...

1) The melodies are easy to <u>sing</u> — audiences tend to prefer songs they can sing along to.

2) The harmony is <u>diatonic</u> — it'll be in either a major or a minor key.

3) The song <u>structure</u> is often <u>simple</u>, with alternating verses and choruses and a middle eight (similar to the structure of a <u>pop song</u>).

| Intro | Chorus | Verse | Chorus | Verse | Middle 8 | Chorus | Verse | Chorus | Verse | Chorus | Outro |

Grabs the audience's attention and sets the mood for the song.

Has new chords and new lyrics — a change of mood to keep the audience interested.

Ties the song off — either loud and brassy or sad and quiet.

4) The chorus is often in <u>32-bar song</u> form. The 32 bars break down into 4 sections of 8 bars each. Sections 1, 2 and 4 use the <u>main theme</u> (sometimes with slight variations). Section 3 has a <u>contrasting theme</u> (middle eight).

5) The chorus has a <u>hook</u> — a catchy bit of lyrics and melody that makes the song memorable. The hook is the bit that gets stuck in the audience's head (so they want to listen to the soundtrack when they get home) and often becomes the title of the song — e.g. '<u>I Feel Pretty</u>' (*West Side Story*), '<u>It's the Hard-Knock Life</u>' (*Annie*) or '<u>And All That Jazz</u>' (*Chicago*).

There are **Four Basic Types** of Musical Song

When you hear a musical song you should be able to identify what <u>type</u> of song it is:

1) ***SOLO CHARACTER SONG*** — a character sings about how they're <u>feeling</u> — in <u>love</u>, full of <u>hate</u>, over the moon with <u>happiness</u>, etc. '<u>Maria</u>' from *West Side Story* and '<u>Maybe This Time</u>' from *Cabaret* are both solo character songs.

2) ***DUET*** — duets are basically the same as solo character songs, except there are <u>two people</u> singing so you get <u>two different reactions</u> to a situation. '<u>I Know Him So Well</u>' from *Chess* is a great example.

3) ***ACTION SONG*** — the words of the song tell you what's going on in the <u>plot</u> — they lead you into the next bit of the story.

4) ***CHORUS NUMBER*** — the whole <u>ensemble</u> get together and have a <u>big old sing-song</u>. For example, '<u>We Go Together</u>' at the end of *Grease* and '<u>Food, Glorious Food</u>' at the beginning of *Oliver!*.

You can also get trios, quartets etc. (i.e. more than one character singing, but not a chorus number).

All these styles of song developed from opera — solo songs are like <u>arias</u>, action songs are like <u>recitatives</u>. The lyrics in a musical song tell part of the story. They're usually <u>written first</u>, so the composer has to fit the music around them.

SUGGESTED LISTENING

It's showtime — let's see those jazz hands...

Listen to the quintet version of 'Tonight' from *West Side Story* — it features Tony, Maria, Anita and the two rival gangs. At one point, all five different parts are sung at the same time.

Film Music

SPOILER ALERT: the next three pages may contain spoilers. Consider yourself warned.

Composers who write **film music** have to write music to **fit** with the **action** already set by the **film makers**.

Look Out for **Leitmotifs** in Most Film Music

'Leitmotif' can also be spelt 'leitmotiv'.

1) A leitmotif is a tune that returns throughout the film (there's often more than one). It represents a particular object, idea or character in the story, and often returns in the background or in an altered form.

2) Leitmotifs are used throughout the *Lord of the Rings*™ films — for example, the one that represents the group of characters who make up the Fellowship of the Ring is heroic, and appears less frequently after the Fellowship falls apart. The leitmotif for the Shire (the home of the hobbits) is a happy melody in a major key. It's light and playful, and reflects the comfort and safety of the Shire.

3) 'Hedwig's Theme' is the main leitmotif in the *Harry Potter*® films — it's repeated in all the films and played by different instruments. It's associated with the world of magic and wizards.

4) Sometimes the leitmotifs give you a hint as to what will happen later in the film — if a character turns out to be a bad guy, their theme might have menacing chords being played in the background.

> In the final few bars of 'Anakin's Theme' from *Star Wars*®: *Episode I — The Phantom Menace*™ (1999), you can hear echoes of 'Darth Vader's Theme' from *Episode V* (also by John Williams). This is a subtle hint that Anakin (who's good in this film) will become Darth Vader.

Composers Use Lots of **Repetition** in Film Music

1) Repeated sections of music can be used to link different parts of the film together — it can remind you of something that happened earlier in the film.

2) A leitmotif can be repeated throughout the film, but might be transformed to reflect what's going on. The instrumentation can be changed, or it can be repeated in a different key (e.g. it might come back in a minor key to show that things have started to go wrong). Sometimes, just the rhythm of the leitmotif is played in the background — it might be so quiet it's hardly noticeable, but it all adds to the drama.

3) Often at the end of the film there's a triumphant modulation of the main theme (as long as the film has a happy ending). It ends in a happy, uplifting key with a drawn-out cadence (see p.42-43), to show that the story of the film has been resolved.

4) Of course, if the film doesn't have a happy ending (or if there's going to be a sequel), the theme may be left unresolved, giving the film a more open or darker ending.

5) Repetition can be used to create tension and suspense — a repeated sequence that's getting louder and louder can really have you on the edge of your seat.

Some Films Use **Pop Songs** to Get **Publicity**

- Lots of films have pop songs as part of their soundtrack — they're usually released in the charts to generate publicity. They're often performed by famous pop stars — like Pharrell Williams' song 'Happy' for the film *Despicable Me 2* (2013). *Barbie*™ (2023) featured songs by a variety of famous artists, including Lizzo, Dua Lipa, Nicki Minaj, Sam Smith, Tame Impala, Charli XCX and Billie Eilish.

- Some films have pop songs over the opening or closing credits — the James Bond films are especially known for this. Sometimes elements of the songs reappear in the film itself — motifs from Billie Eilish's 2020 single 'No Time to Die' can be heard elsewhere in the film of the same name, and the song ends with a distinctive chord heard in many of the Bond franchise's soundtracks.

- A song used as the title track might return in the background later. For example, the song 'My Heart Will Go On' by Celine Dion pops up many times in the film *Titanic* (1997).

A good excuse to watch some films...

Film music is written to create a certain atmosphere. Composers use it to set the scene, create a mood or describe a character. It should help the overall effect of the film and add to the drama of the story.

Film Music

Film composers use music to **set the scene** — it helps you believe it's in a **different country** or **time**.

Traditional Instruments Give You a Feel for Time and Place

1) Music can be used to create the mood of a different <u>time</u> or <u>place</u>.

2) <u>Westerns</u> are set in 19th century North America. They generally tell a simple story and they can often be very <u>dramatic</u> and <u>violent</u>.

3) Westerns use music <u>from the time</u> to <u>set the scene</u>. For example, <u>Ennio Morricone</u> composed some of the music for <u>Django Unchained</u> (2012). He used elements of <u>traditional music</u>, with <u>instruments</u> including the Spanish guitar, banjo, tin whistle, trumpet and percussion.

4) Films set in the <u>70s</u> or <u>80s</u> might use <u>pop songs</u> from the time to set the scene. People will <u>recognise</u> the songs and it'll <u>remind</u> them of that decade.

5) <u>Tim Rice</u> and <u>Elton John</u> composed the songs for Disney's <u>The Lion King</u>® (1994). The songs have a lot of <u>African influences</u> (including <u>drumming</u>, <u>traditional instruments</u> and <u>isicathamiya singing</u> — see p.133), which helps the audience <u>imagine</u> the film's setting. <u>Hans Zimmer</u> composed the <u>orchestral</u> music for the film, and also used <u>traditional African music</u> and <u>singing</u>.

The Music in War Films Creates the Atmosphere

1) The music in war films needs to create an <u>atmosphere</u> for the <u>time</u> and <u>place</u> of the war, as well as showing the <u>action</u> and <u>emotion</u> of the plot. For example, the battle scenes of <u>Gladiator</u> (2000) are accompanied by <u>threatening music</u> (by <u>Hans Zimmer</u>), which creates tension.

2) <u>Sound effects</u> (like <u>explosions</u> and <u>gunfire</u>) can be incorporated into the music to suggest <u>war</u>.

3) <u>Saving Private Ryan</u> (1998) is set in the <u>Second World War</u>. The music (by <u>John Williams</u>) is only heard <u>between</u> the battle scenes (the battles have no musical accompaniment). However, the frequent use of the <u>snare drum</u> is a <u>constant reminder</u> of the fighting (it sounds like a <u>military march</u>). The music is generally quite <u>mournful</u> and <u>reflective</u>, focusing on the <u>cost</u> to life, rather than the <u>heroism</u> of war.

Unnatural Sounds Make Strange Places Seem Even Stranger

<u>Horror</u>, <u>science fiction</u> or <u>fantasy</u> films are often set in <u>strange places</u> or on other <u>planets</u>. Composers need to <u>transport</u> the audience to a <u>weird reality</u>, where nothing is quite what you'd expect.

- <u>Unusual harmonies</u> and <u>time signatures</u> are used when things are a bit <u>weird</u> — they're not what you're expecting, so they sound odd.

- <u>Synthesizers</u> and <u>samples</u> of bizarre <u>sounds</u> often have no relation to what's happening on-screen, but make the audience wonder what's going on and set their imagination racing.

- <u>Instruments</u> or <u>voices</u> can be <u>distorted</u> using <u>computers</u>.

- There's often no clear <u>structure</u> so it's hard to predict what's going to happen.

- <u>Discords</u> and <u>diminished</u> chords make it difficult to listen to.

- <u>Rapid scalic patterns</u> (going up and down scales) and <u>interrupted cadences</u> (see p.43) can make <u>pulse-raising</u> scenes feel more frantic.

- In the famous <u>shower scene</u> in <u>Psycho</u> (1960), the <u>stabbing</u> of the <u>knife</u> is accompanied by (and emphasised by) the <u>violins</u> also <u>stabbing</u> out a <u>high-pitched tritone</u> (p.29). Each chord goes right through you, and makes what you're seeing on-screen feel much more <u>real</u>.

- <u>James Horner's</u> music for <u>Avatar</u> (2009) combines <u>instruments</u>, <u>timbres</u> and <u>textures</u> from music from all over the world to create the <u>music</u> and <u>culture</u> of the <u>Na'vi people</u>.

Music revision can be used to put you in a mood...

There are loads of little tricks that film composers can use to help set the scene and create an atmosphere.

Film Music

Sometimes, film music helps you **understand** what's happening. It can also help to **build tension**.

The **Style** of Music **Changes** With the **Mood** of the Scene

1) The soundtrack for the film *Pirates of the Caribbean®: The Curse of the Black Pearl* (2003) was written by Klaus Badelt.

2) There's a simple love theme to accompany the growing romance between Will and Elizabeth, using string and woodwind instruments playing quietly.

3) In the humorous scenes involving Captain Jack Sparrow, the music is playful to create a light-hearted mood and provides a contrast with the fight scenes.

4) During battle scenes, the mood is tense and dramatic — the music is played by low brass instruments.

Composers Can Keep You on the **Edge** of Your Seat

1) Ostinati keep the audience on edge. For example, in *The Thomas Crown Affair* (1999) an ostinato made up of clapping and a piano motif from Nina Simone's 'Sinnerman' is used to accompany a heist in an art museum.

2) In some sci-fi films there's background music with just drums and bass, generated on computers. It's played throughout the film to let the audience know that the danger is always there.

3) A good example of this is in *Tron: Legacy* (2010), which has music written by Daft Punk. They use computer-generated noises to mimic the sound of high-intensity computer games from the '80s, which helps create the virtual-reality setting.

4) Sustained notes create suspense (e.g. tremolo strings), and minor or dissonant chords make the audience feel uneasy. Suspensions that don't resolve (see p.41) are another good way of doing this.

5) Composers know how to build the tension and make you feel like something bad is going to happen:

> • Dynamics get louder.
> • Tempo gets faster — like the two-note motif in *Jaws* (1975), which speeds up (and gets louder) as the shark gets closer.
> • Pitch gets higher.
> • A tune played earlier in a scary bit sometimes comes back to remind you.
> • Sometimes they use silence before a loud bit just to make you jump.

Diegetic Music is Music the Characters Can **Hear**

1) In most films, the music is extra-diegetic — it's not actually part of the story. It's put 'over the top' of the action to increase the effect of the film. It's for the audience's benefit only.

2) Sometimes film-makers want to include music in the story for the characters (as well as the audience) to hear — this is diegetic music.

> • In *The Hunger Games: Mockingjay — Part 1* (2014), Katniss sings a song for one of her companions. It is recorded and turned into a propaganda video by the rebels, and used as their battle song.
> • In *Inception* (2010), the song 'Non, je ne regrette rien' by Édith Piaf is used diegetically as a plot device. The song helps wake a character up from a dream. Characters in a dream can hear a slowed-down version of the song, while in the real world it's heard at the original tempo. In fact, much of the soundtrack to the film is based on an extremely slowed-down version of the original.
> • In *Baby Driver* (2017), Baby listens to music to counter the effects of tinnitus. Most of the music in the film is diegetic — the audience hears the song that Baby is listening to at that time. The soundtrack is also synchronised to the action seen on screen.

Game Music

From fairly basic origins, video game music has developed into a pretty important genre in its own right.

Early Video Game Music Was Very Simple

1) Due to limited technology, the music for early video games was very simple — it could only have a couple of different instruments or parts, so was often monophonic (or very basic polyphony).

2) The music wasn't usually played throughout the game — it would sometimes just be used as a theme tune at the start, or played in response to something happening in the game (e.g. completing a level).

> Space Invaders (created by Tomohiro Nishikado in 1978) was one of the first games to have music playing continuously throughout the game — it was based on a loop of four descending notes in the bass part, which changed speed to match the movements on screen.

3) Early video game music would often use synthesizers (see p.72), which could be integrated into the video game hardware to create and manipulate synthetic sounds (rather than recording real instruments).

4) MIDI (Musical Instrument Digital Interface) allowed composers to write for a range of instruments that played back consistently on different pieces of equipment (and different types of computer).

5) From the 1990s, video games were able to use higher quality music with more realistic instrumental timbres because of the technological advances in CD audio. Nowadays, soundtracks can be created very effectively using DAW (digital audio workstation) software like Logic Pro or Cubase.

Recent Game Music is More Like a Film Score

1) In modern video games, better technology has led to games with a more intricate plot or complicated mission for the player to complete. Better audio technology has enabled game music to become more like a film score. As well as synthesizers, it frequently uses orchestral and choral elements.

2) As there are often different locations within a game, composers will create music to go with each place or time — using similar methods to film composers (see p.121-122).

3) Games often use motifs (short melodic ideas), which can be developed to reflect the changing actions. Some ways of altering motifs include sequencing, playing inversions or retrograde versions (see p.83), augmentation and diminution (lengthening or shortening all note values or intervals — see p.18). These changes have different effects — e.g. diminution of the note values makes it sound more urgent.

4) Like films, there are different genres of game — e.g. sci-fi, fantasy, war or racing. The techniques that film composers use for these types of film can be used in game music too (see p.122).

5) Some well-known film composers have also written music for games — as a result, some games have full soundtracks. For example, Harry Gregson-Williams composed some of the music for the *Metal Gear Solid*® series of games, the *Shrek* films and *The Martian*, and Gustavo Santaolalla composed music for the film *Brokeback Mountain* and the game series *The Last Of Us*.

- In *Halo*®, the player takes on the role of the supersoldier Master Chief in a fight against an alien religious group called the Covenant. It is set on a range of planets in the 26th century.

- There have been a number of different composers for the games in the series, including Martin O'Donnell (the lead composer), Michael Salvatori, Stephen Rippy and Neil Davidge.

- The main theme opens with male voices singing (like monks chanting — this represents the Covenant), which sounds eerie and mysterious. A driving syncopated drum rhythm (playing an ostinato) builds up the intensity and creates a sense of excitement. Low strings enter playing the melody, which is based on the same rhythmic pattern over increasing intervals (the first time, it's a perfect octave, then a major ninth and so on) — it sounds a bit like a fanfare. Other string parts are introduced, creating a complex layering of orchestral parts and giving the music energy.

I didn't know there was a video game version of Master Chef...

Next time you're playing a video game, pay attention to the music and see what effect it has. Careful not to get too distracted though — you don't want to fail your mission (or your exam).

Warm-up and Exam Questions

Before you get stuck into the exam-style questions, have a go at these warm-up questions first.

Warm-up Questions

1) What does a cappella mean?
2) Name one singer who sings falsetto.
3) When did rock 'n' roll become popular in the USA?
4) Describe four different sub-genres of rock music.
5) What is a concept album?
6) Name three musical styles which appear on Queen's *A Night at the Opera*.
7) List the six different sections in 'Bohemian Rhapsody'.
8) Name the classical instrument played by Brian May in 'Love of My Life'.
9) Give three technological effects that can be heard in 'Seven Seas of Rhye'.
10) How can personality help a solo artist become popular?
11) Name two songs that were hits in the 2010s.
12) What is a musical?
13) Describe 32-bar song form.
14) Name the four main types of songs found in musicals.
15) What is a leitmotif?
16) How is repetition used in film music?
17) Why are instruments from a particular time or place sometimes used in film music?
18) What is DAW software?

Exam Questions

To make sure you really know your stuff, here are a couple of exam questions.

These questions are about 'Seven Seas of Rhye' from the album *Queen II* by Queen.

Unfortunately, we were unable to get permission to include this track on our playlist.

However, it's readily available to listen to online —
you just need to listen from 1:17 to 2:14.

Play the excerpt **four** times. Leave a short pause between each playing.

a) i) Which technological effect is used at the very end of the guitar solo?

   ....

   [1 mark]

   ii) Identify two other musical features of the guitar solo.

   1) ....

   2) ....

   [2 marks]

Exam Questions

b)   Which section of the song is heard when the voices enter?
Circle the correct answer.

   verse   **chorus**   **bridge**   **cross fade**

[1 mark]

c)   The vocals in the excerpt are 'double-tracked'.
Explain the meaning and effect of 'double-tracking'.

....

....

....

[2 marks]

d)   Identify three features of this excerpt that are typical of hard rock.

   1)   ....

   ....

   2)   ....

   ....

   3)   ....

   ....

[3 marks]

e)   Describe the vocal rhythms in the final section.

....

....

....

[2 marks]

Exam Questions

Track 34 is an excerpt from 'Fallin'' by Alicia Keys.
Play the excerpt **four** times. Leave a short pause between each playing.

a) In the introduction of the song, what technique does the vocalist use on the word 'in'?
Circle the correct answer.

   scat   **falsetto**   **riffing**   **belting**

   [1 mark]

b) i) What is the tonality of this excerpt?

   ....

   [1 mark]

   ii) The piano part alternates between two chords.
       On the first two beats of each bar, chord I is played.
       What chord is played on the third and fourth beats of each bar?

   ....

   [1 mark]

c) The bars in the table below are numbered from where the piano quavers start.
   The time signature of the excerpt is $\frac{12}{8}$.

   Read each statement below and put letters in the appropriate box to show
   where each feature is heard.

   • Write the letter A in the bar in which backing vocals are first heard.
   • Write the letter B in the bar in which percussion is first heard.
   • Write the letter C in the bar in which the bass drum is first heard.
   • Write the letter D in the bar in which the bass drum plays 6 quavers
     in the second half of the bar.

1	2	3	4	5	6	7	8

   [4 marks]

d) The solo artist also provides some of the backing vocals herself.
   Which recording technique is used to achieve this? Circle the correct answer.

   sampling   **overdubbing**   **phase shifting**   **reverb**

   [1 mark]

Revision Summary for Section Seven

That's the end of <u>Section Seven</u> — now, let's see which bits you can remember...
- Try these questions and <u>tick off each one</u> when you <u>get it right</u>.
- When you've done <u>all the questions</u> for a topic and are <u>completely happy</u> with it, tick off the topic.

Voices and Instruments in Pop (p.109-110) ☑

1) Describe four different ways backing vocals can be sung.
2) Describe: a) scat   b) riffing
3) Name two electronic effects that can be added to vocal parts.
4) Describe typical lead guitar, rhythm guitar and bass guitar parts in pop music.

Rock 'n' Roll and Rock Music (p.111-116) ☑

5) What were the two main influences on rock 'n' roll music?
6) Write down three things that rock 'n' roll songs were often about.
7) Name three early rock 'n' roll stars.
8) Describe punk rock.
9) Name two rock anthems.
10) What is arena rock?
11) What genre does the album *Sgt. Pepper's Lonely Hearts Club Band* by The Beatles belong to?
12) Name the four original members of Queen and explain their roles in the band.
13) Which instrument is used to create a 'shivering' effect in 'Bohemian Rhapsody'?
14) Describe how a sense of drama is created in the operatic section of 'Bohemian Rhapsody'.
15) Give three elements of pop ballads that are used in 'Love of My Life'.
16) What song is heard at the end of 'Seven Seas of Rhye'? What type of song is it?

Pop Music and Musicals (p.117-120)

17) Name one boy band and one girl band.
18) Briefly describe Britpop.
19) Describe two different solo artists from the 1990s.
20) Describe one effect used on Lady Gaga's 'Telephone'.
21) Give one example of a musical that was based on a book.
22) Name four different composers who wrote musicals.
23) In musical terms, what is a hook?
24) What does an action song in a musical do?

Film and Game Music (p.121-124) ☑

25) How did Tim Rice and Elton John create the African setting of *The Lion King*?
26) What type of films might use music with unusual harmonies or weird time signatures?
27) Describe how the music in *The Pirates of the Caribbean®* films illustrates the different places and characters.
28) How are ostinati used in film music?
29) How do composers create suspense?
30) What is diegetic music?
31) Give three ways that motifs in game music can be altered.

The Blues

You might not associate the blues with 'traditional music', but it took influences from traditional sources and reinterpreted them. It still has an **influence** on jazz, pop and rock 'n' roll music today.

African Slaves in America Started Off the Blues

1) In the 1600s and 1700s, millions of Africans were captured and sold as slaves. Many were taken to work on plantations in North America.

2) To take their minds off their work, which was often brutally hard, they sang work songs, using their tools to give the music a beat. The lyrics were often about the hardship and misery of being a slave.

3) Over the years, African musical styles, such as call and response singing (p.55), blended with features of European music, especially chords. This combination was the beginning of the blues.

4) Even after slavery was finally abolished in the 1860s, life remained hard for ex-slaves living in the southern states. The lyrics and tone of their songs carried on being sad and 'blue'.

5) The traditional blues instruments are the harmonica, guitar, banjo, violin, piano, double bass and voice. They're all acoustic — electric instruments hadn't been invented when blues began.

6) In the early twentieth century, black Americans began to play the blues in bars beyond the southern states. By the 1920s, blues was popular all over America with both white and black audiences.

7) In the 1940s and 1950s a style called rhythm'n'blues (R'n'B) was developed. It's a sped-up version of blues played on electric guitar and bass.

Blues has its Own Scale

- You get a blues scale by flattening the 3rd, 5th and 7th of any major scale. The unflattened 5th is played too.

- The flattened notes are called blue notes. They're not always lowered by a full semitone — sometimes they're flattened by a microtone instead (see p.134).

- Singers and players often slide up or down to blue notes — this is known as pitch bend. This feature comes from the 'bent' notes used in African singing.

- The 2nd and 6th notes are often left out.

Blues scale on C

Blues Melodies have Swinging, Offbeat Rhythms

1) In normal 'straight' rhythm the beats split up into equal halves.

I want chips and egg

I want chips and egg

2) In swung rhythm, the first bit of the beat is longer, as it steals time from the second bit to give the music a swinging feel. The rhythm shown on the left is a special type of swung rhythm called 'shuffle'.

3) Syncopation creates an offbeat sound by avoiding the strong beats — it puts the oomph in unexpected places.

4) A backbeat is when beats 2 and 4 are emphasised.

Please don't make me beg

The blues have influenced almost all forms of popular music...

The blues doesn't have to be mournful, sad and depressing — it just sounds better that way...

The Blues

There are lots of different types of blues, but the most popular song structure is the **12-bar blues**.

Twelve-bar Blues has a **Repeated Twelve-Bar Structure**

12-bar blues uses a set <u>chord pattern</u> that is <u>12 bars long</u>. Singers like <u>Bessie Smith</u> and <u>Robert Johnson</u> made the 12-bar blues structure really popular in the 1920s. It's still one of the most popular styles today.

Chord I	Chord I	Chord I	Chord I
Chord IV	Chord IV	Chord I	Chord I
Chord V	Chord IV	Chord I	Chord I (V)

If the 12-bar structure is repeated, chord V is played in bar 12 instead of chord I, to lead back to Bar 1.

- The only chords are <u>I</u>, <u>IV</u> and <u>V</u>.
- The 12-bar pattern is <u>repeated</u> throughout the song.
- You can make the chords even more <u>bluesy</u> by adding <u>minor 7ths</u> (see p.29).

12-bar blues has had a huge influence on other musical styles including <u>ragtime</u>, <u>jazz</u>, <u>rock and roll</u> and <u>R&B</u>. Loads of <u>pop songs</u> today still use the standard 12-bar structure.

Twelve Bars Break Nicely into **Three Lines of 4 Bars**

The <u>lyrics</u> of a 12-bar blues song usually stick to <u>three lines</u> for <u>each verse</u> of the song.

Lines 1 and 2 are usually the same.

Woke up this morning feeling blue.
Woke up this morning feeling blue.

Line 3 is different, but rhymes with lines 1 and 2.

Feeling sad and lonesome without you.

The words are usually pretty gloomy.

Each line of music lasts for 4 bars, but the words don't always fill up the whole line. The singer's part (the <u>call</u>) is followed by an instrument playing an answer (the <u>response</u>) in the gap before the next line.

There are **Sixteen-Bar Patterns** too

1) Blues <u>doesn't have</u> to use a 12-bar pattern. <u>16-bar patterns</u>, based on the 12-bar structure, can be used.

2) There are a few <u>different versions</u> of the 16-bar pattern. Sometimes the <u>first line</u> of the 12-bar blues is <u>repeated</u> to make a 16-bar pattern. The rest of the pattern then follows the <u>12-bar</u> structure.

3) This variation is the same as the 12-bar pattern, except bars 9 and 10 are repeated <u>twice</u>.

Chord I	Chord I	Chord I	Chord I
Chord IV	Chord IV	Chord I	Chord I
Chord V	Chord IV	Chord V	Chord IV
Chord V	Chord IV	Chord I	Chord I

'Hoochie Coochie Man', performed by Muddy Waters, uses the 16-bar blues.

4) 12-bar and 16-bar patterns can be used in the <u>same piece</u>, for example 16-bar <u>verses</u> with a 12-bar <u>chorus</u>. The 16-bar patterns are also <u>divided</u> into 4-bar lines, so it's easy to <u>switch</u> between the two.

Jazz

Jazz developed from a fusion of African and European influences.

Jazz has its **Roots** in **African American Blues** and **Ragtime**

1) Jazz is a type of music that developed in the USA in the early 20th century. It's a fusion of African and European influences that came from the music of the newly-freed slaves.

2) It started off as Dixieland jazz in New Orleans in the early 1900s. Dixieland jazz is a mix of brass band marches, ragtime (music with lots of syncopated melodies that was often played on the piano) and blues (see p.129-130). Dixieland jazz is polyphonic (different parts move at different times).

3) It was played in bars — one of the few places black musicians were allowed to perform because of segregation (black people weren't allowed to use the same places as white people).

4) In 1920, jazz moved to Chicago. This was the era of the Prohibition (from 1920-1933, alcohol was banned in the United States). Illegal bars (called speakeasies) often had jazz bands playing. Jazz started to get a bad reputation. Some people thought it was immoral.

5) The 1920s were known as 'the Jazz Age' or the 'Roaring Twenties'.

Jazz has **Developed Over Time**

1) Swing music is a type of jazz that can be danced to. It's played by a big band (see below).

1) It's usually quite fast, and rhythms are swung (see p.129). Most pieces are in $\frac{4}{4}$ time. It has regular phrases and an emphasis on the first and third beats of the bar to make it easier to dance to.

2) It was popular because it was played on the radio, which was more accessible and acceptable than going to illegal bars. The radio introduced swing to a wider audience.

3) In the 1940s, bebop (or just bop) developed from swing music. Bebop is fast with lots of improvisation. It has complex harmonies, exciting syncopated rhythms and irregular phrase lengths. Bebop is much less structured than swing.

4) Free jazz developed in the 1950s and 1960s as a reaction against the limits of swing and bebop.

5) It didn't follow the normal rules of tempo and rhythm — players within the same band would play at different speeds to each other. There wasn't a regular rhythm.

6) It involves lots of improvisation (see p.132). Soloists don't follow the chords or structure of the band.

Jazz didn't stop developing in the 60s. There are even more experimental forms of jazz, such as avant-garde jazz, which pushes the boundaries of what's considered "normal".

Trumpets, **Trombones** and **Clarinets** are Used in Jazz

1) A typical jazz band has a trumpet, a trombone and a clarinet on the front row. Later, saxophones were included too. The front row instruments play improvised solos.

2) There's also a rhythm section with piano, drums, a double bass and sometimes a guitar.

3) Big bands are made up of saxophones, trumpets, trombones and a rhythm section. The saxophone section has alto, tenor and baritone saxophones and sometimes clarinets. Some big bands have a singer too.

4) A typical big band has 5 saxophones (2 altos, 2 tenors and a baritone), 4 trumpets, 4 trombones and a 4-piece rhythm section (piano, bass, guitar and drums).

Mmmmmm Jaaazz...

There's loads of different types of jazz out there — the best thing you can do to appreciate it is to listen to as much as you can get your hands on. You might discover that you're a massive jazz enthusiast...

Jazz

Jazz has lots of features that mean you'll **recognise** it when you hear it — for example, it has a **swing** to it.

Jazz is **Swung** and **Syncopated**

1) Early jazz music was based on a 12-bar blues structure (see p.130).
2) The rhythm section played the chords, and the front row instruments would improvise over them.
3) Jazz musicians use call and response and blue notes (see p.129) — key features of jazz and blues.
4) Syncopated and swung rhythms are common in jazz.

Jazz Often **Isn't Written Down**

1) Improvisation is where a performer makes up music on the spot. There are often improvised solo sections in jazz pieces. This means the same piece can be played in radically different ways — even if a piece is played twice by the same people, it won't sound the same.
2) The improvisations aren't totally random though — the soloist will know which chords to improvise over. This is often a 12-bar blues chord pattern (see p.130). Some improvisations use a mode (see page 27) instead of a chord pattern.
3) There are lots of different devices a soloist can use to make their solo interesting:

   • Triplets and dotted rhythms help the tune flow (see p.17).
   • Blue notes (see p.129) are often used in jazz improvisations.
   • Ornaments (like passing notes and appoggiaturas) make the tunes more lively (see p.41).
   • A range of dynamics and accents (see p.20) also bring variety to a solo.
   • Dissonant notes keep the solo interesting.
   • Some performers pinch bits of other tunes in their solos — it keeps the audience entertained when they spot them.

4) Jazz songs are a bit different — the singer has less chance to improvise, but they can use scat (a type of improvised singing with nonsense words and syllables).
5) In early jazz (and some today) the music wasn't written down.
6) The band follows the band leader, so they know when a new section's starting, or the piece is ending.
7) Jazz involves lots of interaction between the soloist and the band, such as call and response — the soloist plays a phrase (the call) and the band answers it (the response), or the other way around.

Jazz is Used in **Lots** of **Fusion Genres**

1) Jazz fusions take any element of jazz and add it to elements of other (often quite different) genres.
2) The elements of jazz that are often used in fusions are the instruments, free rhythms, chords and chord patterns, improvisation and call and response.

   • Salsa is a fusion of Cuban son music with big-band jazz. It uses son rhythms with jazz instruments such as the trumpet and trombone (see p.131).
   • Ska uses jazz instruments and elements such as a walking bass line with rhythms from Jamaican mento music and calypso from Trinidad and Tobago (see p.135).

Improvisation is important in jazz...

...and other genres as well. Make sure you learn the ways a soloist can make their solo exciting and that you can pick them out when you're listening. Oh, and learn everything else too...

African Music

This page is about music in **sub-Saharan Africa**. It's different from North African music (see next page).

Drums Play a Big Part

1) Drums are one of the <u>most widely-played instruments</u> in sub-Saharan Africa.
   They're used to play an <u>accompaniment</u> for <u>singing</u>, <u>dancing</u> and even <u>working</u>.

2) Drums can also be used to <u>call people together</u> for important <u>community events</u> like weddings and funerals — a bit like church bells in Europe. There are <u>different drumbeats</u> for different events.

3) Here are some of the main types of drum from West Africa:

   - The <u>djembe</u> is played with the <u>hands</u>. It comes in different sizes.
     The <u>size</u> of the drum affects its <u>pitch</u> — <u>smaller</u> drums are <u>higher-pitched</u>.
   - Dunduns are <u>cylindrical drums</u> played with <u>sticks</u>. They have a drum skin at each end. There are three types: the <u>kenkeni</u> (a high-pitched drum that keeps the beat), the <u>sangban</u> (a mid-pitched drum) and the <u>dundunba</u> (a large, low-pitched drum).
   - The <u>donno</u> from Ghana is also known as the <u>talking</u> drum. It's played with a stick. The <u>strings</u> round the sides attach to the drumhead. The player can <u>squeeze</u> and <u>release</u> the strings as they play to change the <u>pitch</u> of the drum.

4) Most African music is passed on through <u>aural tradition</u> — it's not written down.

The Rhythms are Complex

1) The music is structured using <u>rhythmic cycles</u> of varying lengths, with <u>accents</u> on particular beats.

2) Rhythmic cycles with <u>accents</u> in <u>different places</u> are often played at the <u>same time</u> — this creates <u>polyrhythm</u> and <u>cross-rhythm</u> (see p.14), and adds <u>tension</u> to the music.

3) Notes that don't fall on a strong beat can be emphasised, giving a <u>syncopated</u> effect.

4) Although the music is based on repeated cycles, individual players introduce <u>small variations</u>. These gradually <u>develop</u> the basic patterns throughout the performance.

This means 'repeat the previous bar'.

A Cappella Singing is a Feature of Some African Music

1) <u>South African</u> all-male choirs (such as <u>Ladysmith Black Mambazo</u>) sing <u>a cappella</u>.

2) There are two main types of South African Zulu a cappella singing:

   - <u>mbube</u> — <u>loud</u>, <u>powerful</u> singing, with <u>high-pitched</u> <u>lead vocals</u> over a <u>four-part harmony bass line</u>.
   - <u>isicathamiya</u> — <u>softer</u> and <u>gentler</u> singing, with <u>four-part harmonies</u> singing <u>call and response</u>.

3) <u>Techniques</u> such as <u>glissandos</u> (slides in pitch, also called <u>portamento</u>), whistles and yodels are used.

African Music

Let's have a look at some more sub-Saharan instruments, before getting onto North African music.

The **Thumb Piano**, **Balafon** and **Kora** are Popular

These are some of the most popular instruments in sub-Saharan Africa.

A balafon is a wooden xylophone. The lumpy things hanging under the keys are dried gourds. They create a warm, mellow sound.

The kora is made and played by the Mandingo people. It's got 21 strings and you play it by plucking — a bit like a harp.

The mbira or thumb piano is really popular — partly because it's pocket-sized. It makes a liquid, twangy sound.

These two are mostly played in West Africa.

The thumb piano is played all over sub-Saharan Africa.

1) In West Africa, the balafon, kora and ngoni (a lute with 4-7 strings) are played by griots.

2) The griots have been around for centuries. They use music to tell stories about the history of the village and region they live in, including recording births, deaths and marriages.

3) They go through years of training to memorise the stories and master their instruments.

4) Senegalese griots play a type of drum called a sabar (a bit like a djembe) at weddings and naming ceremonies. Different rhythms have different meanings in sabar music.

North African Music is **Influenced** by **Arabic** Music

1) North African music is different to music from sub-Saharan Africa.

2) It's strongly influenced by Arabic and Andalusian music. Muslim Arabs came to North Africa from the Middle East and Al-Andalus (Spain and Portugal's name when they were part of the Islamic empire).

3) Arabic and Arab-influenced music is characterised by an emphasis on rhythm and melody, rather than harmony as in Western music. Musicians often improvise over a drone — a continuous bass note.

4) Microtones are also an important feature — they're any size of interval smaller than a semitone.

5) Andalusian classical music has a precise structure — it is performed in nubas (sets of different pieces), which each have a certain mode.

6) Each nuba is performed in five 'movements', called mizan, which each have a different time signature.

A Libyan nuba mode. The flat sign with a line through it means the note is a quartertone flat — it's a microtone.

7) Improvisation is key in North African music — musicians use the modes as a basis for improvising.

Some North African instruments

The ney is a flute made from a type of cane. It has a breathy sound.

The oud is similar to a lute. It tends to have 5 or 6 pairs of strings, with each pair tuned to the same pitch. It has a rich, resonant sound.

The rabab is a bowed string instrument with a small body and long neck. It tends to only have 1-3 strings, so it has been partially replaced by the violin, which has a greater range.

REVISION TIP

It's worth listening to what these instruments sound like...

Have a listen to some African music and try to see if you can pick out the instruments described above. Make sure you learn to recognise features such as call and response.

Caribbean Music

Caribbean music has indigenous, Latin American, African and European influences.
Different styles have developed on different islands, based on what the mix of influences has been.

Caribbean Music is Rich in Variation

1) Caribbean music's diversity is due to its history. People inhabited the islands for centuries before they were colonised by Spain, France, Britain and the Netherlands. The European nations brought millions of Africans to the Caribbean as slaves. Each of these people had different influences on the music.

2) Steel pans are well-known Caribbean instruments. They were originally made from large oil drums, and produce a bright, ringing sound. They're played using sticks with rubber heads.

3) Modern pans are often made from sheet metal. They come in various sizes and are named in line with their range, e.g. a bass pan plays the lowest notes. Oval-shaped dents in the pans give different notes.

4) The instruments reflect the diversity of the music.

Caribbean instruments

Percussion (especially drums) is important in Caribbean music due to the African influence.

The guiro makes a scrapy noise.

Maracas come from the Caribbean.

Types of guitar introduced by the Spanish are common. The tres has 3 sets of 2 or 3 strings, while the cuatro can have 4 or 5 pairs of strings.

 Bongos are paired drums played with the hands. Congas and timbales are also paired drums.

 Claves (wooden sticks) are often used to beat out a rhythm to set the tempo (see p.136 and p.139).

Calypso comes from Trinidad

1) Calypso music has its origins with African slaves who were brought to Trinidad. They used music to communicate with each other. The lyrics had a big role in traditional calypso songs — the songs had funny or mocking lyrics that the plantation owners couldn't understand. They told stories about important topics such as social issues or relationships, and were often improvised.

2) Over the centuries, the island came under the rule of Spain, France and Britain. Calypso music was influenced by the cultures of those countries, in addition to its African roots.

3) The French introduced carnival — it's still held each year, just before the start of Lent (the period before Easter). Calypso plays a big part, and steel pan bands and singers compete for prizes.

4) Calypso bands use a wide range of instruments, mixing the percussion mentioned above with instruments such as guitars, brass and woodwind instruments. Steel pans are important in calypso.

- Calypso music is usually in $\frac{2}{2}$ or $\frac{4}{4}$ time.
- The rhythms are syncopated (see p.129), and mostly follow a 3-3-2 pattern. Each bar has three beats, but the final beat is shorter than the others.
- The songs can have a verse-chorus or strophic structure.
- The texture can be melody with accompaniment, or polyphonic with melodies and countermelodies (see p.47).

These are two calypso rhythms. The square brackets show how the beats are divided.

Cooking with steel pans is not recommended...

Have a listen to some calypso — listening to it will help you remember what the key features of it are.
Try picking out the rhythms and the 3-3-2 pattern, as well as the distinctive sound of the steel pans.

Caribbean Music

You may not be familiar with the styles of music on this page, but they influenced some genres that you've probably heard of — reggae and salsa, among others.

Mento is a Type of Jamaican Folk Music

1) Mento is similar to calypso, and was very popular in Jamaica in the first half of the 20th century.
2) It draws on musical traditions brought by West African slaves, as well as European influences.
3) It usually features acoustic instruments, including:

- acoustic guitar
- banjo — a plucked string instrument with a long neck and small body
- drums
- a rhumba box — a type of large mbira (see p.134) that can be sat on while it's being played

4) The lyrics were often lighthearted and witty, dealing with everyday life as well as political issues.
5) It's in strophic form — all the verses have the same melody (but different lyrics). See p.56 for more.

Son is Music from Cuba

Son is a type of dance music from Cuba. These are its key features:

- A basic repeated rhythm pattern called a clave (pronounced *clah-vey*) is played on claves (*clayves*).
- Other rhythmic patterns are played on instruments such as the maracas and bongos. These parts are often syncopated and form complicated cross-rhythms and polyrhythms against the clave part.
- The melody is played by brass instruments, such as trumpets.
- Call and response between the lead singer (called the sonero) and the chorus (the choro).
- The lyrics in son music often talk about love, or comment on life in Cuba.

Salsa (see p.139) is a mix of son and big-band jazz (see p.131).

Merengue and Zouk are also Types of Dance Music

Merengue is from the Dominican Republic (there's a similar form called méringue from Haiti). It has African and Spanish influences. Caribbean instruments such as the cuatro and tambora (a double-headed drum) and 'Western' ones such as the accordion and saxophone are used to play it. It has a fast $\frac{2}{4}$ or $\frac{4}{4}$ beat, and uses catchy melodies with a simple harmony. It's sung in Spanish.

Zouk comes from the French Antilles

1) The French Antilles are a group of eastern Caribbean islands that were colonised by France.
2) Zouk is a mix of African styles, Caribbean music such as cadence (Haitian pop) and calypso, and American funk (a mix of soul, jazz and R'n'B).
3) It uses gwo ka — a name for both drums from Guadeloupe and the rhythms played on them — as well as the use of synthesizers and backing singers. It tends to have a fast beat.
4) Its modern sound has helped it become popular worldwide, especially in France.

Don't mix up clave and clave...

Phew, there were a lot of different styles on that page. Make sure you're clear on which one is which, and what the key features of each one are. You'll need to know about some of them for the fusions pages.

Fusions

Fusions are a combination of two or more styles of music.
Ska and reggae are two types of fusion that combine Caribbean and American musical styles.

Styles Can Be **Combined** to Create **Fusions**

1) <u>Fusion</u> is when two or more <u>styles</u> of music are <u>merged</u> to create a new style.

2) It can happen <u>gradually</u> and <u>naturally</u> over time as two cultures become <u>mingled</u>, or it can be done <u>deliberately</u> when musicians <u>experiment</u> with different styles.

3) There are <u>different ways</u> of combining styles — e.g. you can mix the <u>rhythms</u> of one with the <u>melodies</u> of another, or use the <u>instruments</u> of one culture to play the <u>melodies</u> of another.

4) Some fusion styles have since been fused <u>again</u> to create even more new types of music.

Ska is a Fusion of **R'n'B** and **Mento**

<u>Ska</u> is a type of <u>dance</u> music that combines <u>rhythm 'n' blues</u> (R'n'B — see p.129) from the United States with rhythms from <u>mento</u> and <u>calypso</u>. It emerged in the 1950s. Here are some of its <u>key features</u>:

- It uses <u>jazz instruments</u> such as trumpets and saxophones with electric guitars, percussion and piano or keyboard — this lineup is influenced by R'n'B.

- There's a <u>walking bass line</u> — usually in <u>crotchets</u>, a walking bass line is improvised by the bassist around the <u>notes of the chords</u> being played. It's common in jazz and the blues.

- It's usually in $\frac{4}{4}$ <u>time</u> with <u>offbeat</u> rhythms, an influence of <u>mento</u>. There's often a drumbeat on the 2nd and 4th beats, and the rhythm guitar plays offbeat '<u>skank</u>' rhythms (see below).

- Ska hits include purely <u>instrumental</u> music as well as <u>songs</u> with lyrics.

Reggae Came **After** Ska

<u>Rocksteady</u> is like a much <u>slower version</u> of <u>ska</u>. <u>Reggae</u> developed from this by mixing rocksteady with <u>new effects</u> and a <u>slightly faster</u> beat, driven by the <u>bass guitar</u>. Reggae tracks tend to have singers.

1) Electric and bass guitars, drum kit and keyboard or an electric organ are usually used. The bass guitar plays <u>riffs</u> — repeated patterns only a few bars long.

2) The lyrics are often <u>political</u>. The songs are usually in verse and chorus form.

3) <u>Simple</u> chord sequences are used. Reggae's played in $\frac{4}{4}$ time:

'Skank' rhythm, played by the rhythm guitar.

The rhythm guitar plays an offbeat pattern. It has a 'choppy' sound created by the guitarist strumming upwards rather than down — known as 'upstroke'.

'Bubble' rhythm, played by the keyboard.

The keyboard plays repeated offbeat chords, alternating between left and right hands. The rhythm above is often used.

- Reggae uses a fair amount of music <u>technology</u> and <u>effects</u>.
- The bass guitar sound is adjusted so that higher frequencies are <u>less prominent</u> and lower frequencies are <u>emphasised</u>, giving it a characteristic <u>heavy</u> sound.
- Remixing techniques are often used, particularly <u>delay</u>. A delay is a bit like an <u>echo</u> — it's a short recording of a bit of music which is then repeated over the top of the piece.
- Reggae musicians began to release versions of their tracks with added effects, in which they used '<u>toasting</u>' — speaking over the top of the music. <u>Hip-hop</u> and <u>rap</u> followed on from this.

4) <u>Bob Marley</u> is one of the most famous reggae artists — his compilation album '<u>Legend</u>', released in 1984, is a great example of <u>reggae music</u>. It includes hits such as '<u>No Woman No Cry</u>' and '<u>Jammin</u>''.

5) <u>Reggaeton</u> is an urban style of music similar to hip-hop or rap. It's dance music, popular in <u>clubs</u>. It's a blend of <u>reggae</u> and <u>dub</u> (a DJ rapping over bass guitar and drums) with American <u>R'n'B</u>, <u>rap</u> and <u>hip-hop</u>, as well as <u>Latin American influences</u>.

Fusions

The musical styles on this page fuse Western music with genres of music from Africa.

Mbalax comes from Senegal and The Gambia

1) Mbalax is a form of dance music from Senegal and The Gambia.
2) It developed from a fusion of the drumming tradition of sabar, played by Senegalese griots (see p.134), Western popular music and Afro-Caribbean influences. Mbalax is also the name for the rhythms used in sabar music.
3) It's characterised by the complex rhythms and the percussion instruments used in sabar music.
4) 'Western' instruments such as electric guitars are used, as well as synthesizers.
5) The lyrics are usually in Wolof (spoken by the Wolof people of Senegal), French or English.
6) Youssou N'Dour made the genre famous with his 1994 duet with Neneh Cherry, '7 Seconds'. The song uses mbalax in the style of a ballad with synth accompaniment.

Raï is Pop Music from Algeria

1) Some Algerian musicians wanted to create something different to North African classical music (p.134) — raï was the result. It developed over time from the early 20th century, but became more popular in the 1980s. Eventually, it got fused with pop, rock and jazz to create a form of popular dance music.
2) Trumpets, saxophones and accordions are used alongside North African instruments (see p.134).
3) Some Western instruments used in raï are fixed-pitch, so they can't produce the microtones common in North African music. This makes the tonality a bit different to the classical music raï comes from.
4) Rock instruments such as electric guitars and drum kit are used as well. Synthesizers, drum machines and techniques such as reverb (an echo effect) are used in raï to create a modern sound.
5) Raï lyrics often discuss everyday life and political issues.
6) Raï is popular in France, which is home to many people with a North African background.

Fusions can be Quite Specific

Fusions can be the work of just one band, or a single track or album.

Afro Celt Sound System

- The band Afro Celt Sound System play a fusion of sub-Saharan African and Celtic music.
- They use traditional Irish and African musical styles (e.g. an Irish air with an African drumbeat).
- They play a mixture of Irish and African instruments (e.g. a bodhrán and a djembe).
- The music's based on pentatonic scales (a Celtic influence) and complex African rhythms.
- An electronic dance beat ties the music together.

Graceland

- Graceland was an album created by the American singer Paul Simon and the South African all-male choir Ladysmith Black Mambazo.
- The songs are a fusion of pop, rock and folk music with a cappella singing (see p.133).
- For example, the song 'Diamonds on the Soles of her Shoes' has isicathamiya singing at the start before the choir is joined by a Western rock band and African drums.

I hope you're not fused out after all that...

With fusions, it's important you know which genres of music were combined to make them and what the main features of these genres are. Then you can spot which bits have been used to make the fusion...

Section Eight — Traditional Music

Salsa

Salsa is a popular form of dance music, particularly in Latin America and the Caribbean.

Salsa Grew Out of Son and Big-Band Jazz

1) Latin American musicians living in New York combined Cuban son (see p.136) with big-band jazz to create salsa in the 1960s and 1970s.

2) Taking the basic structure of son, salsa bands added the harsher, brass-based arrangements of big band jazz. The trombone was a big focus.

3) Salsa also took inspiration from Puerto Rican, Brazilian and African music. It soon became popular throughout Latin America and beyond.

Clave is the Rhythm of Salsa

1) The clave is the basic rhythm of a piece of salsa music. The most common rhythm is the son clave.

2) The son clave rhythm has a group of three notes and a group of two.

It goes like this...   ...or like this...

3) A salsa piece doesn't have to use the same clave throughout. It might switch to a different clave half-way through.

4) All the other parts are built around the clave — the clave is the foundation of the piece.

5) The 'Bo Diddley beat' originates from the son clave rhythm. It is used a lot in rock and pop music.

The Structure of Salsa is Flexible

There are three main chunks in a salsa tune. The three different chunks can appear in any order, and they can all be used more than once.

*   In the verse, you hear the main tune, usually sung by the sonero or played by an instrumentalist.
*   The montuno is a kind of chorus where the sonero or lead instrumentalist improvises and the choro or other instrumentalists answer.
*   There is a break between choruses, called the mambo, with new musical material — e.g. different chords or a different tune. It's often played by the horn section.
*   There's usually an introduction and ending.
*   There could also be a 'break' — a bit where the main tune stops and just the rhythm section plays.

Here's a fairly typical salsa structure:

If only all genres were named after food...

...'salsa' means 'sauce' in Spanish. I guess you can just think of it as a mix of different foods, to remind you it's a fusion. Make sure you're clear on the clave rhythms and the structure — they're pretty important.

Samba

Samba is one of the most popular forms of dance music in South America, and around the world.

Samba Comes from **Brazil**

1) Samba is a Brazilian street carnival dance. Some of the famous Brazilian carnivals, such as the Rio Carnival, have made samba popular all over the world.

2) It's usually in either $\frac{2}{4}$ or $\frac{4}{4}$. It sounds cheery and is played at a fast tempo in a major key.

3) Samba instruments include a big variety of percussion, Portuguese guitar (a bright-sounding guitar with 12 strings), keyboards, whistles and, in larger street bands, saxophones and trumpets.

4) Samba is played by huge bands at carnivals, and by smaller bands for dancing samba-salão in ballrooms, or to accompany samba-canção (samba songs).

The **Samba Beat** Sounds like **Footsteps**

1) The main samba beat is played by a pair of loud, resonant bass drums called surdo drums.

2) The basic surdo rhythm sounds like steady marching footsteps. The surdo players alternately hit the drum with a stick then damp it with the hand. This muting and unmuting gives the effect of offbeat springy notes in between the main beats.

3) Over the basic surdo beat you hear many other complex syncopated, ostinato rhythms, such as this agogo bells rhythm:

4) Other common percussion instruments include: shakers (known as ganzás, caxixis, or shekeres), scrapers (the reco-reco) and tambourines (pandeiros).

The **Whistle Player** is **In Charge** of a Samba Band

1) Large samba bands are controlled by a leader playing a two-toned samba whistle and a drum.

2) The whistle sets the tempo and signals call and response sections. In the call and response bits, the leader plays a rhythm (usually on a drum called a repinique) and is answered by the rest of the band.

3) The call and response sections contrast with the sections where everyone plays repeated rhythms.

4) Sometimes the whole band stops and then starts again. This is called a break.

5) Samba melodies are usually very catchy and repetitive. They also build up — parts get added on top.

Samba has been **Fused** to Make **New Styles**

Because of its popularity, samba has led to many new musical styles.

• Samba is often mixed with other dance styles, e.g. tango and rumba (see next page).

• In the 1950s, samba was fused with jazz to make a style called bossa nova, which has syncopated rhythms and usually features a guitar and vocals.

• It has also been mixed with soul, funk, rock and disco to create a wide range of subgenres and fusions.

Put 2nd December in your diaries — it's Brazil's National Samba Day...

Just like any type of music, the typical rhythms of samba can be changed or added to, so that it doesn't become too boring and repetitive. The rhythms on this page are common, but there are loads of others.

Contemporary Latin American Music

Lots of Latin American music is intended to be danced to, much the same as salsa and samba...

The **Cuban Habanera** Influenced Many Types of Dance Music

1) The habanera is a Cuban dance from the 19th century. It has Spanish and African influences, as well as origins in a European country dance called the contradanza, brought via Haiti.

2) The habanera is usually in $\frac{2}{4}$ and has a distinctive dotted rhythm:
   It's quite slow and deliberate.

3) Lots of other styles of Latin American dance music have developed from the habanera, including:

   • Danzón — a type of dance for pairs, with set steps. The music was traditionally played by an orquesta tipica — a band made up of wind and brass instruments, with a few string instruments as well. The danzón is usually slow and elegant.

   • Cha-cha-cha — a dance style that evolved from danzón in the 1950s. It's a mid-tempo dance (so is slightly faster than the danzón or habanera), in $\frac{4}{4}$ with the 'cha-cha-cha' on beats 3 and 4.

   • Tango — see below.

4) The Cuban rumba is an Afro-Cuban dance, accompanied by percussion (including maracas) and voices. There are a few different types of rumba, each with different rhythms.

Tango is **Dance Music** from **Argentina**

1) Tango has a mix of African, Latin American and European influences, including Italian melodies, Cuban habanera rhythms (see above), milonga (syncopated music from Argentina and Uruguay) and candombe (Uruguayan music with African rhythms).

2) Tango instruments include flute, violin and guitar, accompanied by bandoneons (a type of accordion made in Germany) and a rhythm section of piano, double bass and percussion.

3) Tangos have 2 or 4 beats in the bar. These are some of the basic rhythms:

4) The main melody often uses a slow rhythmic pace with triplets and syncopation (see p.129). Staccato notes (see p.19) give the music precision.

5) Tango has simple harmonies, often in a minor key, based on the tonic and dominant chords (for example, A minor and E major). Prominent and repeating dotted rhythms in the bass often move between the tonic and the dominant notes, as shown below:

The red notes are the tonic, the blue notes the dominant.

This is an habanera rhythm used in early tango music.

Santana Blends **Latin American** and **Rock** Music

1) Carlos Santana was born in Mexico, but he moved to the United States. This influenced his music, which is a fusion of Latin American styles with North American genres such as blues and rock music. He is known for virtuosic guitar playing, and formed the band Santana in 1966.

2) The band includes rock instruments alongside trumpets and trombones — a nod to its Latin influences. They also use Latin percussion instruments and Spanish lyrics in some of their songs. Their music is varied, with jazz, hip-hop, rock and even Classical influences.

3) Santana often use music from other genres and give it a Latin twist — 'Migra' is a cover of a song by rock/raï musician (see p.138) Rachid Taha but with different lyrics, and 'Jingo' is a cover of a song by Nigerian percussionist Babatunde Olatunji.

Esperanza Spalding

In the fusion spirit, these study pieces mix jazz with other genres. You'll study three Esperanza Spalding tracks.

Esperanza Spalding is a **Jazz Singer** and **Bassist** from America

1) Esperanza Spalding is from Portland, Oregon and was born in 1984. She is a bassist — she plays acoustic and electric bass guitar, and double bass. Spalding is also a singer and songwriter, writing in English, Spanish and Portuguese.

2) While best known as a jazz musician, she often writes in a fusion style that incorporates other genres like R&B, classical and Latin American music.

She's won many awards, including five Grammys, and received two honorary doctorates.

3) Spalding often plays live in a distinctive style:

- Her vocal range is alto to mezzo soprano, often in a light, intimate style.
- She is a virtuosic player and can alternate live between bass guitar and double bass.
- There's often counterpoint in her writing, with overlapping instrumental melodies.
- Much of her performance also involves improvisation, scat and freestyling.

4) 'Little Fly' appears on her *Chamber Music Society* album from 2010, while 'I Know You Know' and 'I Adore You' are from her 2008 album *Esperanza*. Most of the songs on these albums are written by Spalding herself and mix lots of different styles — *Esperanza* includes samba, R&B, funk and even flamenco, whereas *Chamber Music Society* has more elements of classical and soul.

5) Although the study pieces fuse several different styles, look out for key features of jazz in each:

| Blue notes | Improvisation | Syncopation | Pitch bends | Riffs | Extended chords |

Extended chords layer extra notes above a 7th.

'Little Fly' Features **Classical String Instruments**

1) The lyrics for this song are from a poem by William Blake. Setting poems to music was typical of Romantic music, and a Western classical style is mixed with jazz here to create a gentle ballad.

Classical Features
- Layered string instruments — Spalding plays double bass accompanied by classical string trio (viola, violin, cello).
- Regular phrasing — generally 4-bar phrases.
- Often a diatonic melody and harmony, mainly using different versions of E and A major chords.
- Clear E major tonality, with occasional B major chords (the dominant) followed by E7 chords to form a perfect cadence (with added 7ths).

Jazz Features
- Vocal melismas with blue notes and chromaticism.
- Seventh chords and chords with added notes (often 6ths).
- Double bass improvisation with pitch bends.
- Riffs (sometimes varied, mostly double bass but heard in other strings too).
- Syncopated rhythms.

2) A laid-back tempo, soft vocals with a bit of reverb, avoidance of the downbeat and regular $\frac{4}{4}$ metre create a lazy feel, suitable for the summer's day setting of the lyrics.

3) The song has an intro, two verses and a coda. While the texture is mostly melody with accompaniment, there is also some polyphony and monophony.

	Esperanza Spalding	Accompaniment
Intro	Double bass plays *pizzicato* riff with double stopping, monophonic first note.	Strings enter *arco* one by one, creating some polyphony. Viola plays a countermelody also heard in V2.
V1	Vocal melody and riff — second half more chromatic with semiquavers.	*Arco* — more chromatic in second half with thicker texture from string chords. Cello briefly doubles bass.
V2	Similar to V1. Longer melisma on some words, altered bass in second half.	Countermelody from introduction in violin — passed around the instruments at the end of the verse.
Coda	Based on verses. Last word monophonic. Bass improvisation, partly monophonic and some closing vocal improvisation.	Tremolo in strings, *pizzicato* riff and *arco* countermelody. Strings end on a major 7th chord.

4) The string tremolo is an example of word-painting (it imitates the buzz of a fly).

Esperanza Spalding

STUDY PIECES

'I Know You Know' Uses **Samba Percussion**

Bass guitar, piano and drums are typical jazz instruments.

1) 'I Know You Know' mixes jazz and samba. It's performed by voice, piano, fretless bass guitar, drum kit, triangle, bongos and samba percussion.

2) There's also elements of R&B, bossa nova and funk — the opening bass riff has a funk influence, and is varied as it repeats.

Samba Elements
- Lots of percussion, including shaker (ganzá) and snare drum (caixa).
- A fast tempo in $\frac{4}{4}$ — samba is dance music.
- Polyrhythms — see p.14.

3) The song generally follows a verse-chorus structure, but with a few variations:

Intro	Verse	Chorus	Verse	Chorus (×2)	Middle 8	Vamp (piano and bass improv)	Chorus (×2)	Verse (freer, + piano improv)	Repeat ad lib (all parts improv)	Outro

4) After the monophonic bass riff in the intro, the texture is mainly melody with accompaniment, with some counterpoint in the improvisation sections. The end of the first chorus is monophonic (a cappella).

5) Much of the rhythm features complex syncopation, and there are off-beat piano chords throughout.

6) The key is ambiguous until the voice enters — the vocal melody is F major, although the accompaniment avoids F chords until the chorus. There's a modulation to B major in the middle 8. The harmony features chords with added notes and extended chords, with a repeating 4-chord pattern in the verses and choruses.

7) Spalding's vocal melody mixes conjunct quaver motion with triadic leaps, and has lots of blue notes. The range is quite large. It's mainly syllabic in the verses and choruses, and melismatic elsewhere.

'I Adore You' Uses **Scat Singing**

1) This piece also mixes jazz and samba. Like 'I Know You Know', there's a piano and drum kit, but there's also a double bass and extra samba percussion (below). There's also salsa influence in the use of congas.

- *shekere* — netting around a gourd which is shaken and twisted
- *cabassa* — chains wrapped around a cylinder, similar effect to the *shekere*
- *surdo* (bass drum)
- *repinique* (two-headed drum)
- *caixa* (snare drum)

2) The piece is long and has a complex form with different sections. There are varied and extended verses, choruses, bridges, an intro, an outro and a solo section. The piece starts and ends with just percussion.

3) In the solo section, the piano, voice and double bass improvise using motifs from earlier sections. The third chorus also has vocal improvisation. As the piece evolves, the piano develops ideas based on motifs and the improvisation becomes more complex as it uses a wider range of pitches and blues notes.

4) A bass riff alternates between G and D, suggesting a G major tonality. The chorus is G Mixolydian (see p.27) but there's also chromaticism throughout. The major tonality and moderately fast tempo create a carnival feel. As with the other pieces, there are extended or added note chords, and some dissonance.

5) Spalding's layered vocals have a samba feel and play an important role:

Spalding improvises scat singing throughout (see p.109), which is a jazz technique.	There are two main vocal hooks which act as upbeats to the verses and choruses.	Technology is used to create a chorus effect. There is double-tracking (recording and playing back the same track) and multi-tracking (see p.109), making it hard to perform the piece live.

6) Syncopation and polyrhythms are the main rhythmic features, with off-beat piano chords in the verses and dotted rhythms in the bassline. The $\frac{3}{4}$ metre is unusual for samba, and it often changes to $\frac{2}{4}$.

7) The texture is melody with accompaniment, but there's some counterpoint, particularly in the last chorus.

REVISION TIP

Doo wop, doobie...zoobie? My scat singing needs work...

Listen to these pieces as much as you can so you can start picking out the jazz features and other styles. Try and spot things like blue notes, samba percussion and improvisation.

Celtic Music

Every country has its own type of folk music, which uses local languages, dialects and instruments.

Folk Music was Played by **Ordinary People**

1) Folk music's still around nowadays, but it used to be <u>much more popular</u>. In olden times, before radios and record players, the <u>only</u> music ordinary people had was music they played themselves.

2) The tunes tend to be quite <u>simple</u> and work with just a <u>few</u> instruments or voices.
   This made them <u>easier</u> for people in the <u>pub</u>, <u>field</u> or <u>factory</u> to learn and play.

3) Folk music was hardly ever <u>written down</u>. It survived through the <u>aural tradition</u>
   — people <u>heard</u> a song or tune they liked and <u>memorised</u> it.

4) Folk music changes over time as people add <u>new ideas</u>. Sometimes they're being deliberately <u>creative</u>, and sometimes they <u>can't remember</u> exactly what they've heard and make up a new bit.

5) The <u>instruments</u> used to play along with folk songs and dances tend to be <u>small</u> and <u>easy to carry</u>.
   The most popular ones are the <u>pipe and tabor</u> (a three-holed recorder and a drum, played together for a one-man band effect), the <u>fiddle</u>, the <u>hurdy-gurdy</u>, the <u>bagpipes</u>, the <u>accordion</u> and the <u>concertina</u>.

6) The main types of folk music are <u>work songs</u> (sung by <u>labourers</u> to help them
   to work as a <u>team</u> and take their <u>minds</u> off their work), <u>ballads</u> (they tell <u>stories</u>
   of <u>love</u>, <u>real-life events</u> or <u>legends</u>) and <u>dance</u> music (see next page).

Folk Tunes are Fairly **Simple**

1) A lot of folk melodies are based on <u>pentatonic scales</u> (see p.27).
   They only have five notes, which makes writing tunes with them a lot easier.

2) A <u>major pentatonic</u> scale uses notes <u>1</u>, <u>2</u>, <u>3</u>, <u>5</u> and <u>6</u> of an ordinary <u>major scale</u>.

3) A <u>minor pentatonic</u> scale uses notes <u>1</u>, <u>3</u>, <u>4</u>, <u>5</u> and <u>7</u> of a <u>natural minor scale</u>.

4) There are <u>no semitone intervals</u> in pentatonic scales. It makes it much easier to
   add a <u>harmony</u> because the notes don't clash. It also makes them <u>easy to sing</u>.

> The <u>structure</u> in folk tunes tends to be pretty simple too. <u>Songs</u> are often <u>strophic</u>
> — the tune stays the same for each verse. Strophic songs can either be a number
> of <u>musically identical</u> verses (with different words), or can have a <u>chorus</u> that's just
> a <u>slight variation</u> on the verse (so the structure is A A' A A' A...). Phrases have even
> numbers of bars — usually <u>four</u>. Often each phrase begins with an <u>anacrusis</u> (upbeat).

Lots of **Celtic Folk Music** Comes From **Scotland** and **Ireland**

1) Lots of places in <u>Western Europe</u> have traditional Celtic folk music
   — like <u>Wales</u>, <u>Cornwall</u> and <u>Brittany</u> in France.

2) Celtic folk music also includes <u>traditional Scottish</u> and <u>Irish</u> music.

3) The songs are often sung in <u>Gaelic</u> — Celtic languages spoken in Scotland
   and Ireland. The two most common forms are <u>Scots Gaelic</u> and <u>Irish Gaelic</u>.

4) Traditional Celtic instruments include <u>fiddles</u> (violins), <u>bagpipes</u>, <u>tin whistles</u> and <u>accordions</u>.
   An Irish framed drum called the <u>bodhrán</u> is also used.

5) <u>English</u> folk is a bit separate from <u>Celtic</u> folk. English folk uses instruments such as the <u>recorder</u>
   and <u>Northumbrian pipes</u> (a kind of <u>bagpipe</u>) as well as many of those mentioned above.

Folk songs were often just passed from person to person...

Folk music is often about simplicity — pentatonic scales, simple structure and instrumentation.
This made it easier to pass on. The use of pentatonic scales gives folk music a pretty distinctive sound.

Contemporary British Folk

This page focuses on folk music that's been mixed with different kinds of popular music to create various fusions. However, there's still a lot of 'traditional' folk around today as well.

Some **Folk** Music is Influenced by **Popular** Music...

1) <u>Modern</u> Irish dance music combines <u>folk rhythms</u> with <u>contemporary beats</u>. It uses both <u>live instruments</u> and <u>MIDI sequencers</u>.

2) A good example of this is the music from <u>Riverdance</u>. It's a sell-out show featuring <u>Irish dancers</u>, a <u>choir</u> and a band using <u>folk instruments</u> alongside other instruments such as the <u>drum kit</u>. It uses techniques such as <u>reverb</u> to enhance the music.

3) Some bands turn folk music into a more <u>modern</u> style by adding a <u>bass line</u> and <u>drum kit</u>.

- The Scottish band <u>Capercaillie</u> combine folk music and instruments with <u>funk</u> bass lines, <u>synthesizers</u> and electric and bass guitars to create a <u>fusion</u>. Capercaillie's album *Beautiful Wasteland* is a good example of Celtic folk rock music.
- Another Scottish band, <u>Runrig</u>, is well-known for its mix of <u>Gaelic folk</u> with <u>rock</u> music. They also use folk instruments with electric and bass guitars and drum kit to create a <u>rock</u> sound. Their lyrics are sung in <u>English</u> and <u>Scots Gaelic</u>. Their rock cover of the song 'Loch Lomond' is very popular.

...and Some **Popular** Music is Influenced by **Folk** Music

Irish pop artists like <u>The Corrs</u>, <u>Westlife</u> and <u>Van Morrison</u> sometimes use <u>elements</u> of Irish music.

- For example, The Corrs use <u>traditional Irish instruments</u> in some of their songs, but their use of <u>music technology</u>, particularly synthesizers, and <u>pop instruments</u> (such as electric guitar) gives their songs a mostly pop music sound.
- Westlife used the <u>Irish</u> tune '<u>The Londonderry Air</u>' (also used in the song <u>Danny Boy</u>) in their hit single '<u>You Raise Me Up</u>'.
- Some of <u>Van Morrison's</u> albums were influenced by Irish music — particularly *Astral Weeks* (his second album) and *Irish Heartbeat*, a collaboration with the traditional Irish group <u>The Chieftains</u>.

English Folk is **Less Well-Known**

1) English folk has often had a <u>lower profile</u> than Scottish or Irish folk. However, there are a few examples of it around in <u>mainstream music</u>. This form of modern folk is often known as '<u>nu-folk</u>'.

2) <u>Mumford & Sons'</u> first two albums are known for their folk-influenced sound, created by their use of instruments such as the <u>banjo</u> and <u>double bass</u>. Their lyrics sometimes reference rural topics such as the <u>harvest</u> and <u>owning land</u>. Many of their songs are <u>ballads</u>, a song format often used in folk.

3) They used to play as the backing band to <u>Laura Marling</u>, a folk-influenced singer. Her music, along with that of the band <u>Noah and the Whale</u>, represented a '<u>folk revival</u>' in British music. They brought folk music to a new <u>generation</u> of listeners.

The group <u>The Imagined Village</u> aims to revive interest in English folk. They bring together a diverse group of musicians, such as <u>Afro Celt Sound System</u> band members (see p.138) and a <u>sitar</u> player. The group takes old folk songs and makes them <u>current</u> — for example, they turned a song about the <u>Napoleonic wars</u> into one about the war in <u>Afghanistan</u>.

Folk fusions usually use folk instruments and melodies...

Have a listen to a traditional recording of 'Loch Lomond' and Runrig's version so you can hear how they've fused the folk melody with rock. It's well worth listening to the other bands too.

Warm-up and Exam Questions

Phew, what a long section. Now it's time to see how much you've remembered. Have a go at the warm-up questions to get yourself in the swing of things, and then try the exam questions...

Warm-up Questions

1) Who first created blues music?

2) What is syncopation?

3) Write out the chord pattern used for 12-bar blues.

4) Name four instruments commonly played by jazz musicians.

5) What is scat?

6) What is a kora?

7) What is a microtone?

8) Which two time signatures are usually used in calypso?

9) Where does mento come from?

10) What is a fusion?

11) What styles of music does ska come from?

12) What technique does the rhythm guitar use in reggae?

13) Where does samba come from?

14) Who wrote the words sung by Esperanza Spalding in 'Little Fly'?

15) Which mode is used in the chorus of 'I Adore You'?

16) What kind of scale is often used in folk music?

17) What is a bodhrán?

Exam Questions

Have a go at these exam-style questions.

These questions are about 'I Know You Know' from the album *Esperanza* by Esperanza Spalding.
Unfortunately, we were unable to get permission to include this track on our playlist.
However, it's readily available to listen to online —
you just need to listen to the first 56 seconds of the recording.
Play the excerpt **four** times. Leave a short pause between each playing.

a) Which **two** terms describe the bass part in the excerpt?
Circle your answers.

polyrhythmic	**swung**	**triplets**	**syncopated**
hemiola	**counterpoint**		**riff**

[2 marks]

Exam Questions

b)   Which of these describes what the piano part plays in the excerpt?
Circle your answer.

   scales   broken chords   chords   octaves

c)   i) Identify **two** features of the excerpt that are elements of jazz.

   1) ....

   2) ....
[2 marks]

   ii) Identify **two** features of the excerpt that are elements of samba.

   1) ....

   2) ....
[2 marks]

d)   Identify **two** features of the vocal part in the excerpt.

   1) ....

   2) ....
[2 marks]

e)   Describe how the texture changes during the excerpt.

   ....

   ....

   ....

   ....

   ....

   ....
[3 marks]

Exam Questions

Track 35 is an excerpt from a piece for steel drums.
Play the excerpt **four** times. Leave a short pause between each playing.

Track 35

Track 35

a) From which region of the world does this style of music originate?
Circle your answer.

Latin America   **Africa**   **Middle East**   **Caribbean**

[1 mark]

b) Which of these rhythms shows the main beat or pulse in the first half of this excerpt?
Tick the box next to the correct answer.

☐

☐

☐

[1 mark]

c) About halfway through the excerpt, the music changes.
Describe the rhythmic differences between the two sections.

....

....

....

....

[3 marks]

d) The title of this piece is 'Carnivale'. Identify **two** features of this excerpt
that make it suitable for a carnival.

1) ....

....

2) ....

....

[2 marks]

Revision Summary for Section Eight

That's the end of Section Eight — put your knowledge to the test by giving these questions a go.
- Try these questions and tick off each one when you get it right.
- When you've done all the questions for a topic and are completely happy with it, tick off the topic.

The Blues and Jazz (p.129-132) ☐

1) What are blues lyrics like?
2) What is the blues scale?
3) Explain the difference between straight and swung rhythms.
4) Why is it easy to switch between the twelve-bar and sixteen-bar blues patterns?
5) Name two different types of jazz.
6) List five devices that could be used in improvisation.
7) What is call and response?

African and Caribbean Music (p.133-136) ☑

8) Name three types of African drum.
9) Describe mbube and isicathamiya singing.
10) Name two features of North African music.
11) Name two types of Caribbean percussion instrument.
12) Write down one calypso rhythm.
13) Give the two definitions of the word 'clave' in Cuban son.
14) What is: i) a sonero?   ii) a choro?
15) Which genres does zouk come from?

Fusions (p.137-138) ☑

16) What type of bassline appears in ska?
17) How is the heavy bass guitar sound created in reggae?
18) Name two features of mbalax.
19) How is a modern sound created in raï music? Give two details.

Salsa, Samba and Contemporary Latin American Music (p.139-143) ☑

20) What is a mambo?
21) What are the typical time signatures of samba?
22) What is the role of the whistle player in a samba band?
23) What two styles make up bossa nova?
24) Describe the origins of the habanera.
25) Give two features of the harmony in tango.
26) Describe how 'Little Fly' paints a picture of a summer's day.
27) Name three musical styles that feature in 'I Know You Know'.
28) Explain how the vocals in 'I Adore You' were recorded.

Celtic Music and Contemporary British Folk (p.144-145) ☑

29) Which notes of a natural minor scale does a minor pentatonic scale use?
30) What is strophic form?
31) List three bands that play folk fusions.

Orchestral Music of Aaron Copland

Aaron Copland was a twentieth-century American composer.

Copland Wrote Several **Well-Known Pieces**

1) Aaron Copland was an American composer who lived from 1900-1990. He studied composition in France for a few years, before returning to America to work as a composer, conductor and lecturer.

2) Although he used different styles in his compositions during his lifetime, such as jazz and serialism (see p.151), he's most well-known for his American-influenced music.

3) He wrote for different ensembles and purposes, including symphonies, ballet music and film scores. His most famous pieces include his third symphony, the ballets *Billy the Kid*, *Appalachian Spring* and *Rodeo*, several film scores (including *Of Mice and Men*) and 'Fanfare for the Common Man'.

> 'Fanfare for the Common Man' is often used for ceremonial occasions in America, such as at the celebrations for the inaugurations of the presidents Bill Clinton and Barack Obama and the opening of the museum commemorating the 9/11 attacks. It's written for a brass and percussion ensemble.

Copland Created Music that Sounded **American**

Copland wanted to create music that had an American sound. It had a more traditional feel than the music of some other 20th century composers, such as Stravinsky or Schoenberg.

1) Copland's music is tonal — it's in a major or minor key. Other music at the time was more atonal.

2) He makes use of simple melodic and rhythmic material, such as American folk tunes.

3) His pieces often celebrate American history and culture. For example, 'Lincoln Portrait' is about the American president Abraham Lincoln, and includes quotes from his speeches alongside the music.

4) Some of his music captures the spirit of the Wild West and America's landscapes. For example, *Appalachian Spring* portrays life in the Appalachian Mountains.

> - Copland's ballet *Appalachian Spring* was first performed in 1944. It's set on the wedding day of a young couple on a Pennsylvania farm.
> - It's written for a small orchestra (only 13 instruments), as that's all there was room for in the orchestra pit of the ballet's original venue.
> - The ballet has a gentle opening, representing dawn. Copland later uses a Shaker hymn called 'Simple Gifts' as the theme for a set of variations (see p.82).

Both Appalachian Spring and Rodeo (see below) have been turned into orchestral versions (without dancers).

Rodeo is a **Ballet** About **Life on a Ranch**

A rodeo is when cattle are rounded up, or a competition in which people show off their horse-riding and animal-handling skills.

1) *Rodeo* is another ballet by Copland, first performed in 1942. It's set in the Wild West (as was Copland's earlier ballet, *Billy the Kid*), on a ranch — a farm where cattle are raised.

2) The ballet is in five sections: 'Buckaroo Holiday', 'Ranch House Party', 'Corral Nocturne', 'Saturday Night Waltz' and 'Hoe-Down'. You can see the influence of the cowboy theme in the names. 'Buckaroo' is another word for cowboy, while a 'corral' is a pen for cattle or horses.

3) Copland used a large orchestra, with lots of brass, woodwind and percussion ('Hoe-Down' uses timpani, xylophone, snare drum, woodblock, bass drum and cymbals). However, he uses fewer instruments in the slower movements, such as 'Corral Nocturne' and 'Saturday Night Waltz'.

4) He often uses American folk tunes in *Rodeo* — for example, the main theme of 'Saturday Night Waltz' is based on the American folk song 'I Ride an Old Paint' (a paint is a type of horse).

A ranch house party sounds like a wild night in...

The first few bars of 'Saturday Night Waltz' sound like an orchestra tuning up. The string section play two or three open strings at once (double- or triple-stopping), as they often do when tuning.

Serialism

Serialism is a twentieth-century method of composition — one of the main composers who developed and used this system was **Arnold Schoenberg** (1874-1951). He invented the **12-tone system** in the 1920s.

The **12-Tone System** Arranges Notes in a **Certain Order**

1) To use the 12-tone system, start by arranging the 12 chromatic notes of an octave into a set order (any order you like), written out horizontally — this is called a tone row.

The initial arrangement is called the prime order:

2) Now rearrange the prime order. There are a few different ways of doing this — the first is to play the notes in reverse order (or retrograde).

3) Take the prime order again and turn the intervals between the notes upside down — this is known as an inversion. E.g. if the prime order goes up a semitone, in the inversion you go down a semitone.

4) For the last type of arrangement, take your inversion and play the notes in reverse order to give a retrograde inversion.

5) These four different tone rows can be transposed — each one can start on any of the 12 different notes. This gives you 48 different tone rows to use in your composition (see below).

6) As it uses all the notes of a chromatic scale, this music is not written in any key — it's atonal.

Use the **Tone Rows** as the **Building Blocks** of the Piece

1) Pick any tone row — the notes can be played in the bass line or melody and in any octave.

2) Once a row has been started, you have to use all the notes in it (i.e. you can't just use half a row). However, rows can be passed between parts and can overlap.

3) Notes can be combined to make motifs — memorable bits of melody that reappear through the piece.

4) Groups of notes can be piled up to make chords. Notes that were next to each other in the original rows would be played all at once by different instruments. This is called verticalisation — notes that were written out horizontally in the rows are written out vertically in the score.

5) The prime order could be designed to create decent-sounding chords with triads, or to create cluster chords with notes really close together.

6) Serialist music is quite complicated to write, so most pieces are only for small groups of instruments.

'Moses und Aron' by Schoenberg and Alban Berg's Violin Concerto are good examples of serialist pieces.

cluster chord

This is an example of verticalisation.

Not to be confused with cerealism — eating your breakfast in order...

Although this page is all about ordering the notes, serialism can order other elements too — such as metres, dynamics or rhythms. Total serialism, which came a bit later, is when every aspect of a piece is ordered.

British Music — Arnold and Britten

There have been lots of **British classical composers** from 1910 to today — but the ones you need to know about for this AoS are **Malcolm Arnold**, **Benjamin Britten**, **Peter Maxwell Davies** and **John Tavener**.

Malcolm Arnold was a Trumpet Player and Composer

1) Sir Malcolm Arnold was born in Northampton in 1921. He played principal trumpet for the London Philharmonic Orchestra before focusing on composition. He died in 2006.

2) He composed a wide variety of music — including symphonies, ballets, overtures, concertos, operas, choral music and film music (he won an Academy Award for the 1957 film *The Bridge on the River Kwai*). He also wrote music specifically for wind bands and brass bands.

3) Arnold lived in Cornwall for a number of years, which inspired some of his compositions — such as *Four Cornish Dances* (he also wrote suites of English, Irish, Welsh and Scottish dances). He composed 'The Padstow Lifeboat' (a brass band march) to celebrate the launch of a new lifeboat.

4) The *Tam O'Shanter Overture* is based on a poem by Robert Burns (it's a piece of programme music — see p.99). It has Scottish elements — for example, the clarinets imitate bagpipes. The drunken Tam is represented by a trombone and bassoons, giving the overture a light-hearted, comedic feel.

5) Arnold's music was quite conservative compared to other composers of the time — he was influenced by late Romantic/early 20th century composers such as Berlioz, Sibelius, Mahler and Bartók (see p.156-158), rather than atonal and experimental styles. His love of jazz also influenced his work.

Arnold Wrote Concertos For a Wide Range of Instruments

1) As well as writing concertos for more traditional instruments (such as cello, piano, flute and horn), some of Arnold's concertos were written for instruments not usually featured in concertos — including guitar, recorder (recorder concertos were more common in the Baroque era) and harmonica.

2) Many of his concertos were written for specific performers — for example, the Harmonica Concerto was written for Larry Adler, and Clarinet Concerto No.2 was commissioned by Benny Goodman:

> Clarinet Concerto No.2 has both typical and non-typical features of a concerto. It has the traditional three-movement, fast-slow-fast structure (the movements are marked Allegro vivace, Lento and Allegro non troppo). However, the concerto is unusual in that it has many jazz influences (see p.131-132), as Goodman was a jazz musician. Arnold uses dissonance frequently, and the third movement is a ragtime piece (it's called the Pre-Goodman Rag). The cadenza is marked with the instruction 'as jazzy and way out as you please'.

Benjamin Britten Wrote Both Vocal and Orchestral Music

1) Benjamin Britten was born in Lowestoft, Suffolk in 1913. He started composing at a young age, and continued until his death in 1976.

There's more on Britten on the next page.

2) Britten wrote a lot of orchestral music — including the *Simple Symphony* (its movements have the light-hearted titles 'Boisterous Bourrée', 'Playful Pizzicato', 'Sentimental Saraband' and 'Frolicsome Finale'). *The Young Person's Guide to the Orchestra* is variations and a fugue (see p.82) on a theme by Purcell, and is often used to teach children about the instruments of the orchestra.

3) He is also well known for his vocal music — he wrote a number of operas and song cycles (see p.102). The sizes of the operas vary — some are written for large companies, while others are written for chamber ensembles. Perhaps his most famous choral work is the *War Requiem* (see next page).

I'm going to call my composition 'Morbid Minuet'...

Have a listen to *The Tam O'Shanter Overture* — the poem that it's based on tells the story of Tam, who's making his way home from the pub when he comes across the devil and some dancing witches. When the witches notice him, they chase him until he escapes on his horse, Meg.

British Music — Britten and Maxwell Davies

You're part-way through the section on music from Britain — and coincidentally, part-way through the section on music by Britten as well. It's time to have a look at a couple of his pieces in a bit more detail.

Peter Grimes is an Opera by Britten

- *Peter Grimes* was first performed in 1945. Britten composed the music, and Montagu Slater wrote the libretto (based on a poem written by George Crabbe in 1810). It tells the story of the title character, a fisherman who is shunned by the people of his town after the suspicious deaths of his two apprentices.

- Britten later arranged the music used in between the acts into a suite called *Four Sea Interludes*: 'Dawn', 'Sunday Morning', 'Moonlight' and 'Storm'. All four interludes are very descriptive (for example, Britten uses horns playing in thirds to imitate church bells in 'Sunday Morning', and frantic low brass and strings to represent the fury of the storm in the fourth movement). All four movements have a sense of doom to reflect the overall mood of the opera.

War Requiem Was First Performed in 1962

1) A requiem is a mass for the dead (see p.103). Britten wrote his *War Requiem* for the opening of the new Coventry Cathedral (the old one was destroyed by a bomb in World War II).

2) He used Latin words from the Requiem Mass alongside war poems by Wilfred Owen (who was writing about World War I). Owen's poems, such as 'Anthem for Doomed Youth' and 'Futility', highlight the hopelessness of war.

3) Britten varies the instrumentation throughout — a soprano soloist is accompanied by a chorus and full orchestra, while a boys' choir is accompanied by an organ. A tenor and a baritone soloist (who sing the war poems) are accompanied by a chamber orchestra. These three groups are combined in the final section for maximum impact.

Peter Maxwell Davies Was Influenced by Different Genres

1) Sir Peter Maxwell Davies was born in Salford in 1934. He was knighted in 1987 and was made Master of the Queen's Music in 2004. He continued composing until his death in 2016.

2) Throughout his career, he explored many different styles of music — including medieval and Renaissance techniques (especially the use of plainsong, a monophonic chant) and serialism (he used sequences of both pitch and note length — see p.151). He was also influenced by expressionism:

> Expressionism is an early twentieth-century artistic movement that followed Romanticism. Artists believed their works should express their inner feelings. To do this, they moved away from conventional forms which they felt were too restrictive. Expressionist music (such as some of Schoenberg's compositions) is characterised by intense emotions, angular, spiky melodies, dissonance and atonality.

3) He composed a large number of orchestral pieces, including ten symphonies and a number of concertos and string quartets.

There's more on Maxwell Davies on the next page.

4) He also wrote a variety of vocal works, such as the chamber opera *The Lighthouse* and the musical drama *Eight Songs for a Mad King*. This is a piece about the madness of King George III — it's written for a baritone and a chamber orchestra of six musicians (who are on stage with the singer and form part of the action).

I prefer the lesser-known 'Six Songs for a Mad GCSE Student'...

A lot of these pieces are 'programme music' — they 'tell a story'. Have a listen to some of the pieces, such as *Four Sea Interludes*, and see if you can pick out how the composer has portrayed the story using music.

British Music — Maxwell Davies and Tavener

You're nearly done with British composers — just a bit more on Peter Maxwell Davies, then a bit on John Tavener as well (not to be confused with the Renaissance composer John Taverner).

Peter Maxwell Davies Was **Inspired** by the **Orkney Islands**

1) Maxwell Davies moved to the Orkney Islands (off the north-eastern tip of Scotland) in the early 1970s. Many of his compositions from the 1970s onwards have Scottish influences (for example, the orchestral piece *An Orkney Wedding, with Sunrise* has a bagpipe solo).

2) He often had strong political opinions — which led him to write *Farewell to Stromness*:

- *Farewell to Stromness* is from a larger work called *The Yellow Cake Revue*, which Maxwell Davies composed in 1980 to protest against a potential uranium mine on Orkney.
- *The Yellow Cake Revue* is a collection of pieces for piano and voice — *Farewell to Stromness* is a solo piano interlude. 'Yellowcake' is the powder taken from uranium ore.
- The piece is slow and gentle, with lilting Scottish rhythms that sound a bit like a Scotch snap (see p.17), though they're written differently.
- It starts with a steady ostinato bass line (see p.83) made up of crotchets — this is thought to represent people having to leave their homes after the mine opened.

John Tavener Wrote a Lot of **Religious** and **Vocal Music**

1) Sir John Tavener was born in London in 1944 and died in 2013.

2) He came from a religious family, and much of his music has religious influences. In 1977, he converted to the Russian Orthodox church, which inspired some of his later music.

3) Whilst at school, Tavener sang in choirs — much of his work is vocal music. He achieved early success with *The Whale* — a cantata that tells the story of Jonah and the whale. A cantata is similar to an oratorio, with arias and recitatives (see p.86) but uses words from books or poems.

4) His *Song for Athene*, a piece for SATB choir, was performed at the funeral of Princess Diana in 1997.

5) Some of his choral works are settings of poems by William Blake — including *The Lamb* (see below).

6) He wrote some instrumental music too — such as *The Protecting Veil*, a piece for cello and strings.

The Lamb is Often Sung at **Christmas**

The Lamb is a four-part choral piece, based on the poem of the same name from William Blake's *Songs of Innocence* (a collection of poems). It was written for Tavener's three-year-old nephew.

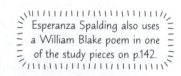 Esperanza Spalding also uses a William Blake poem in one of the study pieces on p.142.

- The score for *The Lamb* is unusual, as it has no time signature and no bar lines (bars are indicated by dotted lines, like in traditional plainsong (see p.85).
- The piece is slow and gentle — the melody is quite simple, and made up of just a few notes.
- It's written for an SATB choir singing a cappella, which adds to the gentle, simple feel. It is quiet throughout (the dynamics range from *pp* to *mp*).
- Tavener creates contrast by varying the texture of the voices — at the beginning, the voices are in unison, then the second part enters in contrary motion (where one part goes up as the other goes down). Finally, all four parts sing in parallel harmony (see p.45).
- In the section in contrary motion, the second part is singing an inversion of the first part (see p.83). This creates dissonance.

 Say Farewell to the British composers...
There's a lot of detail about different pieces on the British music pages. Write down the names of the pieces, then shut the book and note down as much info about them as you can...

Orchestral Music of Kodály

Zoltán Kodály (pronounced 'cod-eye') lived from 1882 to 1967 and had a strong interest in Hungarian folk music.

Kodály Collected Folk Tunes

Kodály was interested in music education — he created a method for learning music.

1) Like many early 20th century composers, Kodály, along with Bartók (see pages 156-158), continued the Romantic trend of expressing his national identity by using folk music in his work.

2) Kodály encouraged Bartók's interest in the genre, and together they collected lots of Eastern European folk tunes. They contributed to ethnomusicology — the study of music from different cultures.

3) Kodály's well-known works include *Concerto for Orchestra*, *Psalmus Hungaricus* (a work for tenor solo, choir and orchestra), the *Háry János Suite* and his *Symphony in C*.

Kodály Mixed Hungarian Folk With Western Classical Music

1) Elements of Hungarian folk music can be seen in much of Kodály's work.

> Hungarian folk melodies are often based on pentatonic scales (see p.27). The texture tends to be melody with accompaniment. The music often contains contrasting slow and fast sections. Dotted rhythms are a distinctive feature.

2) Kodály also took inspiration from Debussy's impressionist music, and introduced Bartók to it.

> Like impressionist art, impressionist music creates an overall impression or mood, rather than focusing on details. Impressionist composers created different timbres or 'colours' by experimenting with new playing techniques and using contrasting combinations of instruments. They moved away from large-scale pieces (such as symphonies) towards smaller works. The tonality tended to be ambiguous, with dissonant harmonies and unusual extended chords.

Kodály was more influenced by the impressionist use of different timbres than the harmony — his music tends to be tonal. Bartók was more experimental with tonality (see next page).

Kodály's Háry János Suite has Elements of Hungarian Folk

> The **Háry János Suite** is a set of six orchestral pieces from Kodály's comic opera of the same name.
> - A large percussion section is used — including a celesta (which sounds a bit like a glockenspiel), tubular bells and a cimbalom. The cimbalom is a Hungarian instrument that's played by hitting its horizontal strings with sticks. The use of contrasting percussion creates lots of 'colour' in the piece — an impressionist feature.
> - The dramatic crescendo to a chord at the start of the first movement represents a sneeze — this refers to the Hungarian belief that a story beginning with a sneeze shouldn't be taken seriously.
> - The fifth movement ('Intermezzo') involves fast, virtuosic cimbalom playing, a rich string sound, variations in tempo, and syncopation — these are all typical of Hungarian folk music.

> Kodály's **Dances of Galánta** includes lots of elements of folk music.
> - *Dances of Galánta* is based on a Hungarian style called 'verbunkos' — this started out in the 18th and 19th centuries as dance music used by the army to encourage people to join up.
> - The piece is in rondo form (see p.93), with a slow andante maestoso section returning in between faster sections. This slow-fast format is also a feature of the verbunkos style.
> - The clarinet has an important part — it has a cadenza in the first movement. It's imitating a type of woodwind instrument called a tárogató, which is often used in Hungarian folk music.

SUGGESTED LISTENING

Kodály, Háry János, Galánta, tóo mány áccents fór my cómpu—...

Listen out for the Hungarian influences in Háry János, like dotted rhythms, cimbalom and ornaments.

Béla Bartók — Hungarian Pictures

Béla Bartók (1881-1945) is another Hungarian composer. The pieces for this area of study are four movements from his *Hungarian Pictures*, a suite (see p.91) of orchestral pieces with features of Hungarian folk music.

Bartók used **Twentieth-Century** Techniques alongside **Folk Music**

1) Like Kodály (see previous page), Bartók collected <u>Hungarian folk tunes</u> and mixed them with <u>Western classical styles</u>. However, he was more <u>experimental</u>. Alongside other <u>twentieth-century</u> composers, he frequently moved away from <u>traditional</u> forms of <u>harmony</u> and <u>structure</u>:

- A lot of early twentieth-century music was <u>atonal</u> (p.26). Bartók sometimes used <u>accidentals</u> (see p.11) instead of <u>key signatures</u>, or <u>made up</u> his <u>own</u> key signatures, e.g. one with a C♯ but <u>no</u> F♯.
- When his music does have a key signature, the harmony is still <u>dissonant</u> and <u>non-functional</u> (it doesn't rely on <u>traditional chord progressions</u> and <u>cadences</u>).
- <u>Classical forms</u> (see p.91-93) had relied on <u>fixed keys</u> to create <u>contrast</u> between <u>different</u> sections. Now fixed keys were gone, <u>traditional structures</u> were used <u>less frequently</u>. For example, the *Concerto for Orchestra* has a non-standard <u>five-movement</u> structure (although the first and last movements do use <u>sonata form</u>).
- Some of his pieces frequently <u>change time signature</u>, and use <u>unusual</u> time signatures such as $\frac{4+2+3}{8}$.

2) Like other modern composers, he <u>experimented</u> with using instruments in <u>new ways</u>. A type of <u>pizzicato</u>, where the string is <u>lifted vertically</u> and <u>released</u> to give a <u>snapping</u> sound, is <u>named</u> after him.

3) <u>Bartók</u> shared Kodály's interest in <u>Eastern European folk music</u>. His *Romanian Folk Dances for Orchestra* are a good example — each movement is based on a <u>Romanian folk tune</u>. He also took inspiration from <u>further afield</u> — his *String Quartet No. 2* was influenced by folk music from <u>North Africa</u>.

Hungarian Pictures are **Orchestrations** of Piano Pieces

The title is sometimes also translated as Hungarian Sketches.

1) The suite is a set of <u>orchestrations</u> of pieces that Bartók composed for piano between 1908 and 1911 (he orchestrated them in 1931). They're an example of <u>programme music</u> — they <u>paint a picture</u>.

2) Bartók uses lots of <u>twentieth-century techniques</u>, particularly <u>non-functional harmony</u> and <u>detailed instructions</u> about <u>dynamics</u> or <u>performance style</u>.

3) The pieces are <u>influenced</u> by the years Bartók spent travelling around the countryside, trying to <u>collect</u>, <u>record</u> and <u>transcribe</u> all the <u>Hungarian folk music</u> he came across.

4) Each movement has <u>important folk elements</u> to look out for:

- <u>Modal</u> melodies
- Clear <u>melody and accompaniment</u> textures
- <u>Folk rhythms</u> (Lombardic or *kanász* — see next page)
- <u>Drones</u> (see p.39)
- <u>Pentatonic</u> scale (movement 1)
- <u>Strophic</u> form (movement 2)

5) The suite was written for a <u>full orchestra</u>, but <u>not all movements</u> use <u>all instruments</u>. There are particular features which give each a different <u>sonority</u> (highlighted in the right-hand column).

There's also a 3rd movement that you don't need to study.

1	piccolo, 2 flutes, 2 oboes, 2 clarinets in A, 2 bassoons, 2 French horns in F, triangle, strings (violins, viola, cello, bass)	Very light brass and percussion
2	2 flutes, 2 oboes, 2 clarinets in A, 2 bassoons, 2 French horns in F, 2 trumpets, 2 trombones, tuba, timpani, snare drum, triangle, xylophone, strings (without violin I)	Xylophone, snare and no violin I
4	2 flutes, 2 oboes, 2 clarinets in B♭, 2 bassoons, 2 French horns in F, 2 trumpets, 2 trombones, tuba, bass drum, strings	Bass drum
5	piccolo, 2 flutes, 2 oboes, 2 clarinets in A, bass clarinet in A, 2 bassoons, 2 French horns in F, 2 trumpets, 2 trombones, tuba, timpani, triangle, bass drum, cymbals, strings	Larger percussion section, bass clarinet

Bartók — a mad scientist of the music world...

Don't think you can just make up key signatures in your compositions — the examiners won't approve...

Béla Bartók — Hungarian Pictures

'An Evening in the Village' Alternates Two Folk-Like Melodies

1) The movement depicts a tranquil evening scene, and Bartók uses a simple melody and accompaniment texture with parallel movement (p.45). A woodwind melody is accompanied by string and horn chords.

2) The time signature is $\frac{4}{4}$ until just before the end, when some bars of $\frac{2}{4}$ and $\frac{3}{4}$ are introduced.

3) F♯ minor acts as a kind of tonic key, but it's emphasised with pedal notes and repetition instead of clear cadences. Melodies are based on the minor pentatonic scale on F♯:

4) The harmony is modal and non-functional, with some minor 7th chords. The piece ends with F♯ minor 7th chords and does not have a clear final cadence.

5) There are two contrasting melodies which alternate in an A-B-A1-B1-A2 structure. A bar of silence is heard before the final A2 section.

Bartók uses a Scotch snap (p.17), also called a Lombardic rhythm, to add to the folk feel.

Lento Rubato melody A (first 2 bars)

Allegretto melody B (first 2 bars)

	Melody	Melody features	Accompaniment features
A	Clarinet 1 in A	Legato, syncopated with p dynamic.	Peaceful muted strings. The bassline moves down the string section as each instrument enters, playing a descending F♯ Aeolian mode (p.27), with upper strings moving in parallel to form triads.
B	Flute 1	Staccato, syncopated, dotted/Lombardic rhythms.	More lively muted off-beat pizzicato strings with clarinet and horn pedals. Tonality moves from F♯m - A - D♯m.
A1	Oboe 1	Rhythm altered slightly to move the strong beats, f.	String chords no longer muted, creating a richer sonority. Begins with D major harmony but ends in F♯ minor.
B1	Piccolo	Embellished with semiquavers and triplets.	Pizzicato strings play on every beat, tonality again F♯m - A - D♯m. There is woodwind ornamentation with horn drones.
A2	Flute 1, oboes, clarinets	In octaves, begins f but ends ppp.	Initially unaccompanied, creating tonal ambiguity. Strings/horns play chords, ending muted.

'Bear Dance' Sounds Rustic and Clumsy

1) Bear dancing was a folk tradition where a bear was trained to 'dance' to an audience. It is considered cruel and is now banned in Europe. Bartók creates an image of an animal moving awkwardly to music:

- To portray the movements of the bear, Bartók uses repetitive ostinato rhythms, *marcato* and *tenuto* markings, and some $s\!f$. He includes the marking *ruvido* for the strings, meaning rough or coarse.

- More coarseness is created by lots of dissonant and non-functional parallel harmony. He uses *poco allargandos* and occasional bars of $\frac{3}{2}$, which feel uneven and clumsy.

- The dance style is shown in the *Allegro Vivace* tempo and simple folk-like melody. Bartók uses an important rhythm from Hungarian *kanász* folk dances (it also appears in movement 4):

The last two minims are often echoed f in the lower brass and timpani.

2) Two similar melodies alternate to give an A-B-A1-B1-A2 structure. This creates a type of symmetrical strophic form (with a few variations in each section).

3) Bartók varies the timbre with *arco* and *pizzicato* — and trumpets and French horns are sometimes muted.

4) The key signature has two sharps and the movement ends in D major, but the tonality sounds ambiguous:

- The A sections have pedal notes on D, but the modal melody is D♯ Aeolian.   *D♯ Aeolian*

- In the B sections, the pedal notes jump to A♭ (up a tritone from D), which creates a dissonant tonal relationship.

- The bassoon melody in the B section uses G♯, which emphasises the tritone between D and G♯ (A♭).

- There are lots of parallel triads and 7th chords, which don't lead to cadences.

Béla Bartók — Hungarian Pictures

'Slightly Tipsy' Depicts Stumbles and Hiccups

1) This piece is meant to portray someone who has had too much to drink. The music is playful, with pizzicato strings and staccato articulation. Techniques like *con sord punta d'arco* (muted, played at the bow tip) and *col legno* (played with the wood of the bow) create an unusual sonority.

2) The piece is in ternary form (A-B-A1) with a chordal texture, but section A1 is developed and has different (more regular) phrasing with a gradual *accelerando*, so the structure feels slightly unbalanced.

3) There are sudden dynamic changes and lots of other ways in which a sense of unsteadiness is created:

- Unexpected accents and 'hiccups' — accented leaps (with brass playing on the last quaver of each for emphasis).
- Irregular phrasing and changes of metre to $\frac{5}{4}$ and $\frac{2}{4}$.
- Syncopation and irregular rhythms — e.g. off-beat pizzicato. Acciaccaturas mean lots of notes land before the beat.
- 'Swaying' as the violins ascend and descend in parallel in the *meno mosso* (slower) bars.
- A 'stumbling' effect before A1 — conjunct chromatic scales passed between instruments and played *rallentando*. There's a 'tumble' in the last two bars with descending strings in octaves.
- Chromaticism and dissonance reinforce the unbalanced feeling, with lots of 7th chords.
- Tempo changes — the opening is *Allegretto rubato*, with lots of *rallentandos* and *accelerandos*.

4) The A sections are major and section B is minor. In section A, although the key signature suggests A♭, the many G♭'s and D♭ chords create tonal ambiguity. At the end of this section, the clarinet plays a descending whole tone scale (see p.27). Section B begins in G minor but is chromatic. The final chord is an open fifth (the tonic and 5th without a 3rd) on F — it's neither major nor minor.

'Swineherd's Dance' is the Only Piece that Uses a Real Folk Song

1) The original folk melody is made up of two 16-bar halves with similar melodic shapes.

2) It's a lively $\frac{2}{4}$ dance with the melody consisting mainly of quavers, semiquavers and semiquaver triplets, marked *Allegro molto*. The two halves are repeated in different ways:

Intro	The clarinet enters playing fragments of the folk song at a *p* dynamic.
A	First half of the folk song heard in full on the flute, still *p*.
B	Second half of the folk song, *f*. Initially flute and clarinet in octaves, piccolo is then added.
B1	Second half, *ff*, *tutti* with ornamented upper woodwind melody. Violin I enters in canon.
A1	First half of the folk song, marked *calmo* and *poco rallentando* as the dance dies down.
B2/ Coda	Variation of second half, dying away before an extended repeat of the semiquavers which close both halves of the song. The *p* dynamic then crescendos to a closing *ff*.

3) The tonality is clearer to sound more like a traditional dance (although there is still some dissonance):

- The melody is Mixolydian on A, and the entire section A is over an A drone.
- B and B1 have drones or pedals on D in the first half and A in the second half.
- The piece ends with a clear perfect cadence in A major.
- However, A1 and B2 have more chromatic harmony with non-functional 7ths.

Mixolydian mode on A

4) Bartók uses many different string techniques (see p.64), including harmonics, double and triple stopping and tremolando, and sometimes even specifies which string should be used to give a particular sonority.

5) The texture is mainly melody and accompaniment. The accompaniment includes a syncopated ostinato pattern in the strings, and the horns also play a syncopated countermelody in the B section.

I have a collection of Hungarian pictures from my holiday in Budapest...

Get to know the character of each piece, and listen out for the folk features. Make sure you're also familiar with twentieth-century stuff like non-functional harmony and tonal ambiguity — Bartók likes those too...

Minimalism

Minimalist music is music that changes a **small subtle bit** at a time. It's all about slow, gradual changes.

Minimalism Builds Music out of Repeated Patterns

1) Minimalism is a <u>Western art music</u> style that developed during the <u>1960s</u> and <u>1970s</u>.

2) It was a <u>reaction</u> against twentieth-century styles such as <u>expressionism</u> (see p.153) and <u>serialism</u> (see p.151) which were <u>atonal</u>, <u>dissonant</u> and <u>complex</u>. <u>Minimalism</u> was a return to more <u>basic concepts</u> — minimalist composers constructed their music from <u>simple</u> note or rhythm <u>patterns</u>, known as <u>cells</u>.

3) The cells are continuously <u>repeated</u>, with occasional <u>slight</u> changes. They're <u>layered</u> on top of each other, so although the individual cells tend to be <u>short</u> and <u>simple</u>, the music can sound <u>complicated</u>.

4) There's often <u>no clear melody</u>. <u>Harmony</u> is created by <u>layering</u> patterns on top of each other. It develops <u>gradually</u> — there are no sudden changes.

5) In contrast to the atonality of serialism, minimalism is usually <u>diatonic</u>. <u>Broken chords</u> are often used to form cells. <u>Common chords</u> (chords shared between <u>multiple keys</u>) are also used.

6) <u>Rhythm</u> is important — some minimalist pieces are <u>purely rhythmic</u>, e.g. *Clapping Music* (see p.162).

Minimalism Uses Musical Ideas from All Over the World

Minimalist composers often borrowed ideas from <u>other countries</u> and <u>cultures</u>.

Minimalism is Often Used in Film Music

1) The short <u>cells</u> of music used in minimalism can work well as <u>leitmotifs</u> in films (see p.121).

2) Minimalism works well as a way of gradually <u>developing</u> a film's atmosphere <u>over time</u>.

3) <u>Film music</u> often involves <u>repetition</u> (a feature of minimalism) — a gradual <u>crescendo</u> through a repeated bit of music is a great way of <u>increasing tension</u>.

4) Even film music that <u>doesn't</u> 'sound minimalist' can have <u>minimalist elements</u>. For example, the '<u>Chariots of Fire</u>' theme features a <u>constant pulse</u> throughout to represent the characters <u>running</u>.

- <u>Michael Nyman</u> and <u>Philip Glass</u> are <u>minimalist composers</u> who have written lots of <u>film scores</u>.
- Philip Glass composed for the film *The Hours*. The film is set in <u>three different time periods</u>, but Glass's music gives it a sense of <u>whole</u> using <u>repetition</u> and <u>layering</u>.

Minimalism

Minimalist composers use different techniques to bring about gradual changes in their music.

The **Cells** Change **Gradually**

There are <u>different ways</u> of <u>changing</u> the cell <u>patterns</u>, as well as the way they <u>fit together</u>. These changes can happen <u>every time</u> the patterns are repeated, or after the same pattern has been <u>repeated</u> a few times.

Gradually adding or taking away notes

The pattern is changed by adding a <u>single</u> note — this is called <u>additive melody</u>.
Another <u>similar</u> idea is to <u>replace one note</u> with a <u>rest</u>, or <u>one rest</u> with a <u>note</u>.

Gradually changing the notes of the pattern

This technique's called <u>metamorphosis</u> — another word for 'changing'.
Small changes to <u>one note</u>, or <u>one bit of the rhythm</u>, are made to the pattern.

The changes often go <u>full circle</u> — the pattern ends up the <u>same</u> or nearly the same as it was at the start.

Adding or removing notes or rests

<u>Two or more</u> performers start with the <u>same pattern</u>.
A note or rest is <u>added</u> or <u>taken away</u> from one of the parts.
They move gradually <u>out of sync</u> and then gradually back in. This is known as <u>phase shifting</u>.

Layering patterns of different lengths together

Cells of <u>different lengths</u>, e.g. a 4-beat cell and a 5-beat cell, are played at the <u>same time</u>. This has a similar effect to phase-shifting — the patterns move <u>apart</u> then come back <u>together</u>.

4-beat cell

5-beat cell

Music Technology Plays a **Big Part** in **Minimalism**

1) Minimalist composers often use <u>music technology</u> to create continuously repeating cells called <u>loops</u>.

2) Composers used to create <u>loops</u> by recording music (or other sounds) onto <u>tape</u>, carefully <u>cutting</u> the bit of tape that contained the music they needed, and <u>sticking</u> the ends together to create a physical loop that could be played <u>continuously</u>. Modern <u>sequencers</u> (p.72) make this process much easier.

3) The <u>different loops</u> are recorded, one on top of another, using <u>multi-track recording</u> (see p.72). This helps create the <u>layered sound</u> of minimalism.

4) The layers can be <u>edited</u> to achieve different <u>effects</u>. For example, two <u>identical</u> loops can be played at the <u>same time</u> but at two slightly <u>different speeds</u> — this effect is another form of <u>phase-shifting</u>.

5) <u>Live</u> performances of minimalist music are often <u>accompanied</u> by <u>recorded backing tracks</u> (p.162).

Riley, Reich and Adams

Terry Riley, Steve Reich and John Adams have all used minimalism in their work.

Riley's In C was One of the First Minimalist Pieces

1) Terry Riley was born in 1935 in the USA — he is one of the founders of minimalism.
2) His influences include jazz (p.131-132) and Indian classical music
   — he studied in India with the singer Pran Nath.
3) Riley's work In C is one of the best-known early minimalist pieces. His other famous works include
   A Rainbow in Curved Air, *Uncle Jard* and *Salome Dances for Peace* (a set of five string quartets).

Riley's Compositions Are Quite Varied

- *In C* can be played by any combination of instruments and/or voices.
- It's made up of 53 cells. The cells are numbered and should be played in order, but each performer can choose how many times they repeat each cell. Some cells are only one quaver in length, but others are much longer. The layering of the cells creates polyrhythm (see p.14).
- Constant C quavers keep the piece together and give it a strong, driving rhythm.
- To finish, all the performers repeat the 53rd pattern together, then each stops when they're ready.

- *A Rainbow in Curved Air* is different from *In C*. Terry Riley performed it by recording each track and then layering them over each other. It has three movements.
- The piece is based on repeated cells of music, but also has more 'traditional' melodic lines.
- It uses a variety of instruments to explore different timbres and textures — it features an electric organ, electric harpsichord, a tambourine and a doumbek (a goblet-shaped drum).

- *Uncle Jard* shows the influences of jazz, blues and Indian classical music on Riley's work.
- In the first movement, influences from Indian music are seen in the modal tonality, singing style and drones (played by saxophones). A harpsichord imitates a sitar (an Indian string instrument).
- In the second movement, syncopated and swung rhythms played on the saxophone and piano create a jazz feel. Riley sings blues-style lyrics over the top (see p.130).
- *Salome Dances for Peace* has these influences, as well as elements of Western classical music.
- It's more melodic than Riley's early music, but still has minimalist features. It has repeated cells of music which are layered over each other, e.g. in the *Ceremonial Night Race* section.

Reich was Influenced by Riley

1) Steve Reich is an American composer who was born in 1936.
2) He did a degree in Philosophy, then studied composition with the experimental composer Luciano Berio. He tried writing serial music (see p.151), but preferred composing tonal pieces.
3) Reich began writing minimalist music, and was influenced by Terry Riley's compositions.
4) His works are also influenced by jazz, music from sub-Saharan Africa (especially drumming — see p.133), Balinese gamelan (tuned percussion music from Indonesia) and Middle Eastern singing.
5) Some of his best-known works are *Clapping Music*, *Electric Counterpoint* and *Different Trains*.

You could try composing a minimalist piece...

...and impress the examiners with something different. However, though minimalist music is repetitive, it's not easy to write — all the cells have to work together and the piece needs shape.

Riley, Reich and Adams

Let's have a look at some of Reich's music in a bit more detail.

Reich Wrote a Piece Based Only on Rhythm

1) Reich's _Clapping Music_ is written for <u>two performers</u> who <u>clap</u> throughout the piece.
   - It's made up of <u>one rhythm</u>. The <u>first player</u> claps this rhythm <u>throughout</u> the piece. The <u>second player</u> claps the <u>same</u> rhythm, but after <u>twelve repetitions</u> they <u>shift</u> so they're one quaver behind.
   - This happens <u>every twelve repetitions</u> until the players end up <u>in sync</u> again. This is a good example of <u>phase-shifting</u>.

2) _Electric Counterpoint_ is for a <u>solo guitarist</u> accompanied by a 14-piece <u>guitar ensemble</u>.
   - It has <u>three movements</u>. For <u>live</u> performances, the <u>solo guitarist</u> often plays along with a <u>recording</u> of the <u>ensemble parts</u> made <u>before</u> the performance.
   - The movements don't have <u>titles</u> — they're just marked ♩ = 192, ♩ = 96 and ♩ = 192. People tend to call them 'Fast', 'Slow' and 'Fast'. The middle movement's <u>half</u> the speed of the others, so there's a <u>constant pulse</u>. There should be no breaks between the movements.
   - It's made up of short <u>cells</u> that are <u>repeated</u> lots of times.
   - Because the guitars all have a <u>similar sound</u>, the <u>timbre</u> (see p.74) doesn't really change. This means the parts all <u>blend</u> together.

   Different Trains is one of Reich's best-known works. It was written as a reaction to the <u>Holocaust</u>. It uses <u>samples</u> of people <u>talking</u> about train journeys, then <u>imitates</u> their voices with <u>instruments</u>.

John Adams Uses Minimalist Elements

1) <u>John Adams</u> was also born in the <u>USA</u>, in <u>1947</u>. He is a <u>composer</u> and <u>conductor</u>.
2) Adams' work is <u>influenced</u> by <u>minimalism</u>, but elements of <u>pop</u> and <u>jazz</u> are also incorporated into his compositions. Some of his pieces are <u>more</u> recognisably <u>minimalist</u> than others.
3) His orchestral works include _Harmonielehre_, _Shaker Loops_ and _Short Ride in a Fast Machine_.
4) Adams has also written a number of <u>operas</u>. Some of these deal with <u>political issues</u> — _Nixon in China_ is about the US President <u>Richard Nixon's</u> visit to <u>China</u> in <u>1972</u> and _Doctor Atomic_ is about the construction of the <u>first atomic bomb</u>.

Adams Uses Music to Paint a Picture

- _Shaker Loops_ was originally written as a <u>string quartet</u> called _Wavemaker_. It features lots of <u>tremolo</u>, which represents <u>ripples</u> on water.
- Adams <u>rewrote</u> it and changed it into a string <u>septet</u> (though it can also be played by a <u>string orchestra</u>). The <u>shaking</u> action used to create <u>tremolo</u> inspired the name _Shaker Loops_.
- It features lots of <u>repetition</u> of <u>short cells</u> of <u>music</u>, and it's <u>tonal</u>.
- It becomes <u>rhythmically complex</u> as different instruments enter, adding more <u>layers</u>.

- _Short Ride in a Fast Machine_ was inspired by a ride Adams had in a <u>sports car</u>.
- The <u>woodblock</u> plays <u>crotchets</u> throughout almost the whole piece — a <u>constant pulse</u> is often a feature of <u>minimalist</u> pieces. The rest of the orchestra is forced to <u>keep up</u>, creating a sense of the <u>tension</u> involved in travelling at <u>high speed</u>. When the pulse <u>stops</u>, the orchestra feels <u>freer</u>.
- The brass play a <u>key role</u>, with some <u>fanfare-like</u> sections. The <u>strings</u> are also important, and combine with a variety of <u>percussion</u> and <u>woodwind</u> to create a number of different <u>timbres</u>. The orchestra is <u>large</u> — it features <u>thirteen</u> different types of percussion.
- Although it has repeated cells, the piece <u>changes</u> quite <u>rapidly</u>. It lasts less than five minutes.

Warm-up and Exam Questions

Well, that was a whistle-stop tour through twentieth-century styles of music. Try these warm-up questions to get yourself in the zone, and then have a go at the exam-style questions.

Warm-up Questions

1) Where is the ballet *Rodeo* set?

2) What is a tone row?

3) Name two musical genres which influence Malcolm Arnold's music.

4) For which occasion was Britten's *War Requiem* written?

5) Describe two features of expressionism.

6) Name a piece by John Tavener.

7) Describe three features of Hungarian folk music.

8) What was Kodály's original *Háry János*, before it was an orchestral suite?

9) What is a Lombardic rhythm?

10) Explain the meaning of the marking *ruvido* in Bartók's 'Bear Dance'.

11) What is the structure of 'Slightly Tipsy'?

12) In minimalist music, what are cells?

13) Give two ways in which cells can be varied to create gradual change in a minimalist piece.

14) Name two pieces by Terry Riley.

15) Which composition by Steve Reich is based only on rhythm?

16) Which technique creates the 'shaking' in *Shaker Loops*?

Exam Questions

Have a go at these exam-style questions.

Track 36 is an excerpt from 'An Evening in the Village' by Bartók.
Play the excerpt **four** times. Leave a short pause between each playing.

Track 36

Track 36

a) Which of the following best describes the tonality of the melody of this excerpt? Circle the correct answer.

major   **minor**   **modal**   **atonal**   **pentatonic**

[1 mark]

b) What is the time signature of the excerpt?

....

[1 mark]

Exam Questions

c) i) Name the instrument playing the melody in the first part of the excerpt.

....

[1 mark]

ii) Describe the string accompaniment to the instrumental melody.

....

....

....

[2 marks]

d) Name the instrument playing the melody in the second part of the excerpt.

....

[1 mark]

e) Describe the texture throughout the excerpt.

....

....

....

[2 marks]

f) Describe how Bartók creates contrast between the two sections in this excerpt, other than the features mentioned above.

....

....

....

....

....

[4 marks]

Exam Questions

Track 37 is an excerpt from 'Hoe-Down' by Aaron Copland.
Play the excerpt **four** times. Leave a short pause between each playing.

a) What are the violins playing in the first section of the excerpt?
   Circle the correct answer.

   the melody   **offbeat chords**   **constant quavers**   **downbeat crotchets**

   [1 mark]

b) Name **two** percussion instruments that play in the excerpt.

   1) ....

   2) ....
   [2 marks]

c) Explain how contrast between the first and second sections of the excerpt is achieved.
   You might want to mention the following musical features:
   • Instrumentation
   • Rhythm
   • Texture

   ....

   ....

   ....

   ....

   ....

   ....

   ....

   ....
   [4 marks]

d) What is the tonality of the second section?

   ....
   [1 mark]

Revision Summary for Section Nine

That wraps up <u>Section Nine</u> — time to put yourself to the test and find out <u>how much you really know</u>.
- Try these questions and <u>tick off each one</u> when you <u>get it right</u>.
- When you've done <u>all the questions</u> for a topic and are <u>completely happy</u> with it, tick off the topic.

Aaron Copland and Serialism (p.150-151) ☑
1) Name two ballets by Aaron Copland.
2) Give two ways in which Aaron Copland created an American feel in his music.
3) Give two ways in which a tone row can be rearranged.
4) Describe the tonality of serialist music.
5) What is verticalisation?

British Music — Arnold, Britten, Maxwell Davies and Tavener (p.152-154) ☑
6) Name one feature of Malcom Arnold's Clarinet Concerto No. 2 that is typical of a concerto.
7) Name the opera by Benjamin Britten that is about a fisherman.
8) The lyrics for Britten's *War Requiem* come from two sources. What are they?
9) Give three details about the instrumentation in *War Requiem*.
10) Why did Peter Maxwell Davies write *The Yellowcake Revue*?
11) In *The Yellowcake Revue*, what does the bass line represent?
12) What is a cantata?
13) How does John Tavener create contrast in *The Lamb*?

Kodály and Bartók (p.155-158) ☑
14) What is ethnomusicology?
15) Give three features of impressionist music.
16) Name two percussion instruments used in Zoltán Kodály's *Háry János Suite*.
17) What is the 'verbunkos' style used in Kodály's *Dances of Galánta*?
18) Give two similarities and two differences between the compositional styles of Kodály and Bartók.
19) Describe the unusual type of pizzicato named after Bartók.
20) Give three features of Bartók's 'An Evening in the Village' that are typical of folk music.
21) Which two of the study pieces from Bartók's *Hungarian Pictures* use the *kanász* dance rhythm?
22) Identify two different transposing instruments used in 'Swineherd's Dance'.
23) Name two modes that Bartók uses in *Hungarian Pictures*.
24) Describe how Bartók develops the folk song in 'Swineherd's Dance'.

Minimalism, Riley, Reich and Adams (p.159-162) ☑
25) What tonality do minimalist pieces tend to have?
26) i) Where does gamelan music come from?
    ii) Which feature of gamelan is used in minimalist music?
27) How many cells is Terry Riley's *In C* made up of?
28) Describe two elements of Indian classical music used in the first movement of Riley's *Uncle Jard*.
29) Name two musical genres which influenced Steve Reich's music.
30) For which instrument is Reich's *Electric Counterpoint* written?
31) Name an opera written by John Adams.
32) How is the idea of travelling at high speed created in Adams' *Short Ride in a Fast Machine*?

General Certificate of Secondary Education

GCSE Music

CGP Practice Exam Paper GCSE Music

Component 1
Understanding Music

Centre name				
Centre number				
Candidate number				

Time allowed: 1 hour 30 minutes

Surname	
Other names	
Candidate signature	

Instructions
- Write in black ink or ballpoint pen.
- Answer the questions in the spaces provided.
- Answer **all 8** questions in Section A.
- In Section B, answer **Question 9** and **one** of Questions 10-12.
- Give all the information you are asked for, and write neatly.
- Do all rough work in this book. Cross through any work you do not want marked.

Information
- The marks are shown by each question.
- The maximum mark for this paper is 96.
- There are 68 marks available in Section A and 28 marks available in Section B.
- For each question in Section A, you will need to play one or more tracks from the online audio. You will be told how many times to play each track.
- You do **not** need to listen to any tracks for Section B.
- Read through the question before you play the track(s).
- Leave a gap between each playing to give yourself time to write.

Instructions for playing the audio tracks:
- The tracks can be accessed via the Online Edition of this book. You can also scan this QR code, or visit cgpbooks.co.uk/tempo.
- There are 8 questions in Section A, covered by tracks 38-50.

Tracks 38-50

Question No.	1	2	3	4	5	6	7	8
Track No.	38, 39	40	41, 42	43, 44	45, 46	47, 48	49	50

- Leave 3 minutes at the start to read through the exam.
- Play one track at a time, stopping after each track.
- Each question will tell you how many times the track should be repeated.
- Allow a short pause between each playing for writing time. After the final playing of each track, allow some time for writing.

Section A: Listening

68 marks
Answer **all** the questions in Section A

1   Area of Study 1: Western classical tradition 1650-1910   7 marks
     For this question, there are two excerpts, track 38 and track 39.
     Play each track **three** times.

(Track 38)

1.1   What type of vocal ensemble is performing this piece? Circle the correct answer.

         Male voice choir   SATB choir   Octet   SSA choir

                                                                                    [1 mark]

1.2   This piece was composed for the coronation of a king.
       Identify **two** features of the excerpt that make it suitable for this occasion.

       1) ....

          ....

       2) ....

          ....

                                                                                    [2 marks]

1.3   What is the cadence heard at the end of this excerpt?

       ....

                                                                                    [1 mark]

Track 39

1.4 Name one of the instruments playing the melody at the start of the excerpt.

....
[1 mark]

1.5 This movement is in $\frac{2}{4}$. Suggest a suitable tempo for this excerpt.

....
[1 mark]

1.6 Which of the words below best describes the texture created by the first
and second violins towards the end of the excerpt? Circle the correct answer.

    unison   antiphony   counterpoint   monophony

[1 mark]

2 Area of Study 2: Popular music   8 marks
Play the track **four** times.

(Track 40)

2.1 What type of voice is singing in this excerpt?
Circle the correct answer.

       bass   tenor   alto   soprano

[1 mark]

2.2 This excerpt alternates between sections in $\frac{3}{4}$ and sections in $\frac{2}{4}$. Circle **two** rhythmic features that can be heard in the excerpt.

     hemiola   swung rhythms   quaver triplets   cross-rhythms   back-beating

[2 marks]

2.3 Describe the texture of this excerpt.

....

[1 mark]

2.4 During this song, the character is excited for the future. Identify and describe
two features of this excerpt that create a feeling of excitement and anticipation.

1) ....

....

....

2) ....

....

....

[2 marks]

2.5   The excerpt is made up of two contrasting sections, each heard twice. Describe **one** difference in the **vocal melody** and **one** difference in the **accompaniment** between these sections.

Vocal melody: ....

....

....

Accompaniment: ....

....

....

[2 marks]

Turn over ▶

3   Area of Study 3: Traditional music   10 marks
For this question, there are two excerpts, track 41 and track 42.
Play track 41 **four** times and track 42 **three** times.

(Track 41)

3.1   Name the family of instruments used at the start of the excerpt.

....
                                                                                   [1 mark]

3.2   Tick the rhythm played by the first drum you hear at the start of the excerpt.

                                                                                   [1 mark]

3.3   Which phrase below correctly describes the device used in the vocal section?
Circle the correct answer.

      a cappella   singing in unison   polyphony   vibrato
                                                                                   [1 mark]

3.4   Name the region of the world this music comes from.

....
                                                                                   [1 mark]

3.5   Some of the percussion rhythms don't fit perfectly into the $\frac{4}{4}$ bars.
What is the technical term for such a combination of rhythms?

....
                                                                                   [1 mark]

Track 42

3.6   What type of bass line is used in this excerpt?

....

[1 mark]

3.7   i)   To which genre of music does this excerpt belong?

....

[1 mark]

ii)   Identify **three** features of the excerpt that are typical of this genre.

1) ....

....

2) ....

....

3) ....

....

[3 marks]

Turn over ▶

174

4   Area of Study 4: Western classical tradition since 1910   9 marks
     For this question, there are two excerpts, track 43 and track 44.
     Play each track **four** times.

   (Track 43)

4.1 What rhythmic feature is heard in this excerpt? Circle the correct answer.

          hemiola   cross-rhythms   Scotch snap   phase shifting
                                                                                              [1 mark]

4.2 Identify **one** similarity and **one** difference between the first and second parts of this excerpt.

     Similarity: ....

     ....

     Difference: ....

     ....
                                                                                              [2 marks]

4.3 Name **one** type of ornament heard in the second half of the excerpt.

     ....
                                                                                              [1 mark]

   (Track 44)

4.4 Circle the word that best describes the harmony provided by the horns.

          dissonance   unison   consonance   suspension
                                                                                              [1 mark]

4.5 About halfway through the excerpt, the violins and woodwind play
     a descending scale. What type of scale is it?

     ....
                                                                                              [1 mark]

4.6 After this scale, the mood of the excerpt changes.
     Describe **three** ways in which this change of mood is achieved.

     1) ....

        ....

     2) ....

        ....

     3) ....

        ....
                                                                                              [3 marks]

5 Area of Study 1: Western classical tradition 1650-1910   10 marks
For this question, there are two excerpts, track 45 and track 46.
Play track 45 **three** times and track 46 **four** times.

Track 45

5.1 This excerpt is from a concerto. What is the name of the part
of the concerto heard in the first section of the excerpt?

....
[1 mark]

5.2 i) To which period of Western classical music history does this piece belong?

....
[1 mark]

ii) Give **one** reason for your answer to part i).

....

....
[1 mark]

Track 46

5.3 Fill in the missing notes in bars 2-3 on the score below,
using the rhythm given above the stave.

[6 marks]

5.4 Describe the tonality of this excerpt.

....

....
[1 mark]

Turn over ▶

6   Area of Study 2: Popular music   9 marks
For this question, there are two excerpts, track 47 and track 48.
Play each track **four** times.

(**Track 47**)

6.1   i) This excerpt comes from a Romantic symphony which is used in a film.
What genre of film do you think this excerpt was used for? Circle the correct answer.

   horror   romance   comedy   action

[1 mark]

ii) Describe **two** features of the excerpt that make it suitable for this genre.

   1) ....

   ....

   2) ....

   ....

[2 marks]

6.2   Describe the texture of this excerpt.

....

[1 mark]

6.3   In the film, this excerpt is actually played on synthesized instruments.
Suggest **one** reason why this might have been done.

....

....

[1 mark]

6.4 What ensemble is playing in this excerpt? Circle the correct answer.

string quartet   chamber orchestra   symphony orchestra   wind band

[1 mark]

6.5 Which of the words below describes the beginning of the excerpt?   Circle the correct answer.

fugue   fanfare   prelude   sonata

[1 mark]

6.6 The beginning of the excerpt includes a canon played between some of the instruments.
Define the term 'canon'.

....

....

[1 mark]

6.7 Suggest an appropriate dynamic for the start of the excerpt.

....

[1 mark]

Turn over ▶

7   Area of Study 3: Traditional music   7 marks
          Play the track **four** times.

(Track 49)

7.1   What is the tonality of this excerpt?

....
                                                                                                                    [1 mark]

7.2   List the order in which the following instruments are first heard
        in this excerpt by writing the numbers 1-4 in the boxes below.

         Percussion   [ ]   Lead vocals   [ ]

         Spanish guitar   [ ]   Trumpets   [ ]

                                                                                                                    [2 marks]

7.3   This excerpt is from a Latin dance track. Identify **one** feature of this excerpt
        that is typical of Latin music, and **one** feature that is typical of dance music.

        Latin music: ....

        ....

        Dance music: ....

        ....
                                                                                                                    [2 marks]

7.4   Describe how the dynamics change in this excerpt.

        ....

        ....

        ....
                                                                                                                    [2 marks]

8 Area of Study 4: Western classical tradition since 1910   8 marks
Play the track **four** times.

(**Track 50**)

8.1 Suggest a suitable dynamic marking for this excerpt.

....
                                                                          [1 mark]

8.2 Describe the rhythm at the beginning of the excerpt.

....
                                                                          [1 mark]

8.3 i) To which genre of 20th century classical music does this piece belong?

....
                                                                          [1 mark]

ii) Describe the features of this excerpt that are typical of this genre.

....

....

....

....

....

....

....

....
                                                                          [5 marks]

Turn over ▶

Section B: Contextual Understanding

28 marks

Answer **Question 9**

9   Area of Study 1: Western classical tradition 1650-1910
This question is about the first movement of Beethoven's *Symphony No. 1 in C major*.

9.1   Describe the structure of the first movement of this symphony.

....

....

....

[2 marks]

9.2   Name **two** different ornaments that are used in this movement.

1) ....

2) ....

[2 marks]

9.3   Identify **two** ways in which Beethoven emphasises the tonic key in the coda.

1) ....

....

2) ....

....

[2 marks]

9.4   Explain how Beethoven creates variety in the first movement
using harmony, sonority (timbre) and/or tonality.

....

....

....

....

....

....

....

....

.... **Turn over** ▶

....

....

....

....

....

....

....

....

....

....

....

[8 marks]

182

Answer **one** of Questions 10-12

10   Area of Study 2: Popular music

10.1 Identify **two** technological effects that were used in the production of 'Bohemian Rhapsody'.

1) ....

2) ....

[2 marks]

10.2 Identify **two** features of the vocals in 'Seven Seas of Rhye'.

1) ....

....

2) ....

....

[2 marks]

10.3 Identify **two** classical features used in 'Love of My Life'.

1) ....

....

2) ....

....

[2 marks]

10.4 Explain how the structure, sonority (timbre), melody and/or texture of 'Bohemian Rhapsody' might have surprised and excited radio listeners in 1975.

....

....

....

....

....

....

....

....

....

183

....
....
....
....
....
....
....
....
....
....
....

[8 marks]

184

11 Area of Study 3: Traditional music

11.1 Identify **two** features of the vocal part in 'I Adore You'.

1) ....

....

2) ....

....

[2 marks]

11.2 Name **two** samba percussion instruments used in 'I Adore You'.

1) ....

2) ....

[2 marks]

11.3 Describe **two** rhythmic features heard in 'I Know You Know'.

1) ....

....

2) ....

....

[2 marks]

11.4 Explain how 'Little Fly' fuses elements of jazz with Western classical music.

....

....

....

....

....

....

....

....

185

....

....

....

....

....

....

....

....

....

....

....

[8 marks]

12   Area of Study 4: Western classical tradition since 1910

12.1   Describe the structure of Bartók's 'An Evening in the Village'.

....

....

[2 marks]

12.2   Identify **two** string techniques used in 'Swineherd's Dance'.

1) ....

2) ....

[2 marks]

12.3   Describe the tonality in 'Bear Dance'.

....

....

....

....

[2 marks]

12.4   Explain how Bartók uses tempo, metre, rhythm, harmony and/or dynamics
       to create an unbalanced mood in 'Slightly Tipsy'.

....

....

....

....

....

....

....

....

....

....

....

....

....

....

....

....

....

....

....

....

[8 marks]

END OF TEST

Answers

Section Two — Reading and Writing Music

Page 15 (Warm-up Questions)

1)

2) A sharp sign raises the pitch of the note (and other notes of the same pitch later in the bar) by one semitone.
A flat sign lowers the pitch of the note (and other notes of the same pitch later in the bar) by one semitone.
A natural sign cancels out a flat or sharp sign in the key signature or earlier on in the bar.

3)

4) Three beats

5) In simple time, the main beats are divided into 2, 4, 8, etc. but in compound time the beats are divided into 3, 6, 9, etc.

6) Regular, irregular and free

Page 15 (Exam Question)

Track 1

a)

(1 mark for each correct note or correct interval between two adjacent notes, up to 8 marks)

b) (see above) *(1 mark)*

c) (see above) *(1 mark)*

d)

(up to 3 marks, one for each different feature identified)

Page 21 (Warm-up Questions)

1) (semibreve)

2) ≡

3) Dotted crotchet, one and a half beats
Quaver, half a beat
Dotted minim, three beats

4) A tie joins two or more notes of the same pitch together.
A slur joins two or more notes of different pitch together.

5) Presto, allegro, moderato, andante, largo

Pages 21-22 (Exam Question)

Track 2

a) dotted notes *(1 mark)*

b) allegro *(1 mark)*

c) forte *(1 mark)*

d) energico *(1 mark)*

Section Three — Keys, Scales and Chords

Page 31 (Practice Questions)

Track 10 a) natural minor   b) melodic minor
c) whole tone   d) major

Track 11 Pentatonic (major isn't wrong, but pentatonic is more accurate)

Track 12 a) unison   b) perfect 5th   c) major 3rd
d) minor 3rd   e) major 7th   f) perfect 4th
g) minor 6th   h) augmented 4th/diminished 5th

Track 13 a) minor 2nd   b) major 3rd   c) perfect 4th
d) octave   e) major 6th   f) perfect 5th
g) minor 7th   h) major 2nd

Page 32 (Warm-up Questions)

1) Eight

2) They tell you what sharps or flats to play.

3) They are relative scales – they have the same notes/ same key signature.

4) Natural, harmonic and melodic

5) Mixolydian

6) Major pentatonic

7) It includes every white and black note on a keyboard.

8) A harmonic interval.

9) Diminished 7th

Pages 32-33 (Exam Question)

Track 14

a) i)   Four *(1 mark)*
ii) Perfect fourth *(1 mark)*
iii) Minor third/augmented second *(1 mark)*

b) C♯ minor *(1 mark)*

c) Tenuto — played full length or longer *(1 mark)*

Page 40 (Practice Questions)

Track 17 a) major   b) minor   c) major

       d) augmented   e) minor   f) diminished

       g) diminished   h) minor

Track 18 a) root   b) 2nd   c) root

       d) 2nd   e) 1st   f) 2nd

       g) root   h) root

Pages 49-50 (Practice Questions)

Track 21 a) perfect   b) plagal   c) interrupted

       d) imperfect   e) interrupted   f) perfect

       g) imperfect   h) perfect

Track 22 a)

       b) first inversion

       c) plagal

Track 23 a)

       b) homophonic

       c) perfect

       d) A

Track 24 a)

       b) F sharp

       c) interrupted

Track 25 a)

       b) (see above)

       c) Relative minor

Track 26 a)

       b) E flat major

       c) G minor

       d) pivot chord

       e) V, III

Page 51 (Warm-up Questions)

1) e.g. piano, guitar

2) I, IV and V or tonic, subdominant, dominant

3) First inversion

4) Block chords, rhythmic chords, broken / arpeggiated chords

5) Diatonic

6) Any three of the following: auxiliary notes, passing notes, appoggiaturas, suspensions, trills or other sensible answer.

7) In the middle of a piece, or at the end of any phrase except the last phrase.

8) Contrapuntal

Pages 51-52 (Exam Question)

Track 27

       a) Piano *(1 mark)*

       b) Alberti bass / broken chords / arpeggios *(1 mark)*

       c) Imperfect *(1 mark)*

       d) G major *(1 mark)*

       e) Accidental *(1 mark)*

       f) Staccato *(1 mark)*

       g) Melody with accompaniment *(1 mark)*

Section Four — Structure and Form

Page 59 (Warm-up Questions)

1) *Conjunct* — melodies move mainly by step. Notes are a major 2nd (a tone) or a semitone apart.

     Disjunct — melodies have a lot of jumps. Notes are more than a major 2nd apart.

     Triadic — melodies made up of the three notes in a triad.

     Scalic — melody moves up and down the notes of a scale.

2) A form where each verse has different music.

3) A repeated bass part, usually four or eight bars long that is played by the left hand on the piano or harpsichord, or by cello and double bass in an orchestra.

Pages 59-60 (Exam Questions)

Track 28

       a) i) D major *(1 mark)*

          ii) Perfect fifth *(1 mark)*

       b) Call and response/question and answer *(1 mark)*

       c) Any three of:

          - Starts off with longer notes (minims and crotchets), then changes to semiquavers.

          - Violin plays chords (double/triple stopping) in the first few bars, then single notes for the semiquavers.

          - Staccato in first few bars, then legato/slurred later on in excerpt.

          - Big intervals between the notes at first (disjunct), then smaller intervals in semiquaver section (conjunct).

          - Short rising and falling semiquaver runs at the end with staccato crotchets.

       (1 mark for each, up to a maximum of 3 marks)

Track 29

a) Baroque period *(1 mark)*

b) Oboe, bassoon, violin, viola, harpsichord, cello, double bass.
(1 mark for each instrument, up to 2 marks)

c) i)

(1 mark for each correct note or correct interval between two adjacent notes, up to 7 marks)

ii) Conjunct *(1 mark)*

d) Basso continuo *(1 mark)*

e) Bassoon / Harpsichord / Cello / Double Bass *(1 mark)*

Section Five — Instruments

Page 76 (Warm-up Questions)

1) E.g. slide — trombone
Single reed — clarinet or saxophone
Double reed — oboe or bassoon
Pizzicato — violin, viola, cello, double bass
Wooden bars — xylophone

2) *Tremolo* — trembling sound on string instrument (fast, short, light strokes with the bow). Guitars can also produce this type of sound.
Con sordino — 'with mute', mute placed on the bridge of string instruments to make them sound further away. Brass instruments can also be muted.
Tenor — higher male voice.
Falsetto — someone with a lower voice singing much higher than their normal range.

3) Acoustic guitar — e.g. played by strumming or plucking six or twelve strings.
Electric guitar — e.g. needs an amplifier and loudspeaker to be heard.
Bass guitar — e.g. has only four strings, is pitched lower than electric and acoustic guitar, needs amplification.

4) Baroque

5) A military band is a marching wind band, with woodwind, brass and percussion. A brass band has brass and percussion. A jazz band can include woodwind, brass, percussion and any other instruments too, and sounds quite different.

6) Piano trio — piano, violin, cello.
Clarinet quintet — clarinet, first violin, second violin, viola, cello.

7) MIDI — musical instrument digital interface
Sampler — record, process and play back samples of music
Remix — mixing together samples of pop or dance music to a fast drumbeat, often sped up
Sequencer — computer program that records and replays many tracks of music together

Pages 76-78 (Exam Question)

Tracks 30 and 31

a) Flute *(1 mark)*

b) Piano *(1 mark)*

c) Shape B *(1 mark)*

d) The left hand of the piano has chords, the right hand melody imitates the flute part. One follows the other around. / The melodies interweave in a two-part texture at a similar pitch. / The parts are contrapuntal.
(1 mark for each sensible comment up to a maximum of 2 marks)

e) Flute, clarinet *(1 mark for each)*

f) Strings *(1 mark)*

g) Chromatic *(1 mark)*

h) Shape C *(1 mark)*

i) Crescendo *(1 mark)*

Section Six
— Western Classical Tradition 1650-1910

Page 104 (Warm-up Questions)

1) There were sudden changes in dynamics (no crescendos or diminuendos).

2) a) A small group of solo instruments.

b) A larger group of accompanying instruments (often a string orchestra).

3) A set of variations played over a repeated bass part (basso ostinato).

4) A repeat of a pattern, but starting on a different note.

5) A note that clashes with a chord, but which is followed by a note belonging to the chord (usually a tone or semitone away from the first note).

6) Treble, countertenor (or alto), tenor, bass

7) A solo vocal piece, backed by an orchestra — it's used to show the thoughts and emotions of the main characters.

8) Handel

9) E.g. clarinet

10) Three movements — first movement in sonata form (quick), second movement in ternary or variation form (slow), third movement in rondo, variation or sonata form (quick).

11) Sonata form. The three sections are:
Exposition, Development, Recapitulation

12) The introduction is slow (*Adagio molto*), but speeds up for the exposition (*Allegro con brio*) and the rest of the movement.

13) (First) Violins

14) E.g. Haydn, Mozart.

15) Approximately 1820-1910

16) In an undertone.

17) A song for one singer and a piano.

18) E.g. *Introit, Dies Irae, Pie Jesu*

Pages 104-107 (Exam Questions)

Track 32

a) Exposition *(1 mark)*

b) Timpani *(1 mark)*

c) Any two of:
- The type of instruments/size of the orchestra are typical of the Classical period.
- The harmony is mainly diatonic.
- The texture is often melody with accompaniment.
- The use of the clarinet, which was a new instrument in the period.
- The movement is in sonata form, which was common for the first movement of a symphony in the Classical period.
(1 mark for each, up to a maximum of 2 marks)

d) Any two of:
- *ff*, loud dynamics.
- Use of repeated quavers (quaver pedals).
- Double or triple stopping.
- Greater use of brass/timpani.
- New melodic material (developed from previous material).
- Melody played in octaves stands out.
- Strong perfect cadence into the new section.
(1 mark for each, up to a maximum of 2 marks)

e) Antiphonal *(1 mark)*

f) Any two of:
- In the first subject, the melody is first played by the first violins. In the second subject, the melody is first played by the oboe and flute.
- The first subject is staccato, while the second subject is legato.
- The melody in the first subject is generally ascending, while the second has descending quavers.
- The melody in the first subject is mainly disjunct, while the second has conjunct quavers.
- There is a sequence in the second subject, but not in the first subject.
- The first subject has a melody with accompaniment texture, while the second subject is antiphonal.
(1 mark for a valid statement about one subject, and 1 mark for a matching contrast with the other subject, up to a maximum of 4 marks)

Track 33

a) i) Requiem *(1 mark)*
   ii) Day of wrath *(1 mark)*

b) The excerpt opens with homophonic chords. — T
The bass drum plays on the off-beats. — T
The choir sing in unison. — F
The strings play ascending runs between the choral sections. — F
(1 mark for each, up to a maximum of 4 marks)

c) Any three of:
- When the orchestra is playing alone, the music is mainly homophonic (playing in chords).
- The sections with choir and orchestra are more polyphonic (the choir are singing overlapping parts, while the brass play fanfare-like melodies underneath).
- The texture is rich and thick throughout.
(1 mark for each, up to a maximum of 3 marks)

d) Quick/lively and agitated *(1 mark)*

e) i) Romantic period *(1 mark)*

   ii) Any four of:
   Instrumentation:
   - The music uses a full choir, with a lot of singers — this has a dramatic impact, which was typical of Romantic music.
   - The choir is accompanied by a large orchestra, with prominent brass and percussion playing accented notes. This is typical of Romantic music — the development of new instruments meant that composers could write for large orchestras, and composers used these to add drama.
   Dynamics:
   - Dynamics are generally loud throughout, with crescendos to increase impact — the use of very loud dynamics (even up to *ffff*) to add drama was common in Romantic music.
   Harmony:
   - This piece involves lots of dissonance/clashing chords and complex harmonies. This was typical of Romantic music — complex harmonies allowed composers to show emotions like pain (which is appropriate for a piece entitled Day of Wrath).
   Pitch:
   - There is a range of pitch — the female voices in the choir sing in a very high range, while the male voices, brass and lower strings are much lower. Romantic composers used a large range of pitch to add drama and emotion to their works. In the instrumental parts, this was often made possible by developments in instruments.
   Tempo:
   - The music is quick — it feels frantic and desperate, which adds drama.
   Mood:
   - This piece is very dramatic and emotional and has a big impact — this is a key feature of Romantic music.
   (Award 1 mark for a correct feature that is typical of Romantic music, and award a further mark for a suitable explanation of the use of that feature, up to a maximum of 8 marks.)

Section Seven — Popular Music

Page 125 (Warm-up Questions)

1) Singing without accompaniment
   (i.e. no instrumental backing).

2) E.g. Michael Jackson

3) 1950s

4) E.g. hard rock — loud and aggressive,
   dominated by distorted electric guitar.
   Glam rock — theatrical and glitzy, with costumes and
   make up. It has a rock 'n' roll feel with catchy hooks.
   Heavy metal — harder and more distorted than
   hard rock, with longer guitar solos.
   Progressive rock — experimental and
   complicated, albums often had a theme.

5) An album with a theme linking all the tracks.

6) E.g. folk, progressive rock, heavy metal

7) Intro, ballad, guitar solo, operatic section,
   rock section, outro

8) Harp

9) Any three from:
   - Multi-tracking
   - Double-tracking
   - Overdubbing
   - Panning
   - Delay / Echo
   - Distortion (electric guitars)
   - Cross fade

10) E.g. It helps them engage with their fans.

11) E.g. 'Someone Like You' by Adele
    'Sing' by Ed Sheeran

12) A lighter, more modern version of opera.

13) 4 sections of 8 bars. Sections 1, 2 and 4 use the
    main theme, section 3 has a contrasting theme.

14) Solo character song, duet, action song,
    chorus number

15) A phrase of music that represents a character,
    place or emotion.

16) E.g. to link parts of the film together.

17) To create the mood of a specific time or place.

18) Digital audio workstation software,
    such as Logic Pro or Cubase.

Pages 125-127 (Exam Questions)

a) i) Delay / Echo / Reverb *(1 mark)*
   ii) Any two of:
      - Complex rhythms (dotted, syncopated)
      - String bends
      - Distortion
      - Virtuosic
      (1 mark for each, up to a maximum of 2 marks)

b) Bridge / Transition *(1 mark)*

c) Recording the same part twice and layering them
   on top of each other *(1 mark)*. This creates the effect
   of having a thicker texture *(1 mark)*.

d) Any three of:
   - Distorted electric guitars
   - Strong drum beat / bass drum / backbeat
   - Loud dynamic / fortissimo
   - Power chords
   - Some high / falsetto vocals
   - Fast/driving tempo
   (1 mark for each, up to a maximum of 3 marks)

e) Any two of:
   - Syncopation
   - Dotted rhythms
   - Rhythmic motif on title lyrics
   - Short note values / quavers / semiquavers
   - Long held note just before the end
   (1 mark for each, up to a maximum of 2 marks)

Track 34

a) Riffing *(1 mark)*

b) i) Minor *(1 mark)*
   ii) V7 (allow V) *(1 mark)*

c)

1	2	3	4	5	6	7	8
		A, B		C			D

(1 mark for each letter in the correct box)

d) Overdubbing *(1 mark)*

Section Eight — Traditional Music

Page 146 (Warm-up Questions)

1) African slaves in America.

2) Syncopation is when the accent is shifted from a strong
   beat onto a normally weaker beat.

3) I I I I IV IV I I V IV I I (V)

4) E.g. trumpets, trombones, saxophones, piano.

5) Improvised singing with nonsense words and syllables.

6) A West African instrument with 21 strings.

7) Any interval smaller than a semitone.

8) 2/4 or 4/4

9) Jamaica

10) When two or more styles of music are combined to
    create a new style.

11) R'n'B, mento, calypso

12) Upstroke

13) Brazil

14) William Blake

15) (G) Mixolydian

16) Pentatonic

17) An Irish framed drum.

Pages 146-148 (Exam Questions)

a) syncopated *(1 mark)*, riff *(1 mark)*

b) Chords *(1 mark)*

c) i) Any two of:
- Use of piano, bass and drum kit / typical jazz instruments
- Funk influence in bass riff
- Improvisation / *ad lib* throughout
- Complex harmony / extended chords
- Blue notes
- Syncopated rhythms
(1 mark for each, up to a maximum of 2 marks)

ii) Any two of:
- Use of common samba percussion instruments
- Fast dance tempo
- Use of polyrhythms
(1 mark for each, up to a maximum of 2 marks)

d) Any two of:
- Conjunct quaver motion
- Triadic leaps
- Blue notes
- Large range
- Mixture of syllabic and melismatic
(1 mark for each, up to a maximum of 2 marks)

e) Any three of:
- Monophonic at the start when the bass plays solo.
- Polyphonic when the other instruments come in.
- Melody with accompaniment when the vocal line comes in.
- Monophony/a cappella briefly at the end of the excerpt when the instruments stop but the singing continues.
(1 mark for each, up to a maximum of 3 marks)

Track 35

a) Caribbean *(1 mark)*

b) The second option is correct. *(1 mark)*

c) Any three of:
- In the first half, the rhythm follows a 3-3-2 pattern.
- In the second half, it has a steady 4-beat pattern.
- The first half has syncopated rhythms.
- The second half has little syncopation/mainly on-beat rhythms.
  The first half has longer notes (crotchets and dotted crotchets).
- The second half mainly has running quavers.
(1 mark for each, up to a maximum of 3 marks)

d) Any two of:
- It's in a major key which sounds happy — this makes it suitable for a carnival.
- It has a bright, lively tempo so sounds fun.
- It's easy to dance to, which is suitable for a carnival.
(1 mark for each, up to a maximum of 2 marks)

Section Nine — Western Classical Tradition since 1910

Page 163 (Warm-up Questions)

1) In the Wild West/on a ranch

2) The twelve chromatic notes in an octave arranged in any order.

3) Any two of:
- jazz
- classical music from the late Romantic period
- early twentieth century classical music
- British folk music

4) The opening of the new cathedral in Coventry.

5) Any two of:
- intense emotions
- angular/spiky melodies
- dissonance
- atonality
- unconventional forms

6) Any piece by Tavener, e.g.: Jonah and the Whale, Song for Athene, The Lamb, The Protecting Veil

7) Any three of:
- pentatonic scales
- slow and fast sections
- dotted rhythms
- melody with accompaniment
- instruments such as the cimbalom
- syncopation
- rich string sound
- triplets
- ornaments

8) Opera / comic opera

9) A 'short-long' rhythm often used in folk music (also called a Scotch snap).

10) Coarsely / roughly

11) Ternary / A-B-A1

12) Short, repeated note or rhythm patterns

13) Any two of:
- additive melody
- metamorphosis
- phase shifting
- layering

14) Any two pieces by Riley, e.g.:
- In C
- Uncle Jard
- A Rainbow in Curved Air
- Salome Dances for Peace

15) Clapping Music

16) Tremolo

Pages 163-165 (Exam Questions)

Track 36

a) Pentatonic *(1 mark)*

b) 4/4 (accept 2/4) *(1 mark)*

c) i) Oboe *(1 mark)*

ii) Any two of:
- chords/chordal
- sustained/pedal notes
- arco
- quiet/*p* dynamic
- playing on the off-beat
- descending in pitch
(1 mark for each, up to a maximum of 2 marks)

d) Piccolo *(1 mark)*

e) The texture is predominantly melody with accompaniment *(1 mark)*, but with some extra woodwind decorations in the accompaniment and a horn drone in the second half. *(1 mark)*

f) Any of:
- Contrasts in tempo (first half slower/lento, second half faster/allegretto).
- Different articulation (first half legato, second half staccato).
- Use of ornamentation in melody of second half, first half has no ornamentation.
- Use of accompanying woodwind chords and embellishments in second half, no woodwind in first half other than oboe melody.
- Faster rhythmic movement/more rhythmic variety in second half (crotchets in strings, some semiquavers in melody).
- Piccolo melody in higher register in second half, compared to lower-pitched oboe melody in first half.
- Use of pizzicato strings in second half, compared to arco in the first half.
(Award 1 mark for a correct statement about one section of the excerpt, and award a further mark for a correct comparison with the other section of the excerpt, up to a maximum of 4 marks)

Track 37

a) Offbeat chords *(1 mark)*

b) Any two of: cymbal, xylophone, woodblock, piano
(1 mark for each, up to a maximum of 2 marks)

c) Any of:
Instrumentation:
- In the first section, only the strings, piano and woodblock play.
- In the second section, the whole orchestra plays.
Rhythm:
- In the first section, strong offbeat chords are played.
- Despite the offbeat chords in the first section, the rhythm is clear/the section is quite rhythmic.
- In the second section, there is a strong downbeat.

- The second section also features some syncopation in the accompaniment.
- The second section melody has triplet flourishes.
Texture:
- The first section is an accompaniment section without a clear melody.
- The second section sounds almost monophonic at the beginning, with nearly all of the orchestra playing the tune and only a few instruments accompanying.
- Throughout the second section, multiple instruments play the melody.
- The second section becomes more homophonic after the start.
Tempo:
- The tempo in the first section is slower than in the second.
Dynamics:
- The first section is quite quiet (*mp/mf*).
- Most of the second section is louder (*f*).
Articulation:
- The first section is mostly staccato.
- The second section is less staccato/more legato.
(Award 1 mark for a correct statement about one section of the excerpt, and award a further mark for a correct comparison with the other section of the excerpt, up to a maximum of 4 marks)

d) Major *(1 mark)*

Page 167-187 — Practice Exam

Pages 168-179 — Section A

1 *Track 38*

1.1 SATB choir *(1 mark)*

1.2 Any two of:
- It's in a major key so it sounds happy.
- The trumpet fanfare sounds celebratory.
- The fast tempo (allegro) makes it sound joyful and upbeat.
- The word 'rejoice' is repeated.
- The timpani make the piece sound grand.
(1 mark for each, up to a maximum of 2 marks)

1.3 Perfect *(1 mark)*

Track 39

1.4 Violin or flute *(1 mark for one correct instrument)*

1.5 Andante (allow adagio, moderato) *(1 mark)*

1.6 Antiphony *(1 mark)*

2 *Track 40*

2.1 Tenor *(1 mark)*

2.2 'Hemiola' and 'cross-rhythms' should be circled
(1 mark for each)

2.3 Melody with accompaniment *(1 mark)*

2.4 Any two of:
- The excerpt has a quick tempo, which gives a feeling of excitement.
- The excerpt is in a major key, which is hopeful, positive and happy.
- There are crescendos on long notes at the end of some sections, which shows building excitement.
- There are loud sections, which sound like the character's excitement bursting out.
- The voice has a breathless quality, which sounds excited.
- Off-beat accents give a feeling of anticipation — they drive the music along as if pushing to the future.
- The lyrics are positive, with words like 'bright' and 'miracle'.
- The accompaniment is light/dance-like, which sounds happy.
- The way the melody rises and falls with rests in between sounds a bit like jumping up and down/ skipping with excitement.
- Accented brass notes add to the excited/triumphant feel.
- There's a long triumphant note at the end of the excerpt, enforcing the idea that something positive is expected.
(1 mark for each, up to a maximum of 2 marks)

2.5 Vocal melody — any one of:
- The first section starts with longer notes then pairs of quavers; the second starts with running quavers then ends with a long note.
- The first section is disjunct, with quite big leaps between some notes, and no repeated notes in a row; the second section starts with repeated quavers on the same note, then is mainly conjunct, with just one bigger leap.
- The first section starts on an anacrusis; the second section doesn't (it starts on the second quaver beat of the bar).
- The first section is in 3/4 (but sounds like 6/8); the second section is in 2/4.
(1 mark. The point about the different time signatures could also be given as a difference in the accompaniment; do not credit for both.)
Accompaniment — any one of:
- In the first section, the accompaniment is played throughout; in the second section, there are just accented quavers, with rests in between them.
- In the first section, the accompaniment is quieter and gentler, with less brass; the second section is louder and more dramatic, with accents and brass instruments playing throughout.
- The accompaniment provides a steady, regular beat in the first section; in the second section, the accents fall on different quaver beats each time.
(1 mark)

3 *Track 41*
3.1 Percussion *(1 mark)*
3.2
(1 mark)
3.3 Singing in unison *(1 mark)*
3.4 (Sub-Saharan) Africa *(1 mark)*
3.5 Cross-rhythm *(1 mark)*

Track 42
3.6 Walking bass *(1 mark)*
3.7 i) Blues *(1 mark)*
   ii) Any three of:
      - blue notes/blues scale
      - swung rhythms
      - syncopated rhythms
      - sad/mournful lyrics (e.g. dead, evil spirits, devil)
      - walking bass
      - the lyrics are 3 lines long with the first line repeated
      - piano finishes off vocal line
      (1 mark for each, up to a maximum of 3 marks)

4 *Track 43*
4.1 Scotch snap *(1 mark)*
4.2 Similarities — any one of:
   - largely the same instrumentation
   - dotted rhythms/Scotch snaps in both
   - string dominated melody
   - crescendos in both parts
   - both use repeated melodies
   - tempo is largely similar in both
   (1 mark)
   Differences — any one of:
   - cimbalom stands out in first half but not in second
   - quavers/triplets in second half, mainly dotted rhythms in first half
   - first half minor, second half mainly major
   (1 mark)
4.3 Any one of: turn, acciaccatura, trill *(1 mark)*

Track 44
4.4 Dissonance *(1 mark)*
4.5 Chromatic *(1 mark)*
4.6 Any three of:
   - The dynamics are quieter.
   - The music is more tonal/less atonal/less dissonant.
   - The strings play a legato melody (they played staccato before).
   - The string melody is more conjunct.
   - The strings play longer notes.
   - The woodwind add light-hearted/bird-like flourishes above the melody.
   - The horns are no longer playing.
   (1 mark for each, up to a maximum of 3 marks)

5 *Track 45*

5.1 Cadenza *(1 mark)*

5.2 i) Classical *(1 mark)*

ii) Any one of:
- The concerto is a common Classical form.
- There is a complicated cadenza for the soloist to show off their skills.
- The soloist is accompanied by a standard Classical orchestra.
- The phrases in the orchestral section are balanced.
- The harmonies are simple.
- The texture is homophonic.
(1 mark)

Track 46

5.3

(1 mark for each correct note or correct interval between two adjacent notes, up to 6 marks)

5.4 Begins major, then modulates to minor *(1 mark)*

6 *Track 47*

6.1 i) Horror *(1 mark)*

ii) Any two of:
- It uses low-pitched instruments.
- It's in a minor key.
- It has a slow tempo.
- Monophony makes it sound empty/scary.
- The tolling bell sounds ominous.
(1 mark for each, up to a maximum of 2 marks)

6.2 Monophonic / playing in unison / octaves *(1 mark)*

6.3 Any one of:
- It makes it sound alien/unnatural/other-worldly.
- It makes it feel like something is wrong.
- It makes it sound more modern.
- It is cheaper/easier to record than live instruments.
(1 mark)

Track 48

6.4 Symphony orchestra *(1 mark)*

6.5 Fanfare *(1 mark)*

6.6 A canon is where the same tune is played by two or more parts coming in at regular intervals and overlapping with each other. *(1 mark)*

6.7 fortissimo/forte/sforzando/loud *(1 mark)*

7 *Track 49*

7.1 Minor *(1 mark)*

7.2 Percussion ☐2   Lead vocals ☐4
Spanish guitar ☐1   Trumpets ☐3
(2 marks for all four correct, otherwise 1 mark for at least two correct)

7.3 Latin music — any one of:
- Traditional Latin instruments e.g. Spanish guitar
- Latin rhythms / syncopation
Dance music — any one of:
- A fast tempo
- Disco beat
(1 mark for a feature from Latin music and 1 mark for a feature from dance music)

7.4 Any two of:
- The guitar and percussion are quiet at the start.
- There is a crescendo just before the trumpets enter.
- It gets louder when the trumpets enter.
- The instruments get quieter as the lead vocals start.
(1 mark for each, up to a maximum of 2 marks)

8 *Track 50*

8.1 pianissimo/piano/mezzopiano/quiet *(1 mark)*

8.2 Any one of:
- Regular, quick rhythm
- Constant/repeated quavers (allow semiquavers)
(1 mark)

8.3 i) Minimalism *(1 mark)*

ii) Any five of:
- Constant pulse/driving rhythm
- Repetitive cell structure/short repeated phrases/ostinatos
- No clear melody
- Gradual build up to complex texture
- Gradual build up to complex rhythm
- Notes gradually added/gradual changes in phrases
- Not atonal/music is modal (accept tonal)
- Diatonic/no dissonance
- No sudden changes in dynamics
(1 mark for each, up to a maximum of 5 marks)

Pages 180-187 — Section B

9.1 The movement is in sonata form *(1 mark)*, with a slow introduction, followed by exposition, development and recapitulation sections and a long coda. *(1 mark)*

9.2 Any two of:
- Trills
- Acciaccaturas
- Appoggiaturas
- Passing notes
(1 mark for each, up to a maximum of 2 marks)

9.3 Any two of:
- Pedal notes
- Timpani rolls on C (the tonic)
- Repeated C major chords
(1 mark for each, up to a maximum of 2 marks)

9.4 Any eight of:
Harmony:
- Introduction creates uncertainty, beginning with F major perfect cadence / chords on the subdominant / dominant / relative minor.
- The tonic key of C major isn't established until the exposition.
- First subject is initially diatonic then heard in a more chromatic version with D minor harmony.
- Diminished chords and chromaticism in the development.
- Circle of fifths / harmonic sequence in the development.
- Unexpected shift to G7 / dominant 7th harmony before the recapitulation.
- The coda returns to the tonic key of C major.
Sonority:
- Much more emphasis on woodwind than was common in a classical orchestra.
- Dialogue / call and response between flute and oboe, and later between woodwind and violins.
- Mixture of string techniques including arco, pizzicato, double/triple/quadruple stopping.
- Variety of articulation — some passages are staccato, some are slurred/legato.
- Contrast between first subject played by the strings and second subject played by the woodwind.
- Brass and timpani used to emphasise cadences and louder passages.
Tonality:
- Contrast between tonic and dominant in the exposition's two subjects.
- Contrast resolved in the recapitulation with both subjects in the tonic.
- Development modulates to a wide range of keys.
- Unrelated/distant keys in the development (e.g. A major, E♭ major).
(1 mark for each, up to a maximum of 8 marks)

10.1 Any two of:
- Multi-tracking
- Overdubbing
- Panning
- Flanger
- Distortion
- Double tracking
- Reverb
(1 mark for each, up to a maximum of 2 marks)

10.2 Any two of:
- Some falsetto
- Wide range
- Loud dynamic
- Vibrato
- (Multi-tracked) backing vocals
- Close harmony in the backing vocals
- Portamentos
(1 mark for each, up to a maximum of 2 marks)

10.3 Any two of:
- Use of harp
- Broken chords in piano
- Pedal notes
- Ornamentation, e.g. trills
- Clear cadences / mainly diatonic harmony
- Counterpoint
(1 mark for each, up to a maximum of 2 marks)

10.4 Any eight of:
Structure:
- Long (almost 6 minutes) — unusual for popular music, especially on the radio, in 1975.
- Lots of separate sections in various distinct styles, including the opera section which is unusual for pop.
Sonority:
- Multi-tracked backing vocals imitate opera chorus — unusual for popular music to have operatic influences.
- Falsetto and high vocal pitches — less common for male vocalists.
- Cymbal crashes and distorted electric guitar create a more exciting sound in the rock section.
- Solo voice uses lots of expressive effects like vibrato and crescendos to build excitement.
- Panning of the vocals creates disorientation.
Melody:
- Syllabic passages emphasise the unusual lyrics in these sections.
- Melismas add expression and excitement.
- Wide pitch range allows more sounds to be explored, keeping the song exciting throughout.
- Pitch bends and contrasts between scalic motion / arpeggios create energy in the guitar solo.
- Chromaticism creates melodic uncertainty / sounds eccentric in operatic section.
Texture:
- Textural contrasts emphasise the different sections (e.g. melody and accompaniment in the ballad, homophony in the intro).
- Call and response/antiphony in operatic section creates tension between different vocal parts.
- Monophony or octaves highlight important lyrics.
(1 mark for each, up to a maximum of 8 marks)

11.1 Any two of:
- Scat singing
- Hooks
- Improvisation
- Layered vocals
- Double-tracked / multi-tracked vocals / backing vocals
(1 mark for each, up to a maximum of 2 marks)

11.2 Any two of:
- Congas
- *Shekere*
- *Cabassa*
- *Surdo* (bass drum)
- *Repinique* (two-headed drum)
- *Caixa* (snare drum)
(1 mark for each, up to a maximum of 2 marks)

11.3 Any two of:
- Syncopation
- Polyrhythms
- Off-beat chords
(1 mark for each, up to a maximum of 2 marks)

11.4 Any eight of:
Jazz elements:
- Vocal melismas
- Blue notes / chromaticism
- Extended / added note chords
- Riff
- Double bass improvisation
- Syncopated rhythms
Classical elements:
- Sets a poem to music (typical of Romantic era)
- Layered string instruments / instruments from a classical string trio, plus double bass
- Regular 4-bar phrases
- Diatonic melody
- Fairly simple harmony used throughout
- Clear major tonality
- Word-painting
(1 mark for each, up to a maximum of 8 marks.
If only jazz elements or only classical elements have
been discussed, award no more than 6 marks.)

12.1 Any two of:
- Two contrasting melodies alternate
- Melodies varied each time they appear
- A-B-A1-B1-A2
(1 mark for each, up to a maximum of 2 marks)

12.2 Any two of:
- Harmonics
- Double / triple stopping
- Tremolando
- Playing notes on specified strings
to give a particular sonority
(1 mark for each, up to a maximum of 2 marks)

12.3 Any two of:
- Ambiguous tonality
- Dissonant tonal relationship
- Tritone between D and A♭
- Pedals on D clash with melody in D♯ (Aeolian)
- Pedals on A♭ in B sections
- Ends in D major
(1 mark for each, up to a maximum of 2 marks)

12.4 Any eight of:
Tempo:
- Use of rubato creates a feeling of unsteadiness.
- Frequent unexpected tempo changes.
- Lots of rallentandos and accelerandos.
Metre:
- Unpredictable changes of metre (mainly 4/4 but some 5/4 and 2/4).
- Time changes disrupt the phrasing / irregular phrasing.
Rhythm:
- Lots of off-beat/syncopated rhythms create an unbalanced feeling.
- Rhythms often irregular.
- Longer notes create a sense of swaying.
- Acciaccaturas move the emphasis off the beat.
Harmony:
- Dissonances sound clumsy.
- Chromaticism and 7th chords disrupt the sense of tonal stability.
Dynamics:
- Unexpected sforzandos and accents support a 'hiccup' effect.
- Sudden dynamic contrasts.
(1 mark for each, up to a maximum of 8 marks)

Index and Glossary

Index and Glossary

blues scale A **scale** made by flattening the third, fifth and seventh of a **major scale**. The unflattened fifth is also played. **129**

Bo Diddley beat An **R'n'B** version of a **son clave**. **139**

bodhrán An Irish framed drum. **67, 144**

Bohemian Rhapsody **114, 115**

bongos A pair of small drums used in Latin American and Caribbean music. **67, 135, 136, 143**

bossa nova A style of Brazilian music based on a fusion of **samba** and **jazz**. **140, 143**

Brahms **102**

brass band Band with **brass** and **percussion** sections. **69**

brass instruments Metal instruments where the sound is produced by 'buzzing' the lips. **62, 69, 71, 74, 80, 89, 94-96, 99**

bridge Section in a piece of music used to link two different chunks together. **58, 92, 93, 97, 116, 118**

Britpop Style of music popular in Britain in the 1990s. **117**

Britten **152, 153**

Broadway A famous theatre street in New York. **119**

broken chord Chord that's played as a series of notes. **39, 90, 100, 101, 110, 116, 118, 159**

bubble rhythm A rhythm often used in **reggae**. **137**

C

C clef A clef that can move up and down the **stave** — the middle point of the clef is always at middle C. **10**

cadence Pair of chords used to finish off a **phrase**. **42, 43, 93, 97, 98**

cadenza Section of a **concerto** where the soloist can really show off. **57, 91, 100, 152**

call and response A short melody (the call), followed by an answering phrase (the response). **47, 55, 58, 97, 109, 111, 115, 129, 130, 132, 133, 136, 140**

calmato Play the music so it sounds very calm. **18**

calypso A style of Caribbean music. **135**

canon Where the same tune is played by two or more parts, each coming in separately and at regular intervals. The parts overlap. Also called a **round**. **46, 98**

cantata A piece of music made up of **arias** and **recitatives**. **154**

carnival **135, 140**

Celtic music **144**

cha-cha-cha A mid-tempo dance that evolved from **danzón**. **141**

chamber choir A small choir. **85**

chamber music Music written for small groups. It was originally played in people's houses. **70, 153**

chamber orchestra Orchestra with small **string** and **percussion** sections, and one or two of each **wind** and **brass** instrument. **71, 80, 85, 153**

choir A group of singers. **68, 85**

Chopin **99-101**

choral music Music written for **choirs**. **68, 85-87**

chord A group of two or more notes all played at the same time. **9, 34-39**

chord progression Repeated pattern of related chords used in bass and rhythm parts, especially **ground bass**. **36**

chorus Piece in an **opera**, **oratorio** or **cantata** sung by the chorus (choir). **86, 87**

chorus effect An electronic effect that gives the impression of lots of singers or instruments. **75, 110**

chorus number A piece in a **musical** sung by the whole cast. Similar to a **chorus** in opera. **120**

chromatic decoration **41**

chromatic scale 12-note scale containing all the notes (**tones** and **semitones**) within an octave. **27**

chromaticism When notes that aren't in the **key signature** are used frequently in a piece. **97, 98, 115, 142, 143, 158**

circle of fifths Madly complicated diagram showing how all the keys relate to each other. **26, 98**

clarinet quintet Small group with clarinet, two violins, viola and a cello. **70**

classical Either any music that's not **pop** (or **jazz**, **folk**, **hip-hop**, **R'n'B**, etc.), or music composed in Europe from about 1750 to 1820. **80-103, 116, 142, 150-162**

clave rhythm The basic rhythm of a piece of **son** or **salsa** music around which the rest of the music has to fit. **136, 139**

claves Wooden sticks used to set the **clave rhythm**. **135, 136**

clavichord An early keyboard instrument. **66**

close harmony Where chords use notes that are close together. **116**

cluster chord Lots of notes all very close together played at once. **151**

col legno For string players — play the string with the back of the bow instead of bowing. **64**

compound time A **time signature** where each main beat can be split into three little ones. **13**

con arco Play with the bow. The opposite of **pizzicato**. **64**

con sordino Play with a mute. **64**

concept album An album where all the tracks are linked by a theme. **114**

concertino The small group of soloists in a **concerto grosso**. **81**

concerto Piece for an orchestra with a soloist, in three movements. **81, 88, 89, 91-96, 100, 152**

concerto grosso A type of Baroque concerto, made up of a **concertino** and a **ripieno**. **81, 88**

concordance Nice sound that you get when notes that fit together are played together at the same time. Also called **consonance**. **34**

conductor The person who controls an orchestra. **71**

conjunct Where the melody is smooth — there aren't big jumps between the notes. **28, 54**

consonance Another name for **concordance**. **34**

continuo Another name for **basso continuo**. **57, 80**

contralto A low-range female voice. **68, 85**

contrapuntal Music with two or more tunes played at the same time and woven together. Also called **polyphonic**. **45, 46, 47, 80, 116**

contrary motion Where one line of music goes up at the same time as another goes down. **45, 154**

Copland **150**

coronation anthem An **anthem** performed at coronations. **87**

countertenor A high-pitched male voice. **68, 85**

country and western **111**

crescendo Get louder gradually. **19**

crotchet A note that lasts for one beat. **12, 16**

Cubase A piece of software used as a **sequencer**. **124**

cyclic form Where a common **theme** runs throughout the movements, usually in a large-scale work. **56**

Index and Glossary

Index and Glossary

H

habanera A 19th century Cuban dance with a distinctive dotted rhythm. **141**

hammer-on A guitar technique that allows you to play notes quickly and in a **legato** style. **65**

Handel 80, 81, 87

harmonic A technique on stringed instruments (including guitars) that produces a high, ringing note. **64, 158**

harmonic interval The difference between two notes played at the same time. **28**

harmonic minor scale 8-note scale using notes from the **minor key** except for the seventh note, which is sharpened by one **semitone**. **25**

harmonic progression A series of chords. Another name for a **chord progression**. **36**

harpsichord A keyboard instrument shaped like a small grand piano. It was popular in the **Baroque** period. **57, 66, 80, 89**

Haydn 81, 88-91, 94

heavy metal A type of **rock music** that uses a lot of **distortion**. **113**

hemiola When the music feels like it's in triple time when it's actually written in duple time, or vice versa. **14**

heterophonic In heterophonic music all the parts have different versions of the tune. **45**

hip-hop Popular music with African-American and Caribbean influences. It features rapping, **DJing** and **beatboxing**. **137**

home key The key that a piece of music starts and ends in. **44**

homophonic Where the tune is accompanied by chords, keeping to roughly the same rhythm. **45, 47, 88, 90, 115, 116**

hook A catchy tune used in pop music and musicals. **110, 111, 113, 116, 118, 120, 143**

Hungarian Pictures 156-158

I

I Adore You 143

I Know You Know 143

imitation A phrase is repeated with little variation. Could be one instrument or voice, or two or more imitating each other. **46, 83, 87**

imperfect cadence A **cadence** that usually moves from chord I, II or IV to chord V. **42, 43**

impressionism Late 19th and early 20th century music that focuses on the mood of music. **155**

improvisation Music that's made up on the spot by a performer, often based on a given chord progression or set of notes. It's used a lot in jazz. **57, 91, 109-111, 131, 132, 134, 135, 137, 139, 142, 143**

incidental music Music written to be performed as part of a play. **119**

Indian classical music 114, 159, 161

instrumental section 111

interrupted cadence A **cadence** that moves from chord V to any chord except chord I. **42, 43**

interval The gap in pitch between two notes, played one after another or at the same time in a chord. **28, 29**

inversion (chord) Using a chord in a position other than its **root position**. **37, 38**

isicathamiya A type of South African Zulu **a cappella** singing. **133, 138**

J

jazz Music with lots of **syncopation**, **improvisation** and quirky harmonisation. Influenced many different musical styles, such as **hip-hop** and **salsa**. **69, 111, 119, 131, 132, 137-143, 152, 161, 162**

Jenkins 103

K

kanász rhythm A rhythm used in Hungarian folk dances. **156, 157**

key signature Sharps or flats just before the **time signature**, to tell you which key the music's in. **11, 24-26, 44**

Kodály 155, 156

L

Ladysmith Black Mambazo 133, 138

larghetto 60-66 beats a minute. Broad and slow, but less so than **largo**. **18**

largo 40-60 beats a minute. Broad and slow. **18**

layering Using technology to record several parts separately and layer them one on top of another. **46, 109, 143**

ledger lines Extra lines added above or below the stave, to write high or low notes. **16**

legato Play smoothly. **19**

leitmotif A phrase or piece of music that represents a person, place, time or emotion in film music or musicals. **121**

libretto The words of an **opera**. **86, 153**

Lied A **Romantic** song for one singer and piano. The lyrics are often in German. **102**

Liszt 99, 100

Little Fly 142

Logic Pro 124

Lombardic rhythm Another name for a **Scotch snap**. **156, 157**

loop Section of music repeated over and over. **46, 75, 160**

Love of My Life 116

M

major key A **key** using notes from a **major scale**. **24, 26, 90**

major scale Series of eight notes. The **intervals** between them are: **tone**, tone, **semitone**, tone, tone, tone, semitone. **24**

major triad A **triad** with an **interval** of four **semitones** between the bottom and middle notes, and three semitones between the middle and top notes. **35**

male voice choir A **choir** made up of two groups of **tenors** as well as **baritones** and **basses**. **68**

mambo A break between choruses in salsa music. **139**

mass Piece of music sung as part of the Catholic church service. **85, 103**

Maxwell Davies 153, 154

mbalax A fusion of **sabar**, **pop** and Afro-Caribbean music. **138**

mbube A type of South African Zulu **a cappella** singing. **133**

melismatic A single syllable of text is sung over a succession of notes. The opposite of **syllabic**. **87, 109, 115, 117, 142, 143**

melodic interval The difference in pitch between two notes played one after another in a tune. **28**

melodic inversion Version of a tune where the intervals between notes are the same but in the opposite direction (e.g. up instead of down). **83**

melodic minor scale A **minor scale**. Like the **natural minor** but with the 6th and 7th notes raised a **semitone** going up and reverting back to the natural minor coming down. Used for composing melodies in **minor keys**. **25**

melody with accompaniment
A type of musical **texture** where the melody has a different rhythm to the **homophonic** accompaniment. **45, 97, 115, 116, 142, 143, 155-158**

Mendelssohn 86, 100

mento Type of Jamaican folk music. **136**

merengue Type of dance music from the Dominican Republic. **136**

Messiah 87

metamorphosis Technique used in **minimalism** where small changes are made gradually. **160**

mezzoforte, mf Fairly loud. **19**

mezzopiano, mp Fairly quiet. **19**

mezzo-soprano A female voice that sings the top part of the alto range and the bottom part of the soprano range. **68, 85**

microtone An **interval** between two notes that's smaller than a **semitone**. **129, 134, 138**

middle 8 Eight bars, in the middle of a song. Has different chords and/or tune to keep you interested. **58**

MIDI Stands for Musical Instrument Digital Interface — a way of connecting different electronic instruments. **72, 118, 124, 145**

military band A type of **wind band** — they usually play marches. **69**

minim A note that lasts for two beats. **12, 16**

minimalism Mid-20th century music that is based on very gradual changes to repeated patterns. **159-162**

minor key A **key** that sounds sad. Uses notes from the **minor scale**. **25, 26, 90**

minor scale Series of eight notes (the first and last notes are the same). The **intervals** between them are: tone, semitone, tone, tone, semitone, tone, tone in a **natural minor** scale. **Melodic** and **harmonic** minor scales are slightly different. **25**

minor triad A **triad** with an **interval** of three **semitones** between the bottom and middle notes, and four semitones between the middle and top notes. **35**

minuet and trio Third movement of a **sonata** or **symphony**. Two sections in **ternary form** — the minuet and the trio — are put together so the overall structure of the piece is ternary too. **93**

mixing When different tracks are mixed together. **75**

Mixolydian mode A **mode** following the pattern created by the white notes, starting and ending on G. **27, 143, 158**

mode Seven-note scale following a particular sequence of **tones** and **semitones**. **27, 156-158**

moderato 108-120 beats per minute. Not too fast, not too slow. Moderate speed. **18**

modulation When music shifts into another **key**, usually a related one, e.g. the dominant or **relative minor**. **44, 80, 81, 92, 97, 98**

monophonic Music with a tune and nothing else — no backing, rhythm or harmony. **45, 47, 142, 143**

montuno The chorus in a **salsa** tune. **139**

mood The overall feel of a piece. **18**

mordent An **ornament** commonly used in Baroque music. **84**

motif A little bit of music that's often repeated. **97, 98, 102, 116, 118, 121, 123, 124, 143**

Mozart 81, 88-91, 95, 103

multi-track Recording system that allows you to record different parts separately then play them all back together. **72, 109, 115, 116, 143, 160**

musical A popular, lighthearted version of **opera** that's been around since the 1920s. Has more talking and more dancing. **119, 120**

mute Wooden, rubber or metal gadget used to dampen the sound of **brass** and **string instruments**. **62, 64**

N

natural A symbol that cancels out a **sharp** or a **flat**. **11**

natural minor scale A minor scale using the notes of the **minor key** (and no funny accidentals like the **melodic** and **harmonic** minors). **25**

non-functional harmony Harmony that doesn't rely on traditional **chord progressions** and **cadences**. **156-158**

North African music 134

nuba A North African set of pieces, each with a certain **mode**. **134**

O

octave The distance from one note to the next note up or down with the same letter name. **28, 29**

octave effect An electronic effect used to create octaves higher or lower than the note played. **75**

octet Piece in eight parts, or a group with eight players or singers in it. **70**

open fifth A chord that has a tonic and a 5th, but no 3rd. Often called a **power chord** in rock music. **158**

opera Drama set to music. **85-87, 91, 115, 119, 153, 155**

opera buffa A type of **opera** with light, everyday themes. **86**

opéra comique Form of **opera** with some spoken **recitatives**. **86, 119**

opera seria A type of **opera** with serious, often mythological themes. **86**

operetta A small **opera**. **86, 119**

oratorio Bible stories set to music. Oratorios are **sacred**. A bit like **opera**, but not acted out and with a religious theme. **85-87**

organ A large keyboard instrument that makes sound by blowing air through pipes. **66, 80**

ornament Short extra notes that add some **decoration**. **84, 88, 92, 98, 116, 132, 157, 158**

ostinato A musical pattern which repeats over and over again, like the bass part in **ground bass**. **57, 82, 83, 123, 124, 157, 158**

overdubbing Recording a track over another pre-recorded track. **115, 116, 118**

overture A one-movement piece for orchestra, usually written as an introduction to an **opera** or ballet. **91**

P

Paganini 102

panning A way to separate sounds and send them through different speakers. **110, 115, 116**

parallel motion When two or more parts move with the same interval between them. **45, 87, 154, 157, 158**

passing note A type of **decoration** — a note that links the two notes before and after it. **41**

patron People who paid composers to write music. **89, 94, 96**

pause A rest in the music, usually more than a beat long. **18**

Index and Glossary

Index and Glossary

Index and Glossary

MUAS43